RIGHTS ON TRIAL

Arthur Kinoy during his campaign for state senator
in New Jersey on Citizens Party ticket, 1981.

RIGHTS ON TRIAL

The Odyssey of a People's Lawyer

ARTHUR KINOY

HARVARD UNIVERSITY PRESS
Cambridge, Massachusetts, and London, England

This book is printed on acid-free paper, and its binding materials have been chosen for strength and durability.

Library of Congress Cataloging in Publication Data

Kinoy, Arthur.
  Rights on trial: the odyssey of a people's lawyer.

  Includes index.
  1. Kinoy, Arthur. 2. Lawyers—United States—
Biography. 3. Civil rights—United States. 4. United
States—Constitutional law. I. Title.
KF373.K525A37 1983 349.73′092′4 [B] 83-10878
ISBN 0-674-77013-7   347.300924 [B]

Designed by Gwen Frankfeldt

To James Dombrowski, Samuel Gruber,
Fannie Lou Hamer, and Ben Smith

Their lives and their commitment to
people in struggle taught me much about
the responsibilities of a people's lawyer.
May their spirit live on and continue to
inspire us in the difficult days ahead.

Contents

Illustrations

Illustrations

Mississippi Freedom Democratic Party Convention, August 1964. *Guardian.*

Empty seats of disputed Mississippi delegation at Democratic National Convention in Atlantic City, August 24, 1964. *UPI.*

Martin Luther King addressing supporters of MFDP delegation in Atlantic City, August 24, 1964. *Joanne Grant, Guardian.*

Victoria Gray, Annie Devine, and Fannie Lou Hamer, MFDP congressional contestants in the Mississippi Challenge, January 1965. *UE.*

following page 296

Arthur Kinoy dragged from HUAC hearing by federal marshals after Representative Joe Pool ordered his removal, August 17, 1966. *Ken Feil, Washington Post.*

Arthur Kinoy announcing appeal of his conviction for disorderly conduct at HUAC hearing, August 19, 1966. *Wide World.*

Adam Clayton Powell with his attorneys Herbert Reid and Arthur Kinoy after Supreme Court overruled his exclusion from Congress, June 1969. *Wide World.*

Arthur Kinoy and daughter Joanne Kinoy after grand jury hearing at Foley Square courthouse, New York, January 4, 1971. *Jim Hughes, New York Daily News.*

Arthur Kinoy arguing before Court of Appeals in Chicago Seven case, with Leonard Weinglass and Bill Kunstler, February 24, 1972. *Verna Sadock, WMAQ-TV Chicago.*

Acknowledgments

There are many people to whom I am indebted for urging me to write this book and aiding me in its completion.

John Anthony Scott and Susan Moger were invaluable colleagues from the earliest days, helping me to write and rewrite every section of the book. Their guidance and expertise were critical to me in making the leap from the oral to the nonlegal written arena.

Some of the most important early encouragement to think through the experiences and lessons of the past as a people's lawyer came from John Ratcliff, Anne Lancellotti, and Lenore Hogan of the Oral History Research Office at Columbia University.

It would have been impossible to unearth all the old buried files crucially needed over the past five years of writing without the enthusiastic help of many students at Rutgers Law School. Their dedication in pulling together the events of the past was vital to the process. As they know, my inability to remember names has become part of the folklore of the school. So rather than omitting anyone by name, I give deep thanks to all Rutgers law students, past and present, who worked with me in the research.

I am very grateful to the Lillian Boehm Foundation, the Samuel Rubin Foundation, the Funding Exchange, the Louis M. Rabinowitz Foundation, and the Harry Wright Jr. Charitable Trust for their help in meeting the expenses involved in the writing.

Acknowledgments

It would have been impossible to finish the book without the untiring assistance of Irene Yarrow, the project coordinator of the Constitution in Crisis Project. Her daily work in editing and preparing the manuscript was essential to its completion. And without the constant help and enthusiastic support of Elizabeth Urbanowicz, the administrator of the Constitutional Litigation Clinic of Rutgers Law School, who has labored side by side with me as a legal worker and friend for many years, the book would never have been completed.

Elaine Markson and Geri Thoma, my literary agents, have been very supportive throughout the period of writing and rewriting.

Marilyn Clement, executive director of the Center for Constitutional Rights, and Bernard Mazel of Brunner Mazel, Inc., were especially helpful in the final stages of arranging publication.

To Virginia LaPlante and Aida Donald of Harvard University Press my most special thanks for the thoughtful and intensive assistance I received from them in the final editing.

I am especially grateful to Barbara Webster, my wife, for her support, encouragement, and deep insights into some of the most difficult periods of the past, flowing from her own experiences as an activist and organizer in the antiwar and women's movements. And to Mary Lutz and Peter Kinoy, my son, and Mark Weber and Joanne Kinoy, my daughter, my thanks for the ongoing support received from them in so many ways over the years as I struggled with the ups and downs of the work.

Finally, my deepest thanks and gratitude go to those many dear friends in the peoples' movements, past and present, who have steadfastly urged upon me the responsibility of taking the time and spending the energy to set forth the experiences I have had in coming to understand the serious nature of the tasks of a people's lawyer in this country.

RIGHTS ON TRIAL

1

Wiretapping and Watergate

Few events have had as cataclysmic an impact upon the course of American history as did the days of Watergate in the early 1970s. And yet no period remains quite so clouded, so little understood. To this day the true explanation for the extraordinary developments which rocked the country remains hidden behind the self-serving accounts written by the participants. There were moments, however, when the layers of camouflage were torn away and the underlying truth lay exposed, revealing a frightening reality which had brought the nation closer to the brink of disaster than any turn of events since the rebellion of the southern slave states over a hundred years earlier. Such a moment of truth was the argument on February 24, 1972, before the United States Supreme Court of a case with the strange name of "United States against the United States District Court for the Eastern District of Michigan."

I found myself in the center of the unfolding developments of that case and shared, with a few others, a sudden frightening view into the reality it exposed. As the years pass, any real explanation for the underlying facts of that era becomes more and more hidden. As the social forces responsible for that nearly successful experiment, which could have been fatal to all of our democratic institutions, once again appear to be quietly edging in that direction, I find myself from time to time thinking about that case and realizing how close to the heart and center of the Watergate explosion it was.

When I was first approached to come into the case, in October 1971, I was in a mixed and moody frame of mind, with all kinds of problems stewing inside of me. William Bender and Linda Huber came to see me at home to propose that I join them in working on the appeals briefs and argument in a case they had been hard at work on for several months, which was scheduled to be heard by the Supreme Court later that winter. Bill Bender, a lawyer, was the administrative director of the newly formed Rutgers Law School Constitutional Litigation Clinic, an experiment in merging the teaching of legal theory with the actual experience of students participating in the preparation of ongoing cases of constitutional importance. Linda Huber, a recent graduate from the University of Washington School of Law, was also working in the clinic.

As they started to describe the case to me and the reasons for my joining them in the work, I found myself experiencing the deepest reluctance even to consider the possibility. For the past seven years I had been teaching full-time at Rutgers University School of Law, where I had helped found the clinic in which they were working. In addition, I was still very much committed to the work as a people's lawyer that I had been involved in since the late 1940s. Many lawyers in the legal profession choose to utilize their skills and talents in representing the powerful political and corporate interests that control and dominate the life of the nation. In contrast, the people's lawyer represents movements of people who throughout the history of this country have struggled to protect and advance their elementary rights and interests against attempts by the government or big business to undermine or derail them. As I was to realize over and over again throughout the years, this means that the life of a people's lawyer is filled with intense and exhausting experiences in seemingly endless battles.

This ongoing responsibility as a people's lawyer, now intermingled with my daily activities as a teacher of law, was often overwhelming. Only a few weeks before, Doris Peterson and Helene Schwartz, two extraordinarily committed lawyers, and I had finished writing a mammoth 547-page appellate brief in the Chicago Seven case, involving the appeals of leaders of the anti-Vietnam War movement from their conviction on the charge of conspiracy, flowing from their participation in massive demonstrations outside the Democratic Party convention in Chicago in 1968. This was probably the largest brief ever filed in the history of the country in a political trial involving the ideas and activities of opponents of the establishment. It had just been served on the government, and I was anxiously awaiting their reply. I felt drained. Mixed feelings of exultation and total fatigue always engulf me at the completion of a major appeals brief. Everything inside of me resisted moving once again into the pressurized atmosphere of deadline-controlled conceptualization and analysis that a major constitutional appeal requires.

More than this, during the summer I had started on a new path. I had begun to write, uneasily and with some hesitation, about ideas that had been ripening inside me for a long time as to the political road that lay ahead for this country. I was convinced of the need for organizing a new type of political party which might recapture the old vision of people controlling the government and their own lives. For me, working on this paper was a sharp departure from years of thinking and acting primarily as a lawyer. As I sat and listened to Bill Bender and Linda Huber describe this case they wanted me to throw myself into, resentment surged up in me against their effort to lure me back into the world of legal struggle. The political concepts I was writing about seemed to demand priority. But as they talked on into the night, strange and nagging questions began to form, which slowly chipped away at the barriers of resistance within me to becoming involved in another consuming legal struggle.

The case had begun in a federal courtroom in Detroit early in 1970, where three young men were awaiting trial on serious federal criminal charges. The three—John Sinclair, Lawrence "Pun" Plamondon, and John Forrest—were leaders of an organization in Michigan called the White Panthers, which was involved in community organizing work, primarily among white working class people in and around Detroit. The defendants, like many of their contemporaries at the end of the sixties, were committed to

3

participating in and organizing demonstrations, meetings, and other community activities expressing the opposition of millions of Americans to the seemingly endless Vietnam War.

Like other antiwar organizers from different parts of the country, these young people from Detroit had been hit in 1969 by a wave of "law and order" measures launched by the new Nixon administration for the purpose of cutting off the antiwar movement. They found themselves suddenly charged with the crime of "conspiracy." Simultaneously all over the country that charge appeared. In Chicago it was a "conspiracy" to start a riot at the Democratic National Convention. In Harrisburg, Pennsylvania, it was a "conspiracy" to kidnap Henry Kissinger. And here in Detroit, it was a "conspiracy" to bomb a Central Intelligence Agency building. In retrospect, it is clear that these charges of conspiracy were thrown together by the Nixon administration with little or no relationship to truth or reality, in a desperate attempt to muffle the anger flowing from the developing mood of opposition of millions of people to the Vietnam War. None of these conspiracy charges against the leadership of the antiwar movement has survived the test of time. But at that moment the charges were serious. The prospect of long imprisonment for the defendants—anywhere from ten to twenty years—and, perhaps even more important, the potential destruction of their movement hung over their heads.

But as Bill Bender and Linda Huber described what had happened at the beginning of the trial in Detroit, I suddenly began to feel that something very strange was going on here. This was not just the opening of yet another wave of repressive political trials similar to those that had characterized the McCarthy years of the 1950s. Something new was in the air. Prior to the trial, the lawyers for the defendants had prepared a whole host of pretrial motions, raising every conceivable question challenging the legality and the propriety of the prosecution. Lawyers always have a batch of these motions ready to go. Familiarly called "boiler plate" motions, they are traditionally made to preserve a point for appeal. Although they are thrown into the hopper without any real expectation that the trial judge will even consider them, they have to be made because, years later, they may end up as a foot-

4

note in an appeals brief which may move some appellate judge to decide in the appellant's favor.

In Detroit, one of these boiler plate motions was a request that the government inform the defense as to whether the case involved any wiretapping of the defendants in violation of the Fourth Amendment to the Constitution. This amendment, written into the Bill of Rights, guarantees the right of the people "to be secure in their persons, houses, papers and effects, against unreasonable searches and seizures." The amendment commands further that "no Warrants shall issue, but upon probable cause, supported by Oath or affirmation, and particularly describing the place to be searched, and the persons or things to be seized."

These are the words of the eighteenth century. The Supreme Court in the 1960s had come to the conclusion that, within the context of modern life, "few threats to liberty exist which are greater than those posed by the use of eavesdropping devices." Accordingly, the Court held that wiretapping was a "search or seizure" within the meaning of the Fourth Amendment. It followed from this proposition that government officials could not engage in wiretapping without obtaining in advance the same kind of specific warrant from a judge which would be required to authorize a physical "search" or "seizure." The conclusion that flowed from this updating of the Fourth Amendment to meet the realities of the twentieth century was that criminal proceedings which were in any way based upon wiretapping engaged in by government officials without a warrant had to be dismissed as "tainted," meaning that if the government engaged in this type of illegal conduct, it lost the right to prosecute. This reflected the Court's concern that nothing is more dangerous to the existence of constitutional government than wrongdoing by the government itself. The opinions of the Court which insisted upon this result invariably quoted the words of Justice Louis Brandeis in the 1920s, that "in a government of laws existence of the government will be imperiled if it fails to observe the law scrupulously."

The "routine" wiretap motions which were filed by the defense lawyers in Detroit were based squarely upon these Supreme Court decisions applying the Fourth Amendment to the contemporary realities of life, but they were filed without the slightest expectation of any effect upon the trial. The defense lawyers knew, as did others familiar with the practices of the Federal Bureau of Investigation and the Department of Justice since the earliest days of the Cold War in the 1950s, that wiretapping without warrants was going on constantly but was never acknowledged. This was one of the facts of public life that no one would openly admit. Every now and then, if the wiretapping involved a nationally known figure, it would leak out in a newspaper column. Sometimes it showed up through bungling by the wiretappers. I remember picking up my own telephone and listening in astonishment to a conversation between two FBI agents discussing the changing of reels on the tap on my phone. People knew that this tapping was going on, but defense lawyers could rarely, if ever, prove its existence in a courtroom. Invariably the government lawyers blandly denied the presence of any such wiretapping when challenged by the defense at the beginning of a political trial. This denial ended the matter. No federal judge would challenge the veracity and integrity of government lawyers. The question of whether the case had been tainted by illegal wiretapping remained, at best, a minor issue for an appeal if the defendants were convicted, and routinely the appellate courts accepted the assurance of government lawyers that no such wiretapping had occurred.

It was against this background that what happened in Detroit seemed unbelievable. When the wiretapping motion was perfunctorily presented, the United States Attorney stepped forward and informed the court that the government was prepared to concede that in this case there had indeed been wiretapping without a warrant—that one of the defendants, Plamondon, had been overheard by a government agent when he called someone whose phone was being tapped, without a warrant having been obtained.

Before the defense lawyers could recover from the shock of this unexpected admission and demand to see the transcript of what appeared to have been conceded as an illegal wiretapping, the government lawyer, to the astonishment of both the defense lawyers and the sitting judge, Damon Keith, argued that the wiretapping actually was legal, despite the written mandates of the Fourth Amendment. In support of this contention, he produced what may be one of the most arrogant documents in American constitutional history. It was an affidavit made out by John Mitchell, the Attorney General of the United States, stating simply and directly that he had authorized the secret wiretapping because, in his sole judgment, acting for the President of the United States, he had determined that the wiretap was "necessary to protect the nation from attempts of domestic organizations to attack and subvert the government." The government argued in a fully prepared supporting memorandum that, even though a prior judicial warrant had not been obtained, the authorization of the Attorney General as representative of the President was sufficient to make the surveillance legal, regardless of the warrant requirements of the Fourth Amendment. This power to brush aside the constitutional provisions, in effect to suspend the written Constitution, flowed, according to the government, from the President's "inherent power as Chief Executive officer of the United States" to "protect the security of the nation." The United States Attorney then instructed the federal judge that any determination to ignore the provisions of the Fourth Amendment was solely a matter of presidential concern and that the "courts should not question the decision of the Executive Department."

As the defense lawyers handling the trial prepared their response to this sweeping assertion, they began to realize that this development in Detroit was no accident. In at least two other political trials Mitchell had assumed the same posture, radically departing from the prior position of the Department of Justice. In a 1969 affidavit Mitchell had conceded a warrantless wiretapping in the case of the Chicago Seven. A year later in an appeal in California involving the conviction of a member of the Black Panthers, Mitchell unexpectedly disclosed in court that the conviction had in fact involved warrantless wiretapping. What happened in Detroit thus appeared to be part of a national pattern, a sudden change in position. With the advent of the new Nixon administration in 1969, the Department of Justice had decided to assert openly what had been hidden in all previous administrations—the existence of widespread warrantless wiretapping involving surveillance of individuals and organizations considered to be a threat to "domestic security."

As Bill Bender and Linda Huber described the Detroit devel-

7

opments to me, placing them within the context of the parallel situations in Chicago and California, a puzzling question began to bother me, as it obviously did them. I had of course known about the Mitchell affidavit in the Chicago conspiracy trial, where to no one's surprise the trial judge, Julius Hoffman, who had supported the prosecution at every turn, accepted the government's rationale as to the legality of the warrantless tappings. That issue then became lost in the appeal among the hundreds of other critical points raised by the 32,000-page transcript of the mammoth trial. We had written a short section in our appeals brief brushing aside what appeared to be a totally unsupportable legal position involved in the Mitchell doctrine of "inherent power," but the underlying unanswered question as to why the Department of Justice had forced the wiretap question into the open instead of following the older, easier path of simple denial did not become pressing until the Detroit case.

Judge Keith considered the government's arguments carefully and on January 21, 1971, in a terse written opinion, denied Mitchell's contentions that the President could disregard the provisions of the Fourth Amendment by relying on a mystical reservoir of inherent power. Judge Keith's opinion was a curt rebuke: "The Court cannot accept this proposition for we are a country of laws and not of men." As for the assertion that the President had some loosely defined power to protect the national interest in whatever way he saw fit, even if it meant ignoring the written commands of the Constitution, Judge Keith replied sharply, "Such power held by one individual was never contemplated by the framers of our Constitution and cannot be tolerated today."

This should have ended the matter. The wiretapping of Plamondon was clearly illegal under the most binding decisions of the Supreme Court, and Judge Keith very properly ordered the government to turn the logs of the intercepted conversations over to the defense lawyers, so that a hearing could be held as to whether the tapping tainted the prosecution in any way, requiring a dismissal of the case. But at this point Mitchell and his Department of Justice made a strange move. Instead of turning over the logs and then arguing that the tapes were really not related to the pending prosecution—a position they had urged in other cases in which wiretapping was accidentally disclosed as a result of some blunder by a government agent or a United States Attorney— they embarked on a course of action that seemed incredible, if considered solely within the four corners of the Detroit case itself. They announced that instead of going ahead with the trial, they were taking a direct appeal to the Court of Appeals for the Sixth Circuit, the court that supervised Judge Keith's activities in Detroit as a district judge. Since appeals during an actual trial are rarely permitted, the only way they could do so was by using an ancient procedure from English common law known as suing out a "writ of mandamus." This required the government to name the trial judge as defendant and ask a higher court for an extraordinary order directing him to reverse himself. The case then became known as *United States of America v. United States District Court for the Eastern District of Michigan, Southern Division, and Hon. Damon J. Keith, presiding; and John Sinclair, Lawrence "Pun" Plamondon, and John Waterhouse Forrest.* The White Panther defendants, being the real parties in interest, remained defendants in the mandamus proceeding. In looking back on this strange development in the case, I have often thought that the "caption," the name of the case, was deeply symbolic. It should have given me a clue into what Mitchell and his cohorts were secretly planning. The United States against its own district court? The seeds of their underlying plan were right there.

The court of appeals gave short shrift to Mitchell's position. In an opinion written by Chief Judge George Edwards, the appeals court again struck down the contention that the President had "inherent power" to allow his representative, the Attorney General, to authorize wiretapping without regard for the prohibitions of the Constitution. In words that permitted no evasion, Judge Edwards said, "The government has not pointed to, and we do not find, one written phrase in the Constitution, in statutory law, or in the case law of the United States, which exempts the President, the Attorney General, or federal law enforcement from the restrictions of the Fourth Amendment in the case at hand."

In pressing the inherent power argument in the court of appeals, Mitchell's representatives, under the direction of William Rehnquist, then Assistant Attorney General, had dredged out of old English case books examples of the assertion by British monarchs in the fifteenth, sixteenth, and seventeenth centuries of their "inherent power" to take action deemed necessary by them to protect the nation. Judge Edwards underscored the irony of these arguments: "It is strange, indeed, that in this case the traditional power of sovereigns like King George III should be invoked in behalf of an American President to defeat one of the fundamental freedoms for which the founders of this country overthrew King George's reign." As for the concept that this mysterious reservoir of inherent power gave the President authority to take any action required to protect the national security, Judge Edwards, in blunt words rarely found in a judicial opinion, called this an "argument *in terrorem*" which "suggests that constitutional government is too weak to survive in a difficult world and urges worried judges and worried citizens to return to acceptance of the security of 'sovereign' power." It is chilling to consider in retrospect how close the judge came in that observation to the underlying assumptions of the administration in power.

Again, this should have closed the matter. The case normally would have gone on to trial, and the opinions of Judge Keith and Judge Edwards would have ended up as interesting footnotes in some ponderous treatise on presidential power. But as Bill Bender and Linda Huber pointed out to me that evening, Mitchell and the Nixon administration had something else in mind. Instead of proceeding with the Detroit trial, as was conventionally expected, the Department of Justice announced in April 1971 that it was taking the wiretap issue to the Supreme Court for a "definitive ruling." And on June 12 the Court agreed to hear the case. Mitchell and the Nixon administration were pushing the issue all the way up.

What was behind it all? What were they up to? Why the sudden unexpected admissions of wiretapping as the Nixon administration took over? Why the unconventional appeal to the Court of Appeals and then to the Supreme Court? What was really going on? These questions built up a pressure in me which probably more than anything else edged me into agreeing to undertake the Supreme Court appeal with Bill Bender and Linda Huber.

As we began to put together the pieces of the appeal in the winter of 1971–1972, reading and rereading the positions of the Department of Justice in the district court and the circuit court of appeals, slowly an answer began to emerge which rocked us in its implications for the present and the future. Carefully and consciously the Nixon administration was using the case to advance an extraordinary claim of power, the claim that the President, acting through his representative the Attorney General, had the power, "inherent" in the office of President, to disregard the limitations of the written Constitution whenever in his sole and unfettered judgment the national security of the country required him to do so. Put in its bluntest terms, Nixon, Mitchell, and the men who surrounded them were driving hard for an authoritative statement from the highest court in the land that the President had the power to suspend provisions in the Constitution whenever he unilaterally determined it was necessary. Whatever we touched in the case exposed this underlying assertion of a power unparalleled in its potential sweep.

The implications of this claim to power were so terrifying that we found ourselves dissecting and redissecting the government briefs and arguments in an atmosphere of disbelief and skepticism. But there it always was, naked and direct. The wiretap issue was beautifully structured to thrust the claim of power to suspend the Constitution directly into the center of judicial attention. The Fourth Amendment, the government conceded, would require, if applied to these wiretaps, a judicial warrant in order to comply with its provisions. But the Nixon administration representatives insisted that the President, in his sole discretion, could determine that the national interest permitted him to suspend this provision of the amendment and permit warrantless wiretapping without court review. Over and over again the one sharp demand emerged, that the courts, and finally the Supreme Court, the institution which in the eyes of the people represented the fount of legality, sanction the concept that the President had the power to ignore and suspend provisions of the Constitution whenever in his sole judgment he found it necessary to do so.

Out of the maze of technicalities and legal phrases that jammed the briefs, there emerged a still broader message. The Nixon administration wanted, and was acting as if it expected to receive, a

11

legal sanction from the highest court in the land to undertake wholesale actions that would otherwise fly in the face of specific constitutional prohibitions. Nixon was seeking a stamp of legitimacy for a sweeping strategy of governmental lawlessness—for the suspension, if not the abandonment, of the elementary forms of constitutional protection. As we approached the day of argument, I had a sinking feeling that what was at stake here was a bid to establish a legal "cover" to sanction wholesale experimentation with the abandonment of constitutional government.

It was not until later that the real story of what was involved was revealed for all to see. When the facts were known, our most extreme fears were substantiated. The Nixon-Mitchell thrust was deadly serious. It had been carefully structured and orchestrated by three members of the so-called Arizona gang whom Senator Barry Goldwater had originally brought to Washington. There was William Rehnquist, the chief theoretician and architect of the inherent power claim during the years he had functioned as Assistant Attorney General under Mitchell, who in 1971, only a few months before our argument, was suddenly elevated to the High Court itself. Today he remains the only member of the inner Nixon power elite unscathed by the post-Watergate holocaust, still sitting in his position of power and influence on the Supreme Court. Next there was Richard Kleindienst, Deputy Attorney General under Mitchell and the first public spokesperson for Rehnquist's theory of the President's inherent power to suspend the Constitution, with which he had attempted to justify the wholesale arrest and mass detention in May 1971 of almost 15,000 antiwar demonstrators in the capital, in total disregard of any elementary constitutional protection. Finally, at the center was Robert Mardian, who headed the section of the Justice Department euphemistically known as the Internal Security Division, which was dedicated to the destruction of the left and all organized dissent. Heir to a large construction company in Phoenix and campaign manager in the western states for Goldwater in 1964 and for Nixon in 1968, Mardian had been brought in by Mitchell as a lawyer for the Health, Education, and Welfare Department. He was then moved to the Department of Justice as chief of the Internal Security Division, where, together with

12

Rehnquist, over a three-year period he fashioned the machinery of both open and covert operations designed to evade and ultimately ignore the basic constitutional protections of citizens' liberties.

The full dimensions of these covert operations—their evolution from the Mardian-directed "interdepartmental intelligence unit" that had been set up by Mitchell to coordinate the so-called intelligence-gathering activities of the different branches of government, into the notorious Huston plan to launch widespread secret operations by the FBI, the CIA, and the military against every section of the people's movements, and finally into the full-scale operations of the so-called "plumbers" unit which culminated in the wiretapping of the Democratic National Committee Watergate headquarters—were not known to us at the time, nor to anyone uninvolved in their secret discussions. But we were aware of the scope of the open operations that Mardian and Rehnquist were masterminding throughout this period—the long list of dragnet conspiracy indictments against the leadership of the antiwar movement and the persistent use of a network of federal grand juries to hound and harass those who were raising their voices in political opposition.

In January and February of 1972 as we prepared for the argument, we were still not privy to any of these secret plans and covert actions of the Nixon administration. We could only imagine and speculate as to what it had in mind in the wiretap case. But to demand the right to suspend the Constitution, to disregard the commands of the Fourth Amendment and the other fundamental guarantees of the Bill of Rights, was to demand the right to abandon government through constitutional forms and to substitute at will government without law.

We discussed the word to describe where this all might be heading. There was a word, but we were all reluctant to use it. It had fearful connotations for most Americans. It was a word out of European experiences which most Americans, including ourselves, were loath to put into an American context. That word was "fascism." My own sensitivity to the normal paranoia which I knew we long-time movement lawyers understandably developed, as a result of years of fighting in political trials, inhibited

13

somewhat the conclusions I was prepared to draw as to what really lay behind this move on the part of the Nixon administration.

Then one morning I remembered a phrase repeated often during the 1930s by that master of American experimentation with the forms of repression, Governor Huey Long of Louisiana. He had said with great insight, "When fascism comes to America, it will come wrapped in an American flag." As I worked on the argument, it dawned on me that the Nixon administration was seeking to wrap its plan for governmental lawlessness in a mantle of legality. This was to be the "American" way—not the "foreign" path via the coup d'état.

It was a brilliant move. From the very beginning in the Chicago courtroom, then in the California and Detroit courtrooms, and up to the Supreme Court itself, the plan had been deliberately structured and fashioned to maneuver the courts into placing the stamp of legitimacy upon moves to destroy constitutional government. Too often in the wake of Watergate, one tends to forget the skillfulness of some of the Nixon administration moves. This was the most skillful move of all, masterminded from its inception by that astute tactician and theoretician, William Rehnquist.

As I wrestled with the last stages of the argument, I also thought of the words of advice from David Scribner, general counsel of the United Electrical Workers, that wise and experienced union lawyer with whom I had first worked after graduating from law school. He used to drum into me the warning, "Never underestimate the opposition," and he particularly cautioned, "Never underestimate the lawyers from the head office of the company." Well, the "lawyers from the head office of the company" had set this one up skillfully and with care. The legitimization of warrantless wiretapping was in the deepest sense wholly incidental to what they were after. If this had been all that was involved, they could have just continued the wholesale wiretapping they were doing anyway and the bland lying about it when challenged at the beginning of a trial. What was involved was much more serious. The importance of this move was primarily as a vehicle for propelling to center stage the claim of ultimate, unchecked executive power itself. The stakes were enormous. This is why the government lawyers had rushed the issue to the High Court. The issue far transcended the "legality" of domestic security wiretapping. It went to the very "future of the Republic," as the Fourth of July speeches used to express it, only now it was for real.

These were sobering thoughts. How was I to make them reach the members of the Court? How was I to discuss what was really involved? Two paths lay open. One was in the direction of professionalism and scholarship. A "perfect" legal rebuttal could be prepared, addressing the many sophisticated nuances of the government's argument and dissecting the past precedents of the Supreme Court, which the government had miscited and misused, in the quiet, confident tone of the scholar and law professor. A number of people urged this approach to the argument.

The other path lay in a different direction: in the words of the leaders of the southern civil rights movements of the 1960s, "to tell it like it is," to inform the Court of the blunt realities of what the Nixon administration was after. Unless the Court understood fully the enormous implications of the administration's grab for power, the case might become swamped in the technicalities of search and seizure law, and we could easily lose such an argument. The Nixon court was already shifting—five-to-four, six-to-three—away from the guarantees of due process of law, in the direction of strengthening law enforcement. Unless the Court saw the ominous passages that opened up beyond the administration's position, the case was lost. And yet to appear "political" or "unlawyerlike" was dangerous: it could lose the conservatives and might alienate the middle-of-the-roaders. Then again, they might be lost already. These conflicting thoughts surged through me during those terrible last days of preparation. Their final resolution was not to come until the actual moment of argument.

In a way, it may have been the last-minute discussions with William Gossett, the lawyer for Judge Keith, which placed the issues in sharpest perspective. Gossett was an unusual lawyer for me to be sharing an argument with before the Supreme Court. He was the general counsel for the Ford Motor Company, a former president of the American Bar Association, and a ranking Republican. His original entrance into the appeal was one of those strange twists that set this case apart from the very beginning. After the Nixon administration had decided on the unusual technical course of making Judge Keith a defendant through use of the writ of mandamus, the judge responded sharply by asking the Michigan Bar Association to appoint a lawyer to represent him in the court of appeals. The bar association selected Gossett, one of Michigan's most prominent attorneys.

Two days before the Supreme Court appearance, scheduled for February 24, 1972, Gossett, Bill Bender, Linda Huber, and I met in Washington to plan the division of the argument. Gossett had suggested that we work in one of the private offices in the ABA building set aside for past officers. As I walked into the office, troublesome thoughts surfaced in my mind. What in the world was I, a movement lawyer, doing preparing to share an argument with Gossett? This was the first time in my life I had been in the inner sanctum of the ABA, the citadel of establishment law, whose reactionary policies I had fought for years. Gossett was general counsel for one of the most powerful corporations in the country. I had seldom appeared on the same side of the counsel table with corporate lawyers of any kind; they were generally across the way. What brought us together that morning in Washington?

After a few minutes, it became clear why we were together and why a cooperative sharing of the argument not only was possible but could be important in presenting the issues effectively to the Court. Gossett seemed fully to understand the case. He had prepared, together with Professor Abraham Sofaer of Columbia Law School, a powerful and effective brief supporting Judge Keith's opinion. He took with dead seriousness the implications of the assertion of sweeping power the administration was making. He said to us that morning, as he was later to say openly to the Court, that the claim of inherent power in the President was deeply dangerous to the written constitutional liberties of the people, that he was very disturbed as a lawyer and as a citizen by the thrust of the administration in this case. Let there be no mistake. Gossett's frame of reference was not ours; his background and experiences were certainly not ours; and we were poles apart in every respect except one, our growing common apprehension that the thrust for

16

power which we were about to contest was no lawyer's ploy to win a case but was rather a serious effort to obtain sanction from the High Court for a course of conduct perilous to the future of constitutional democracy. And such an outcome, perhaps for wholly different reasons at that moment, neither we nor Gossett were prepared to accept.

Gossett told me at one point during our preparatory work about a discussion of his with Republican friends back in Michigan who could not understand why he had gotten into this kind of a case. His answer captured the tone and flavor of the argument he would soon make to the Court. He said to his skeptical friends, "I am a conservative, and I believe in conserving the fundamental values of the Constitution."

Another insight developed into what was moving Gossett when he said half-jokingly, but perhaps with more seriousness than we understood at the moment, that he was not quite sure which side a lot of his clients would take in the case. In a real sense he was reflecting the inner pull of his own commitment to the values of the system of written constitutional government, which sometimes ran contrary to the needs and strategic perspectives of powerful corporate clients.

And then there was the intensely human aspect of Gossett's excitement at being in the center of a constitutional struggle. At a particularly difficult moment late in the final evening of preparation, he turned to me and said, in a reflective mood, that of all the cases he had worked on over the years, many involving millions of dollars, this was the most important and the most interesting. It was, he added, the heaviest responsibility as a lawyer he had ever felt. It was this combination of an almost overpowering sense of responsibility and a high excitement which infected all of us as we separated that last evening before the argument.

On the morning of February 24, 1972, which dawned bleak and gray, Barbara Webster, an activist and organizer of the people's antiwar movement, and I walked down the street toward the Supreme Court building, where we were to meet Bill Bender, Linda Huber, and Bill Gossett. It was an exciting moment for me to be approaching this critical confrontation with Barbara Webster by my side. Two years earlier we had begun a relationship which would culminate in marriage six months after the Supreme Court argument. In many ways, this relationship represented a total change in my personal life, and to be walking with Barbara toward the morning showdown with the power structure gave me a feeling of strength and confidence. But as the pillars that front the Court came into sight, the feelings that welled up inside me became complex and conflicting. I was frightened, and I felt the fear run through me. I held tightly to my briefcase with the notes for the argument in it, as if to reassure myself. I was facing head on an ominous bid for unlimited power by the top forces in the ruling establishment, and it was overwhelming.

As we hurried down the street, I thought about the Court, and the fear grew within me. This was the Nixon Court, after all. The clever strategy might well succeed. The administration had all but remade the Court in its own image, so many of us thought. First came Warren Burger, to replace Earl Warren, and then Harry Blackmun, to replace Abe Fortas. Burger and Blackmun were beginning to be called the Minnesota twins because of their similar views. Then came Lewis Powell, a southern conservative. To clinch it, Rehnquist, the mastermind of the doctrine of inherent power, had been appointed three months earlier, replacing Hugo Black, the champion of the written Constitution. At his Senate confirmation hearings Rehnquist had admitted publicly that he had fashioned the entire theory of inherent power for the government's Supreme Court brief in this very case. And Byron White and Potter Stewart, the traditional middle Justices of the Warren Court, who had swung so often from liberal to conservative positions, could hardly be counted on to withstand the emotional impact of the national security argument. Would Justices Marshall, Brennan, and Douglas remain the only ones on the Court to support our position? Maybe Mitchell, Nixon, Mardian, and Rehnquist were unstoppable. They might well have the Court in their pocket. Maybe it was all over. I began to wonder what I was doing there, walking to disaster, small, helpless, against the strength of the administration and its Court.

As we neared the building, my mood suddenly changed. Long lines of people were queued up on the marble steps of the Court. More than a hundred and fifty law students from Rutgers had arrived in the early hours of the morning. When they saw us approaching, they began to call out friendly greetings. Some raised their fists in the traditional Black Power salute. It was a reassuring and strengthening moment. I suddenly felt that we would not be entirely alone when we took on the Nixon administration that morning.

Then just as abruptly, my mood shifted again. As we walked through the heavy metal doors into the long hallway leading to the courtroom, we were thrust back into the ominous atmosphere which had haunted the case from the start. For the first time in my experience with the Supreme Court, and for the first time in the history of the Court, barriers had been set up across the hallway. Security guards stood beside them, demanding to inspect our briefcases before we entered. I felt not only harassed but menaced. As a result of the growing tensions, security measures had become common in recent years in courtrooms throughout the country, but never in the Supreme Court of the United States. Who were they afraid of? Us? Angrily the words of custom and ancient usage of members of the bar of the Supreme Court came to me, and I snapped at the guard who reached for my briefcase, "I am counsel for the day. I am a member of the bar of this Court." I brushed past him, closed briefcase in hand. No representative of the other side, I told myself heatedly, was going to see my notes for the argument.

Why was I so outraged? I was certainly more nervous and apprehensive than usual about this appearance before the Supreme Court. That alone would have made me touchy. But more than that was involved. It was not only my own integrity that was being attacked by this peremptory demand to hand over my briefcase but, more important, the integrity of the legal profession itself and what it was supposed to represent in a "system of laws, not men." I felt for a moment the way I had six years earlier in this same city when I had refused to be silenced by Chairman Joseph Pool of the House Un-American Activities Committee during a hearing at which I was representing young members of the antiwar movement. After objecting to his refusal to permit me to cross-examine hostile witnesses, which had been a long-standing problem for lawyers at HUAC hearings, I was at his order choked

19

and wrestled out of the room by three federal marshals. While being dragged out, I shouted at them, "Don't touch a lawyer."

I have mixed feelings about my instinctive reaction on both occasions. On the one hand, it revealed an elitist, privileged feeling about the status of the legal profession. On the other hand, it reflected the special sense of violation that attaches to the use of force, or even the threat of it, against lawyers who are themselves supposed to be representatives of a system of authority which is grounded in laws and the courts that administer them. Hence, when lawyers, the "officers of the court," are subjected to violence, surveillance, or other forms of abusive treatment, it threatens the very fabric of our democracy. Given the threatening atmosphere that already surrounded this case, it was no wonder, then, that I was upset by those guards and their command.

I began to wonder what was really going on that morning. Had some Justice, or even the Chief Justice, arriving early at the Court, been alarmed by the lines of students waiting to get in? Had he called the marshals and ordered the barriers? Inwardly I shivered. Was this an omen of what was to happen in the argument? Was it a mindless fear of students, of long hair, of tieless shirts, of Blacks and women—instead of the traditionally quiet, well-groomed tourists on their daily tour through Washington? At that moment the words of Judge Edwards earlier in the case drummed through my head. The government was about to make once more its *in terrorem* argument, raising the specter of lawlessness to mesmerize the Court into constructing a sanction for lawlessness, persuading the Court to legalize illegality. At the very entrance to the Court, an hour before the case was to be heard, the *in terrorem* argument was already being played out in life. Legal words were turning into the reality of barriers and guards. This was the heart of the Nixon-Mitchell-Rehnquist-Mardian formula. Invoke the magic incantation of national security in order to sanction the suspension of constitutional government, and then themselves create the acts that would transform the words "national security" into a reality, which in turn would force an alarmed public to accept and even applaud as necessary the violation of constitutional rights.

The placement of a security blockade in the highest court in the land, in order to create an atmosphere that would imperceptibly set the stage for the Court's acceptance of the concept of unlimited power invoked by the words "national security," was in its own way a microcosm of the pattern unfolding all around us: the fabricated "plots" and "conspiracies" in Chicago, in Detroit, in Harrisburg, in a dozen different courtrooms throughout the country, the "plans" of arson, bombings, and kidnapings, which were often woven by secret agents of the prosecution or the FBI and deliberately instigated at the highest levels of the Department of Justice. All of this would then give substance to the increasingly insistent drive to obtain legal and public approval, in the name of national security, for a policy of repression which might well end in the total abandonment of constitutional government. These somber thoughts preoccupied me as I walked through the already crowded courtroom to the table reserved for counsel.

At this point, something happened which again placed the coming confrontation into troubling focus. Just across the aisle, four or five grim-looking men, immaculate in dark business suits, carrying briefcases, swept into the area reserved for our adversaries. The government's team had arrived. I immediately looked for their most prominent member, the one wearing the traditional long morning coat that government lawyers invariably wear when arguing before the High Court. This uniform would mark the representative of the government, our physical opponent in the battle to come. I expected to see Erwin Griswold, the Solicitor General and a former dean of Harvard Law School, who was respected for his scholarship and integrity even by those of us who increasingly found ourselves in deep disagreement with the positions he had been advancing in the Supreme Court, in his role as chief legal representative for the Johnson and now the Nixon administrations, to justify the growing repression of the antiwar movement. Instead, I saw an unfamiliar man, tall, dark, and scowling, wearing the morning coat. I turned to Gossett and whispered, "It's not Griswold!" "No," answered Gossett, "it's Mardian." Then suddenly we realized that the rumors of the past several days were true. Griswold would not appear for the government in this case. This had seemed unlikely to us, because the Solicitor General traditionally argued the most important cases for the government. And regardless of one's position on the issues of this case, it was likely to be one of the most important cases of that term. Yet here was Mardian taking Griswold's place.

Then something even stranger happened. Griswold walked into the courtroom and sat down in the seat reserved for the Solicitor General, as though to make it clear to the Court that he had not withdrawn because of illness or scheduling conflicts, but for some other reason. He sat there quietly throughout the argument, as if he were constantly saying to the Court through his physical presence, "I am not arguing this case. Just remember that."

As I waited for the case to begin, playing with the old-fashioned quill pens on the counsel table which are traditionally provided by the Clerk, perhaps to remind lawyers a little too impressed with their own importance that they rise before an institution which finds its roots in our remote past, I asked myself a number of questions. Had Griswold had a falling out with Nixon, Mitchell, and Mardian about this case? If so, how deep did the split go? What were the differences really about? In the mid-1950s during the ravages of the Cold War, when thousands of citizens were subpoenaed before the McCarthy and the HUAC committees, Griswold had written an article defending the Fifth Amendment privilege against self-incrimination as a "cornerstone of American liberty." Did he see something in this case which frightened him, bringing back echoes of the past and making him refuse to argue the administration's position? Had he himself glimpsed a future of planned lawlessness and abandonment of constitutional government which we ourselves were only beginning to see, lying just beyond the claim of unlimited presidential powers? Did he actually know of the administration's plans for an abandonment of constitutional government? I have often, since then, wondered about these questions, and only Griswold himself could answer them.

Regardless of whatever internal struggle in the Justice Department may have preceded the Supreme Court argument, the architects of its underlying strategy were now in firm control, as evidenced by the appearance of Mardian to argue the case himself. Mardian was much more than a legal craftsman and political technician. He was one of those leaders of the reactionary right who are committed to destroying all opposition to the establishment. Over the years I have run into many lawyers in the Department of Justice who are "just doing a job." Not so Mardian. He had a fervor, an ideological intensity, which set him apart. Later that morning when the Court adjourned for lunch and the opposing counsel were escorted by a marshal to reserved tables in the Court's cafeteria, Mardian refused to engage in the conventional amenities between members of the bar but stalked past us as if we did not exist. Someone standing next to me muttered, "All he needs is the jackboots." The remark seemed apt. At that moment we were reminded of those in Germany who tragically shaped the course of history in the early 1930s, their consuming hatred of political opponents, dissenters, minorities, and nonconformists resulting in the death of millions.

These thoughts left me suddenly as the Chief Justice intoned the ritual words, "We will hear argument in No. 70-153, United States against the District Court and others. Mr. Mardian, you may proceed." As the lawyer for the petitioner, he was the first to speak. I tensely awaited what he would say. Would he actually make the bid for power? Was the administration so confident of "its" Court that it would arrogantly press its demand for power to suspend the Constitution? A few moments after Mardian rose, the answer was evident when he spoke these words: "The stakes, as far as the government is concerned, are high." I said to myself, "My God, he is going to go the whole way. He is really shooting the works."

And so he did. Drowned by the later revelations of Watergate, the events of that February morning in Washington in 1972 have been buried and forgotten. Yet in Mardian's argument the whole strategy became clear. It was one of those rare moments when for an instant the outer wrappings of rationalization are peeled off and, like a flash, the truth is revealed. Without hesitation or apology, Mardian demanded from the Court judicial approval for a course of conduct that would place in the President, in Nixon, the unreviewable and absolute power to suspend the provisions of the written Constitution, the fundamental law of the land. The Court itself was being pressed to preside over the demise of constitutional government, to legitimate its own ultimate destruction as an institution, to wrap the "flag" and "truth" and "law and order" around plans to exchange the absolute rule of one man for the government of law embedded in the written Constitution that the Court was sworn to preserve. It was one of the most dangerous moments in the long history of the Supreme Court.

As Mardian spoke, the reality of this bid for power began to break through to the judges themselves. At one point in his argument Mardian sought to invoke the constitutional oath of office of the President to justify the President's inherent power to disregard the written Constitution when domestic security required it. The President, he argued, takes an oath "to protect the principles under which the Constitution was adopted, and the rights guaranteed by that Constitution." This was too much for one of the Justices, who interrupted abruptly to ask him, "Do you think that argument helps you in this case?" There was a moment of stunned silence as Mardian reshuffled his notes, looked down at the rostrum, and then blandly continued to insist upon the claim of absolute power.

For five or ten minutes more Mardian pressed his argument, dwelling upon the many laws reflecting the fear of domestic violence and rebellion against the authority of the United States which are scattered throughout the legislative history of the country, on which he was basing the need for unlimited presidential power. Suddenly Justice Marshall spun around in his chair. "Mr. Mardian," he said. "You keep ducking the Fourth Amendment. Are you ever going to get to it?" This cut like a knife through the rhetoric. Mardian was indeed ducking not only the Fourth Amendment but the entire constitutional structure. In place of the written Constitution, he was bluntly demanding judicial sanction for a system which reposed "responsibility in one man and one man alone." These incredible words of Mardian, which extended the issue far beyond the immediate context of electronic surveillance, acknowledging at last the administration's real motivation for pressing this appeal, visibly jolted the listeners.

Toward the end of Mardian's argument the basic implications of his thrust for power came clear. One of the Justices put the question to Mardian directly. What were the protections for ordinary citizens if the express words of the Constitution could be disregarded at will by the executive? Mardian paused and replied, "This Court must, as a coordinate branch of government, rely almost entirely on the integrity of the Executive Branch." There it was, on the line. The "integrity of the Executive Branch." On this was to rest our freedom as a people. Not on the written guarantees of the Constitution. Not on the Bill of Rights.

When Mardian spoke these words, echoes of past attempts to substitute lawlessness for even the most limited constitutional protections rang in my ears. What I did not then fully know was the extent of the present danger. The very administration that was asking for total reliance on its "integrity" was at the same time, it was later revealed, already involved in secret meetings at the Department of Justice, hardly a stone's throw from that courtroom. In these meetings, John Mitchell, the Attorney General and the President's chief political representative; John Dean, the President's counsel; and Jeb Magruder, the deputy director of the Committee for the Re-election of the President, had been discussing with G. Gordon Liddy, a White House aide, a $1 million plan for mugging squads, kidnaping teams, sexual scandals, and surreptitious electronic surveillance to deal with the opposition in the forthcoming national election. On February 4, less than three weeks before Mardian's statement to the High Court, they had met again in Mitchell's office to discuss a more "practical," less expansive, and less grandiose plan, which settled for illegal entries, wiretapping, and undercover photography. At this secret meeting, the Democratic National Committee headquarters at the Watergate had been selected as one of the top-priority targets for the covert break-ins and secret surveillance. And here, only two weeks later, the representative of the President was asking for the sweeping power to suspend the Constitution, based solely upon faith in the integrity of the executive branch.

Scarcely two years after that statement before the Court, not even the most intransigent supporters of the Republican Party would have dared to rest any argument upon an invocation of the integrity of the Nixon administration. But as I rose to argue on that morning in February 1972, I was not at all sure what the impact of Mardian's bold position would be on the Court. Reliance upon the integrity of the executive branch had been demanded at other crises in our history by Presidents who wished to sanction a momentary suspension of constitutional rights in time of war. Two of our greatest Presidents had done so. Abraham Lincoln had used this argument to suspend the writ of habeas corpus during the Civil War, and Franklin Roosevelt had used it, with the wartime sanction of the Supreme Court, to justify setting up concentration camps for Japanese-Americans in World War II. Both of these actions eventually aroused considerable disapproval in the courts, but years after the crises had ended and the damage resulting from these policies had been done. The words "integrity of the Executive" invoked by Mardian, coupled with the emotion-charge symbols of "national interest" and "domestic security," might still sway a majority of this Court, particularly if the Nixon appointees, who had sat almost silently through Mardian's argument, supported the administration's assertion of its right, responsibility, and need to exercise this arbitrary power.

So as I walked to the wooden rostrum from which lawyers argue to the Court, I was still filled with deep uncertainty as to what I ought to do. Bill Gossett's opening argument had already laid out, smoothly and effectively, the requirements of the Fourth Amendment and the existing congressional statutes in respect to the necessity for a warrant in our case. For days I had been wrestling with the central question of what the strategy for my own argument should be. Increasingly I had come to believe that only one approach was possible. Legal technicalities, sophisticated distinctions, would be disastrous. The Court must be made to understand the full reality of what the administration was seeking. Nothing else would move them. But this required an open, frank exposition of the real motives behind the case, putting them not only as sharply as possible but in essentially political rather than legal terms. Part of me still held back, even to the last minute, from this approach. Every ounce of formal conventional knowledge of the art of appellate advocacy weighed in the scales on the side of a careful, scholarly, academic, professional argument. But something else within me said no, this was wrong.

This moment was very different in tone and quality from the last time I had appeared before the Court in the final days of the Warren Court, in June 1969, to argue against the exclusion of

Representative Adam Clayton Powell from the House of Representatives. That argument had called for an emphasis on history, on precedent, on legal theory. The Court had to be persuaded that it had the power, the authority, the duty, to intervene in the decisions of Congress. Today's argument, though no less critical, no less difficult, seemed to demand another, less academic approach. It called for a frank statement of reality, an open denunciation of the hidden aims of the administration. There could be no holding back, no professional niceties. But would I have the chance to do this? I had to be prepared for the possibility of answering dozens of hostile questions on technicalities that could derail me.

After I opened the looseleaf binder in which I always sketch out the notes for an argument and spoke the traditional words of opening, "Mr. Chief Justice and members of the Court," I glanced for a moment at the faces of the Justices across the bench. The rostrum for the arguing lawyer in the Court is set up so that the lawyer is only two or three feet from the Justices. This was a very different Court from the one I had last looked at. There were the familiar faces of Justices Brennan, Marshall, Douglas, White, and Stewart, but also the new faces of Powell, Blackmun, and Burger. Would they be cold, hostile, unfriendly? The two faces of Black and Warren were sadly missing. Then, for an instant, I was startled to see only eight Justices—one empty seat—until I remembered that of course Rehnquist was not there, having left the courtroom as soon as our case was called. As the initial formulator of the claim to power that Mardian was demanding and as one of the writers of the government's appellate brief, he could not sit in judgment on his own creation. But in a way I felt his presence as I looked at the new faces across from me.

I know of no experience for a lawyer comparable to arguing before the High Court. For an instant in time you are cut off from the rest of the courtroom—from the rest of the world—standing alone, talking directly to the Justices. The very physical arrangements, the rostrum that places you at eye level with the sitting Justices, adds to this feeling of sudden isolation, along with a strange feeling of intimacy, which is simultaneously overwhelming and equalizing.

I opened with a blunt accusation that "the government has seen

27

fit to use this case as a vehicle for propelling a claim of executive power so ominous in its implications and sweeping in its dimensions that it has transformed this appeal into a case which, as this Court has said, touches the bedrock of our political system." The court was facing "an openly expressed and frank attempt by the Executive to use this case to obtain the imprimature of this Court for a program of domestic espionage and surveillance of political opponents unprecedented in our history." And then I began to spell out the implications of the administration's claim.

Suddenly, I realized with a shock that I had been talking without interruption for almost ten minutes. Something was wrong. A Supreme Court argument is traditionally scattered with interruptions from the bench and always becomes a dialogue. Yet I had gone through ten of my allotted thirty minutes without a question from the Justices. A ghastly thought shot through my mind. Was my approach so out of line that no one was even listening? In an instant of panic, I glanced up and found myself looking directly into the face of Justice White. He seemed to smile slightly, as if he knew what was rushing through my mind, and he nodded imperceptibly. Then I saw his lips move, and he seemed to be saying softly, "Keep going."

Whether he actually did or not I may never know. But when I looked around from Justice to Justice on the bench, I was suddenly at ease. They were all looking intently at me. I said to myself, "All right. Keep going. If they are listening, keep talking." And they were listening. One can always tell when people are listening, whether it is in a classroom, or a mass meeting, or a conference, or a courtroom. There is something in the air, a bond, an electric current. And so I kept talking. For the full thirty minutes.

Then another odd thing happened. The red signal flashed which requires counsel to stop talking, even in the middle of a sentence. But I disregarded it, perhaps not really seeing it, and talked on for five or ten more minutes. And the Chief Justice sat there and let me continue. After I had finished, the awesome nature of being permitted to put the issues steadily and fully without a single interruption began to dawn on me. The eight Justices had sat throughout in silence. After the argument was over, the Clerk of the Court, Michael Rodak, told me that he had never before seen this happen in the Court, a wholly uninterrupted argument.

I have since tried to understand why my argument developed in the way it did. In a curious way, my own predilection for exaggeration in the interest of driving home a point led me unknowingly to an argument which laid bare the real nature of the case. Two weeks before the Supreme Court argument, H. R. Haldeman, the White House chief of staff, had attacked the leadership of the Democratic Party, including Senator George McGovern, for statements critical of the administration's policies in the Vietnam War. He said these leaders were in effect "aiding and abetting the enemy of the United States." It had occurred to me, in going over my notes the night before the argument, that I might be able to illustrate the potential, if totally unlikely, danger in the unlimited power demanded by the Executive by asking, rhetorically, whether the power claimed by the administration might even include warrantless wiretapping of these Democrats. However, I had decided not to use this example; it seemed too farfetched. Such an unlikely and bizarre idea could destroy the argument itself. So it sat there, buried among my notes.

The next day, however, as my argument unfolded and the Justices let me develop all my points and take them where I would, I suddenly decided to use the Haldeman episode as an example, no matter how absurd it might seem, of how far the arbitrary power demanded by the administration might go. I opened with known realities. The power sought by the administration "would legitimize a widespread dragnet of secret surveillance of domestic political opposition," and "already the Attorney General's suspicion falls on leaders of the antiwar movement, Black militants, Catholic activists, pacifists, advocates of youth culture." The danger to the country was that this claim of power could include "anyone who speaks out." To illustrate, I cited "the recent suggestion from high quarters in the executive department that critics of the proposals made by the President of the United States in respect to the Vietnam War . . . are consciously aiding and abetting the enemy of the United States." And then I asked, "Would these critics be included within the scope of this domestic surveillance? They are aiding and abetting the enemy of the United States. You mean their phones can be tapped?"

29

Tap the Democrats? I could almost hear my colleagues at the counsel table muttering under their breath, "There goes Arthur again. He just can't resist fanciful exaggerations." In his rebuttal, Mardian jumped to his feet and indignantly repudiated the inference that the administration might even contemplate such an outrage. He assured the Court that "neither this President nor any prior President, to my knowledge, has authorized electronic surveillance to monitor the activities of an opposite political group." Listening to him, I wondered whether I had overdone it.

What we did not know that morning, of course, was that less than three weeks before, the Attorney General of the United States, in a secret meeting in his office, had in fact "authorized electronic surveillance . . . of an opposite political group," namely the Democratic Party, and that the real response to my outrageously hypothetical question, "You mean their phones can be tapped?" had already been answered affirmatively by the highest representatives of the administration.

Almost three years of scheming, planning, and maneuvering by the administration had come to a head that morning in Washington before the High Court. This was the ultimate move in a game in which, to use Mardian's own words, "the stakes were high." If the Court accepted the administration's position and approved the power to suspend constitutional guarantees—then the perfect cover had been constructed for experimentation with governmental activities which openly violated the constitutional system and were repugnant to the traditions of a free people: break-ins to private homes and offices, kidnapings, wholesale wiretapping of political opponents. All of this would be legal and proper if the administration won this case. Both the secret break-in to a California psychiatrist's office in an attempt to obtain information from his files derogatory to a critic of the Vietnam War, Daniel Ellsberg, and the wiretapping of the headquarters of the Democratic Party in the forthcoming national elections would be protected under the mantle of legality if the claim of inherent power to suspend the provisions of the Fourth Amendment in the interests of domestic security were to be sustained in this case. But much more than this, the secret Huston plan to use wholesale illegal methods to crush any domestic political opposition would be legitimized. Even the hesitations of that past master of covert activity, J. Edgar Hoover, would be put to rest. Finally, if the Fourth Amendment could be suspended here today for one reason, it could as easily be suspended tomorrow or next year to permit midnight raids without warrants all over the country, or roundups of political opponents, or imprisonment without bail or trial. Detention camps could be authorized by presidential decree under a suspension of the Fourth, then the Fifth, then the Sixth Amendment in the sacred name of national security.

Far-fetched? Absurd? Impossible? So seemed my example of potential wiretapping of the Democratic Party that February morning in 1972. But when the revelations of the years to come, resulting from both the Watergate upheavals and the exposure of FBI files, are examined in the context of Mardian's argument that day, they indicate clearly what the Nixon administration was heading toward. Once the cover of legality was established for the suspension of the constitutional guarantees of individual liberty, the road was open, at the sole discretion of the President, to utilize the lists, carefully compiled by the FBI, of hundreds of thousands of citizens who were potential dangers to the establishment. Secret documents even then specified the concentration camps that could be used. No warrants would be required for wholesale roundups of these security dangers, and they could be held, by executive decree, without bail or trial. Fascism would have arrived, in Huey Long's words, "wrapped in an American flag."

It is now absolutely clear that the Nixon administration was seeking this legal cover for experimenting with the abandonment of constitutional government and the substitution of forms of rule which were, in the words of Justice Stewart in *Shuttlesworth v. Birmingham,* a case arising out of efforts by the southern white power structure in the 1960s to destroy by force and terror the rising Black civil rights movement, "the hallmarks of a police state." Attempts of those who rule society to experiment with the substitution of forms of terrorist rule for the more limiting forms of constitutional government historically characterize a period of transition to fascism. History teaches that the nature of the transition to fascism varies greatly, depending on the political, social, cultural, and economic traditions within a particular country.

This transition does not necessarily have to take the form of the classic coup d'état or military seizure of power. The President of the Weimar Republic turned over governmental power to Adolf Hitler in 1933 legally, under the cover of constitutional propriety.

The crafters of the 1972 plan had learned the lessons of history well. They had studied carefully the American tradition and were using it to construct a stamp of legitimacy for the imposition of a rule of lawlessness as sweeping in its potentialities as the regime of a Hitler, a Mussolini, or a Franco. The height of irony, that wry twist which sometimes lurks behind the most frightening events of history, was that the Supreme Court, in its own words the "ultimate guardian of constitutional government," was to be the instrument for creating their stamp of legitimacy. The Court itself was to be maneuvered into sanctioning the abandonment of the constitutional system, As Chief Justice Burger intoned the traditional thanks to the participants at the close of the argument, I thought to myself that Mardian was right—the stakes that afternoon were indeed high.

As the weeks went by, my apprehensions grew. Every Monday, when decisions of the Court were announced, the steady erosion of the former Warren majority continued. Time and again the Court backed away from its strong civil liberties and civil rights positions of the sixties. My hopes, which had been raised during the dramatic turns of the February argument, began to sink. May went by—no decision. Then the first two weeks of June. Finally only two decision days remained, the 19th and the 26th. I was restless, confined to bed since May with a slipped disk, with too much time to think and worry. A bedridden perspective on the outside world is bound to be pessimistic.

On Sunday morning, June 18, a strange article appeared in *The New York Times,* bearing the headline, "5 Charged with Burglary at Democratic Quarters." I read on. The burglars were "five well-dressed men carrying electronic surveillance equipment." Someone was wiretapping the Democratic headquarters—and of course I thought I knew who. I was momentarily overwhelmed by the thought that my seemingly impossible prediction in February was actually coming true, but as the day wore on, all I could think about was that the next morning was another decision day.

At about 11:30 the next morning, I called the Court, as I did every Monday, the familiar knot of anxious anticipation tightening as the call went through. The operator told me that the Clerk of the Supreme Court was on the line. Rodak's voice came on. In measured tones, he said, "Mr. Kinoy, there is a decision today in *United States v. United States District Court.*" I stopped breathing. He continued, "Mr. Justice Powell wrote the decision for the Court." I died. Powell was the Nixon appointee. It was all over. Rodak paused, and I asked haltingly, "Are there any dissents?" He replied firmly, "Justice Powell wrote for the whole Court. No dissents." I could not contain myself and almost screamed into the phone, "Not even Justice Douglas?" And then he laughed as he said, "You don't understand, Mr. Kinoy. You won. It's a unanimous decision. You won."

It was almost impossible to believe. The whole Court, except Rehnquist of course. Even Nixon's Chief Justice. It took days to sort through the implications of this extraordinary event. There was the immediate pleasure of sharing the joy of victory with Bill Bender, Linda Huber, Bill Gossett, and the defendants. But there were also the more sober and reflective moments of recognizing that something profoundly important in the life of the country had occurred. A *New York Times* editorial suggested this the next morning when it observed, "The Supreme Court has delivered a sharp rebuke to those ideologues of the executive branch who consider the President's 'inherent powers' superior to the Constitution." The unanimity of the decision, according to the *Times,* emphasized the sharpness of the rebuff that the Court had administered to the Nixon administration: "The Supreme Court, ignoring the usual division between 'liberal' and 'conservative,' has now reminded the Government that it is just because its powers are so awesome that their exercise cannot be left to the discretion of men without precise restraint of law, under the Constitution."

The careful scheme to use the Court to legitimize the suspension of constitutional forms had run into a barrier which the conspirators had not counted on: the Court itself. In upholding the Fourth Amendment and striking down the policy of warrantless wiretapping in the name of domestic security, Justice Powell wrote for the Court: "History abundantly documents the tendency of Government—however benevolent and benign its motives—to view with suspicion those who most fervently dispute its policies. Fourth Amendment protections become the more necessary when the targets of official surveillance may be those suspected of unorthodoxy in their political beliefs. The danger to political dissent is acute where the Government attempts to act under so vague a concept as the power to protect 'domestic security' . . . The price of lawful public dissent must not be a dread of subjection to an unchecked surveillance power. Nor must the fear of unauthorized official eavesdropping deter vigorous citizen dissent and discussion of Government action in private conversation. For private dissent, no less than open public discourse, is essential to our free society." This was Powell, not Douglas or Brennan or Marshall.

This decision was a disaster for the administration, the full impact of which was not felt until Nixon's resignation. Nixon, Mitchell, Mardian, Rehnquist, and Kleindienst, a clever and resourceful band of lawyers, had designed a plan which would have legalized everything, including not only the Watergate bugging and the break-in at the office of Daniel Ellsberg's psychiatrist, but also the full sweep of the Huston plan of operations. All of the covert activities already engaged in, and those still on the drawing boards, would have been "lawful" and "proper" if the Court had adopted the theory advanced by Mardian that morning in February. What tripped them up was their inability to perceive that their claim of unlimited inherent power to suspend, if not ignore, the Constitution threatened the existence of the Supreme Court itself. In the earliest days of the Court's history, Chief Justice John Marshall, the conservative Federalist, had fashioned the Court's power to stand against the Jefferson-controlled executive branch and Congress through his skillful use of the concept that the Court, and the Court alone, was the "ultimate interpreter," the "guardian," and the "enforcer" of the written Constitution. This was the source of the Court's power over the other branches of government, which was to be used often throughout history to protect the interests of the rich and mighty against abolitionist, populist, or other radical challenges. But now this source of institutional power of the Court itself was severely threatened by the administration's demand for the unrestrained right to suspend and ignore the written Constitution. The recognition that the special prerogatives and influences of the Court itself were at stake had dominated the February proceedings, and it had eventually united the conservatives Powell and Blackmun with the liberals Marshall, Brennan, and Douglas, and had probably won over the pivotal swing Justices. It had even forced the Chief Justice to "concur in the result," as uncomfortable as that must have been to the administration's chief representative on the Court. Thus the elaborately contrived cover for the plans to experiment with massive illegality was blown apart by the very agency selected to create the cover. Nixon and his staff, speaking for the most conservative forces in American society, had stubbed their toes on the institution fashioned by one of the first and most effective conservatives in American history, Chief Justice John Marshall.

The Court's decision that Monday morning left the administration in total disarray. If the case had gone the other way on June 19, the wiretapping of the Democratic National Committee would have been "legal" and "proper," and could have been openly acknowledged as "authorized by the Attorney General" on behalf of the President. Now there was no longer any available legal cover for the accidentally disclosed operation at the Democratic National Committee headquarters. The actual authorization of the Attorney General and, through him, the President, which could have been the saving justification if the decision had gone the other way, was suddenly turned into its opposite, and the authorization had to be hidden at all costs. The conspirators were not prepared for this turn of events. They had expected a totally different result. Consequently, in haste and panic, files had to be deep-sixed or cleaned out, and the silence of wiretappers had to be bought. In place of the Supreme Court cover, this new, difficult, and ultimately disastrous "cover" of denial was the only alternative. The one thing which up until the June 19th decision it had been essential to show—presidential authority for the covert acts in violation of the Constitution—afterward became the one thing which had to be hidden at all costs.

One aspect of those June days continues to haunt me—the

strange coincidence of events, which has never been explored, of the Watergate break-in on Saturday evening, followed by the Court decision on Monday morning. There are puzzling, unresolved questions about the Saturday break-in. For example, why did it occur at all? The bugs and microphones had been installed successfully on May 28. On June 16 the break-in team of Bernard Barker, Eugenio Martinez, Frank Sturgis, and Virgilio Gonzalez had been recalled from Miami, where they were engaged in other secret operations, to Washington, where they were met by James McCord, a former CIA official and currently a security consultant for both the Republican National Committee and the Committee for the Re-Election of the President; G. Gordon Liddy, a White House aide; and E. Howard Hunt, formerly a high official in the CIA. Why did they go back into the Democratic National Committee office at the Watergate the next morning? The only explanation ever publicly offered has been that one of the bugs was faulty. But why did five men have to go in to make a repair that could have been done by one? Further, why was this risky adventure carried out at all in light of the known imminence of the Supreme Court decision which would affect so intimately the planned legal cover for the covert operation? Even to the police on the scene the whole affair was strange. One officer in charge of the initial investigation told a reporter that the operation was "bungled too badly" and there seemed to be "three or four more" people there than the operation called for. And finally, why, when the men were arrested on the scene, were they found with *all* of the electronic equipment removed from the ceiling and in their hands, instead of just the one tap that was allegedly not working?

No one has ever explained this incredible aspect of the June 17 break-in. Only one explanation seems to me to make sense out of the whole situation. The Supreme Court case was the culmination, the apex, of the carefully constructed cover of legality. If the case had been won and the Watergate wiretapping was later accidentally exposed, the Attorney General, acting for the President, could openly acknowledge his authorization, and the entire affair would be covered with the mantle of legality. But if the case had been lost, and the wiretapping was subsequently exposed or discovered, there would be no explanation at all available to the administration. Suppose, therefore, the following sequence of events occurred. Suppose that sometime prior to the Watergate break-in, someone in a high position of responsibility, privy to the secret meetings at which the Watergate wiretapping operation was discussed and finally authorized, heard in some way that the decision in the Supreme Court case had gone the other way—the wrong way—against the administration? Suppose this person, in panic and concern because the cover of legality was about to be blown, told whoever was in charge of the Watergate operation to get in there and clean it out, remove everything from the Democratic headquarters fast, *before* Monday, the day on which the decision was coming down. The whole team would then be needed for a swift, total removal job. Suppose they went into the Watergate late that evening to clean it out, only to be caught in the act. Absurd? Ridiculous? Impossible? Perhaps. But no more absurd than the hypothetical question I blurted out in the excesses of oral argument on February 24: would the administration be able to tap the phones of the Democrats, its political opponents? This is the only explanation for the break-in that makes any sense. There is no other conceivable reason for the use of the entire team, and for the fact that they were discovered by the police holding all of the electronic equipment in their hands, not just one faulty tap.

Nothing is supposed to be more sacred than the secrecy of the process of decisionmaking in the Supreme Court. Decisions in pending cases are carefully guarded from premature disclosure. No one is informed of the decision in a case until the actual reading of the opinion in open court. Only the Justices themselves, their clerks, and essential court technical personnel are ever supposed to be aware of a decision prior to the public announcement. However, on rare occasions throughout history there have been leaks of information from the High Court as to impending decisions. The most startling instance was the leaking of the first draft of the 1857 Dred Scott opinion to President James Buchanan, which changed the course of history. He exerted pressure on the Court to shift that tentative decision, which was restricted to deciding the case on narrow technical grounds, to a sweeping decision totally favorable to the slaveholding powers, providing a full constitutional rationale for the institution of slavery itself.

Whether the White House conspirators got news of the impending wiretap decision may never be known. Whether someone within the institution of the Court, privy to the decision, informed them, or whether the chambers of the Court itself were bugged, as Justice Douglas himself charged during his last years on the bench, may remain one of those haunting, unanswered questions of history. And whether the never explained eighteen-minute erasure of the confidential Nixon tapes of that Monday morning involved an explanation to the President of the real reasons for Saturday night's break-in, and its relation to Monday morning's Supreme Court decision, may also never be known. But one fact emerges sharp and clear beyond dispute. The conspiracy that was involved in the strange events of those June days was not a relatively simple conspiracy to "obstruct justice" or to "cover up" White House involvement or to buy an election through corruption and bribery. What was fundamentally involved was a conspiracy to move away from American constitutional government. It was a conspiracy which had at its heart the creation of a legal sanction for experimentation with a brand of fascism to be clearly marked "Made in America, 100 per cent pure," based on the theory designed by Rehnquist that there is inherent power in the President to suspend the Constitution.

That the American public has little understanding that this was the real, the underlying Watergate conspiracy is a sobering thought. The deadly thrust of the administration's plan has been lost sight of amid a welter of irrelevant controversies concerning Nixon's specific responsibility for this or that surreptitious blackmail payment or his refusal to hand over this or that tape recording. Buried beneath the shocking admissions of corruption and obstruction of justice lies the irrefutable evidence of his participation, with his closest associates, in a nearly successful plan to experiment with the betrayal of constitutional government. This was a conspiracy more dangerous to the future of the Republic than any event since the firing on Fort Sumter by the southern slaveholding power more than a hundred years ago.

David Scribner (left) and James Matles of the UE at congressional committee hearing in the 1950s.

James Matles (left) and Julius Emspak at union meeting in the 1950s.

A moment after the federal judge found James Matles not guilty of contempt of Congress, 1952. Front row from left: Arthur Kinoy, Matles, Dave Scribner, Alan Rosenberg (Boston attorney). Rest of group are UE members and organizers.

Protesting wife of blacklisted UE shop steward after being shoved back into her seat by U.S. marshal (right) at GE-McCarthy committee hearing in Albany, New York, February 1954.

*James Matles (right) blocked from entering union membership meeting
during raid on Schnectady UE local, 1954.*

James Matles' denaturalization hearings at federal district court in Brooklyn, New York, February 1957. From left: Matles, Sam Gruber, Frank Donner, Albert Fitzgerald, and two UE members.

2

Education for a People's Lawyer

As I put down the telephone that June morning in 1972 and the words echoed through my head, "You won, Mr. Kinoy, you won," one thought emerged through the general wave of exultation. "You were wrong, Arthur," I heard myself saying, "dead wrong that morning in February when you walked to the Supreme Court feeling small and helpless in the coming confrontation with all the strength and power of Nixon, Mitchell, Mardian, Rehnquist, and the governmental machinery they controlled. No, you were not alone. You rose before the Court that day as a representative of one of the proudest traditions of the American bar."

In this country, I reminded myself, from the earliest revolutionary days and through all the tides of our history, one section of the profession has always chosen to identify with the people rather than with the entrenched power of aristocracy, wealth, and privilege, using their skills and talents to help in the struggle of workers against their employers, the poor against the rich, Black and other oppressed people against the white power structure. The long history of the people's lawyer runs from colonial lawyers like James Otis, who before the King's judges fought the hated writs of assistance which allowed the soldiers of the King to break into homes of the colonists and ransack their possessions, and Sam

Adams, who helped to organize the Sons of Liberty, the first American revolutionary organization dedicated to the overthrow of imperial rule, to nineteenth century lawyers like Wendell Phillips and Charles Sumner, who placed their abilities at the service of those men and women, Black and white, who dared to stand up against the southern slave power that dominated every institution of national life. Then there were lawyers like Clarence Darrow, who left a lucrative practice to defend the rights and liberties of labor organizers and working people, and Carol King and Harry Sacher, who in the thirties and forties threw themselves into the legal conflicts arising from the upsurge of unionization that was sweeping the nation. I found strength in the recognition that all of them had discovered their own ways of merging a mastery of legal skills, techniques, and concepts with the movements of popular struggle. No, I said to myself that happy morning of victory, the lawyer who stands up against the power of the establishment is not alone, even within a profession so traditionally controlled by the industrial and financial power structure.

My own life as a people's lawyer began in a very strange way, on a walk around the reservoir in Central Park in New York City in the spring of 1945. It was a walk I shall never forget. I had just been discharged from the Army, after three years of combat duty in Africa and Italy in a chemical mortar batallion attached to the infantry, when I heard from an old friend, Leo Marx. He had gone through Harvard College with me in the late 1930s and had also just been discharged from military service. We had not seen each other or been in touch during the war years, although we had been very close as undergraduates. So when we met for the first time since leaving college and decided to take a walk around the park reservoir, each of us opened up to the other about what we had decided to do with our lives now that the war was behind us.

I described to Leo Marx how immediately after my discharge, I had gone back up to Cambridge to visit old friends. I had spent a good deal of time with two members of the faculty who were most influential in shaping our thinking during our undergraduate years, F. O. Matthiessen, whom we all knew as "Matty," and Perry Miller. Both were revered figures to us undergraduates working in their field of American history and literature. And both had suggested to me the possibility of becoming what was called at Harvard a junior fellow. This position, much prized and sought after by graduate students, was offered by the university only to those few young people who were expected to become members of the faculty at either Harvard itself or one of the other top universities in the country. It was the road to formal academic scholarship on the highest level.

Both professors pressed me to accept the offer, although Perry Miller took the initiative in the discussion. Matty supported his position but remained unusually quiet and reserved, and in the years that followed I often wondered whether he had already begun to feel the deep depression which, coupled with the pressures of the Cold War, led him five years later to that terrible moment of suicide after having been subpoenaed before the House Un-American Activities Committee. In putting forth their case, Perry Miller talked about the senior honors thesis I had written in 1941 on George Ripley, the founder of Brook Farm and one of the first American utopian socialists. He called it an "exciting and creative" piece of work. Then he paused and said sharply that it was "unfinished." He repeated the word, "unfinished." I had a responsibility, he argued, to complete this creative academic research, and the position of junior fellow would give me that opportunity.

I told Leo Marx that I had argued as strongly as I could with Professor Miller, protesting that since college I had changed a great deal. Particularly after my intense experiences in the war, in the landings at Salerno and the Anzio beachhead, I had a growing feeling that the theoretical, intellectual, conceptual world of academia was not the real world of struggle, toward which everything within me had always tugged. Perry Miller was familiar with this pull within me; it had showed up clearly in my activities in the radical student movement at college. In my junior year I had been elected the secretary of the John Reed Society, that group of Harvard students who had banded together during the 1930s in an attempt to recreate the symbol John Reed had become to the entire world after his account of the Russian revolution, *Ten Days That Shook the World.* John Reed, the only graduate of Harvard to be buried in the wall of the Kremlin with revolutionary leaders from all over the world, was the symbol of a different Harvard, one that could break from the class elitism of the Boston financial aristocracy and identify itself with working people rising in revolt. Perry Miller reminded me of the impact on the whole university when in 1939 we in the John Reed Society decided to "go public," to "come out of the closet" and be open students of Marxism within the university world. Up to this point the organization had kept a relatively low profile and was not officially registered with the university as a recognized student organization. It had shaken the aristocratic structure from top to bottom when we proclaimed, sometimes in strident tones, the necessity of breaking from the intellectual mold of an upper-class institution and searching for ways to put student abilities, talents, and skills at the service of oppressed and struggling peoples.

Once again Perry Miller made clear to me, as he had in my undergraduate years, that intellectually he did not necessarily agree with the philosophical theories we had then been exploring concerning the relationship between an analysis based upon Marxist principles of scientific socialism and the study of American history and literature. But he also made it clear, as he had always done in earlier days, that he fully respected my explorations in that direction. Then he spoke the words that catalyzed my decision to return to Cambridge and follow the academic road: "Accept the fact that the contributions one can make within the world of the intellect, the world of conceptions, are important. Accept the fact that this ought to be your role, and recognize that we within the academic institution, controlled by those who rule society, need rebels inside that world. That's your role. Accept it."

As I later told Leo Marx on the walk in Central Park, that did it. Professor Miller's analysis of a useful, social, even a radical, role within the academic world put it all together for me. In addition, many other factors pulled me in the same direction. This was quite a piece of business for a Jewish youngster from Brooklyn to be offered Harvard's elite status, and in a way the oldest influences of my childhood were pushing me to accept. All my grandparents were working class people. My grandfather on my

42

mother's side was a shoemaker. My grandfather on my father's side was a tinsmith. Both of my grandmothers had raised families of twelve or thirteen children in the New York Jewish ghetto in the lower East Side. And from my grandparents flowed a powerful drive which had shaped my parents and which in turn shaped me as a child growing up in Brooklyn. This was the drive, which an oppressed people develop out of centuries of discrimination and exclusion, to grab and use the tools of knowledge and learning that are normally controlled by the rulers of society. So from my grandparents, rooted in the traditions of the Jewish past, came an insistent message that to understand knowledge, science, and culture is, in and of itself, an essential way out of oppression.

To my grandparents, the fact that my mother and father went to college was an incredible achievement. When my parents both became teachers, nothing more noble and honorable in my grandparents' view could happen. Of course, there was the irony that all my uncles on both sides, mainly small businessmen, made so much more money than my parents, who were "only" schoolteachers. But all that suddenly shifted one day in October 1929 when my parents came home and said in shocked tones, "They're jumping out of the buildings on Wall Street." When the Depression hit, my father and mother started supporting everyone else in the family because only schoolteachers were getting paid.

And so a feeling of exultation overcame us all— my grandparents, my mother and father, and myself—when the unbelievable happened, and I was accepted as a student at the college attended by America's aristocracy. I can remember the pride in my grandparents' eyes when my parents took me to their home in the East Bronx to tell them the astounding news: their grandson had been admitted to Harvard. This pride was born out of both a striving to achieve knowledge, to use it, as my grandfather said, "for the people," and a need to achieve protected status within existing society and, in so doing, to show "them," the upper crust, that a Jewish boy from Brooklyn could do as well as New England aristocrats.

Leo Marx laughingly reminded me that it was probably this underlying anger and desire to "show them" that had led me to do the strange thing at Harvard which my closest friends in the radical student movement always found difficult to understand. It all started during my freshman year, at the same time as I was moving toward radical activism in the John Reed Society, the American Student Union, which was involved in building an antiwar and antifascist movement throughout the colleges, and the Young Communist League, which was then the center of most student radical activity. In the midst of all this swirling activity the other drive, to "show them," to fit in, asserted itself. I was sitting in my room in Matthews Hall, a freshman dormitory, when there was a knock at the door. An older man stood in the hall with two students. I could tell at once that the students were from the eating clubs, Harvard's high society, the private sanctuary of the aristocrats. What in the world were they doing coming to see me? Then the older man introduced himself. He was Tim Bolles, coach of the Harvard crew. When I caught one of the other names, I almost gasped. It was J. P. Morgan II. Then Bolles said, "How would you like to try out for crew?"

"This must be some gag," I thought to myself. I was all of five feet four. My entire life I had struggled with the fact that I was too small and never any good at athletics. All I could ever do in high school athletics was to manage the teams. Sure, I could "manage" things, but I could never go out for the teams. "I can't, I'm too small," I told them. They smiled and replied, "We looked up the records. You're the smallest and lightest member of the class. We need you as coxswain." When I asked, "What's that?" they really laughed. "Come down tomorrow and we'll show you."

The next day I went down to the boathouse, looked around, and started to leave. I did not belong there, with all of the elite from Groton, Exeter, and Andover. There was not a Jewish student in sight, and certainly not a Black. As I turned away, Bolles came over to me and started to describe what was happening in a racing shell that lay in the water. It had eight rowers, and there at the back sat a little person who not only steered, he explained, but "ran the race." That hooked me, and I agreed to try. The "cox," as they called us, had to run the show. We coxes figured everything out. We worked out the strategy. We analyzed the weak points of the individual crew members and studied their psychology, so as to know when to yell at the rowers to goad them on.

44

So there was I, the little Jewish youngster from Brooklyn, yelling at America's elite, telling them off, running the show. Then, after a practice row down the Charles River, I would leave the Morgans, the Peabodys, and the Eliots behind in the boathouse and rush up to Harvard Square to meet my friends in the office of the Student Union, where we would grab the leaflets about the next antiwar rally and start handing them out on the street. If I happened to hand a radical leaflet to one of the crew members walking up the street, he would stare strangely at his coxswain and walk on. Right there all of the inner conflicts that my background had set in motion were tied together in one complicated knot in Harvard Square.

These contending pressures had come to a head in dealing with my decision whether to accept the position of junior fellow and all it meant for my future. Now, walking around the reservoir with Leo Marx, I told him firmly that I had decided to accept the junior fellowship and head straight for the life of scholarship, teaching, and research in American history. To finish the book on George Ripley, I assured him, as Perry Miller had persuaded me, would be a contribution in and of itself to the advancement of the struggle. To dig into the roots of a socialist tradition in American history, which was where the study of Ripley would lead, was not merely an academic exercise but an important part of the present social movement.

When I finished, Leo Marx opened up to me. He had decided not to go back to Harvard and enter the academic world. His experiences in the war had convinced him that, if there was to be an end to the horror, misery, and brutality in the way human beings treated each other in modern society, if there was to be an end to the experiences of death and slaughter we had both gone through, "some of us," as he put it, "are going to have to be much more active in our lives. We don't have the luxury of living in the academic world, of quietly solving intellectual and academic problems, as important as they are." He turned my arguments upside down. As persons committed to activism and the social struggle, we had a responsibility, he felt, to use the skills and talents we had been trained to develop in a far more active arena than academia. He planned on going to law school. By becoming a lawyer, he believed, he could reconcile this conflict within the world of social action. As a lawyer, he could use the skills and techniques of intellectual perception directly in the daily struggle of the people.

I was stunned. We debated and argued for more than two hours as we walked around the reservoir. I used every argument I could think of to justify my decision to go back to Harvard and follow the path of academic studies. He used every argument he could think of to justify his decision not to return to Harvard but to go to law school to train himself for the active life.

Then an incredible thing happened. Leo Marx and I, to this day, look back on that episode with amazement. By the time we left Central Park that afternoon, he had persuaded me, and I had persuaded him. The walk around the reservoir had led me to the decision to turn down the junior fellowship and head for law school. The same long path had led Leo Marx to turn away from law school and head back to the academic world. He called up Professors Miller and Matthiessen and returned to Cambridge. It took me a few days to clear my head, after which I took the subway up to 125th Street and registered for the next semester of the wartime-accelerated program at Columbia Law School. Today Leo Marx is one of the most creative teachers and students of American history and literature in the country. And I am a people's lawyer.

Law school whirled by in two years by virtue of the wartime acceleration. The necessity of condensing the normal three years into two hardly left a moment to breathe, much less to think through the implications of that choice in Central Park to utilize the skills of the lawyer in the struggle for social justice. There was just barely enough time to begin to grasp the full dimensions of the law's conceptual sweep, thrown at us with such rapidity by the outstanding teachers of law gathered at Columbia in those days—such teachers as Richard Powell, Elliot Cheatham, Jerome Michaels, Walter Gellhorn, Richard Dowling, Paul Hays, and Herbert Wechsler. But I quickly discovered that, with notable exceptions, this faculty could not be expected to give any specific guidance in fulfilling my own fundamental need to learn how to use the skill and knowledge of the profession to advance the aims of social movements. Within the four walls of Columbia Law School, one of the leading centers in the country for the training of establishment lawyers, this question was not to be answered directly.

But what the school did offer was invaluable. Through exposure to the thinking of its brilliant teachers of law, I obtained one fundamental insight which was to serve me in good stead in the years to follow, and which became my basic tool in fashioning legal concepts into weapons of struggle with the establishment. This was the realization that flowed from the in-depth analysis of teachers like Richard Powell, who constantly stressed that all concepts of law are in a constant process of growth, development, and change, that nothing in law is written in stone, including, he pointed out with a wry smile, even the Ten Commandments. The art of the lawyer is to understand these dynamics. By comprehending the processes by which legal ideas are shaped and changed, the lawyer can play an active rather than passive role in fashioning and shaping these concepts. From Richard Powell, Elliot Cheatham, Jerome Michaels, and Walter Gellhorn, despite differences in their social perspectives, came this important insight into the fundamental role of the lawyer. It departed from the widely accepted view which was expounded to the general public by the establishment and by the bar itself, that the lawyer is a skilled technician who merely invokes the inflexible principles of an immutable legal structure.

A recognition that the lawyer is in reality an activist, shaping the ideas and concepts of bodies of existing law to serve the needs of the forces that the lawyer represents, was the most valuable lesson to emerge from my years at Columbia. It led me to ask a fundamental question. If skilled lawyers for the corporations and for the government understand this fact and function this way in the interests of their establishment clients, why cannot lawyers for the people also fashion legal concepts into weapons of struggle to meet the needs of their clients? This question was to live with me for years, and the answer to it was forged in the reality of experience, not in the relative isolation of the classroom or the law library.

The more pressing question at that time, however, was what to do after graduation. Where was I to plunge into what appeared to be the real classroom, practical work itself? During my last year at law school I discussed this subject with several members of the faculty with whom I was fairly close. The same conflict that had emerged so sharply in my walk around the reservoir with Leo Marx continued to haunt me. When Elliot Cheatham, an outstanding teacher and scholar in the area of conflict of laws, called me into his office shortly before the end of my last semester, my heart sank as he told me excitedly about potential teaching appointments that he had worked out for me at three schools around the country. At once I understood what he was really saying. The three schools he mentioned were among those referred to at the time in baseball lingo as the minor leagues, in which one "prepped" for the major leagues—Columbia, Harvard, or Yale, the big three among law schools.

Professor Cheatham was paying me a great compliment, but I knew what I had to do. I blurted out in embarrassment, "It's not for me." The expression on his face suddenly changed, and he asked incredulously, "What in the world do you mean?" Here he had opened up entry for me into the highest, most sought-after level in the world of legal scholarship, and I had bluntly turned him down.

The discussion that followed was troubled. My position, that I was not yet ready to teach law because one could not teach without a background of years of experience in the reality of practice, touched a raw nerve. Somewhat upset, Professor Cheatham attempted to justify the traditional barrier that existed at that time between the teaching and the practice of law in every major American law school. Finally, though, he accepted the fact that I saw it differently and that the legal academic road was simply not for me at that point. Not until many years later was I willing even to consider the academic path, and then under vastly different circumstances. As I summed it up to Professor Cheatham, "I have got to be in active struggle. I've got to be in active life. I'm not ready to teach." The path around the reservoir was still clear.

The necessity of finding an answer to the basic question of whether this dream of using the skills of the lawyer against the oppression of the system had any reality was momentarily postponed when, through channels of the school administration, I was asked whether I would be interested in a one-year appointment as law clerk to one of the most respected liberal members of the Supreme Court, Justice Wiley Rutledge. This I was excited about. The experience of functioning at the highest level of the legal system would give me insights into the shaping of legal concepts that might prove invaluable in the future. The proposal was both exciting and flattering. So I said yes, and the proposal was made to the Justice by the school. There was tentative agreement, subject to an interview in Washington. But fate intervened with a heavy hand when the sad news came in that Justice Rutledge had died.

I was back to the basic question. As I studied for the New York bar exams, scheduled for a few weeks after graduation, I explored the possibility of some sort of job with lawyers involved in representing labor unions. But before I could move in that direction, certain grim considerations stopped me dead. It was the summer of 1947. Political changes had begun to develop within the country, and we were feeling the first icy winds of the Cold War. The House Un-American Activities Committee had opened up a broadside attack on progressive writers and actors in Hollywood, in the first move toward blacklisting these individuals, and President Harry Truman by executive order had set in motion a gigantic witchhunt and purge of radicals of any complexion throughout the federal government.

These were ominous signs. I began to hear stories that the character committee of the New York Bar Association was suddenly holding up applicants for membership who had any sort of radical background. This caused me considerable concern. My record as an activist and radical at college was fully public, and I was in no mood to hide it or deny it, even if that had been possible. I began to fear that I would have to spend the next ten years fighting the Bar Association for the right to be a lawyer instead of functioning as a lawyer in the interests of the fighting people.

Then a friend who had recently gone through the ritual of bar admission gave me some hope. It appeared, he said, that if an applicant were working for a "respectable" Wall Street law firm at the time of application, and if one of that person's supporting affidavits came from the firm, the committee would take a more flexible view toward a radical student background. The Cold War had not yet completely rigidified the admissions procedure; the hysteria against radicals had not yet reached the full force it would in years to come. An audacious thought occurred to me. Why not immediately get a job with such a firm? Then, assuming the character committee did not hold up my application, I could consider my long-range plans after admission to the bar.

Everything fell into place. After the grueling experience of taking the bar exams, I was offered a position as an "associate," the polite professional term for a beginning clerk, with an eminent Wall Street law firm. To my surprise, the firm sent me down to Washington to work in their branch office as an assistant to a new senior partner who had just come out of the administration. Working with Frank Shea was in actuality a fascinating experience for me, far beyond the necessity of waiting out the processes of the character committee. It allowed me to see at first hand the close interrelationship between the top governmental bureaucracy and the large corporate law firms. Shea, for example, having once been Assistant Secretary of the Interior, where the utilization of the power of eminent domain was a prime responsibility, was an expert in the legal process of setting prices for land the government took over for its own use. This ability was made to order for a law firm whose major corporate clients were involved in suits to increase the prices to be paid for land taken over from them by the government. Who could do this better than a former Assistant Secretary of the Interior? What was more natural than this sudden shift in roles from a condemnation expert for the government to a condemnation expert for the corporations? Even to my young and inexperienced eyes it was clear that Shea was making millions for the firm's clients in fighting the awards of a department he had only recently administered. Over lunch, he explained to me that this was simply the way it was everywhere: there was a constant exchange back and forth between high administrative and policymaking officers in the government and personnel of the major Wall Street law firms. "It's good for everyone," he pointed out.

The work with Shea, which brought me into a world I had

never dreamed I would be so close to, lasted all of three months. Shortly after I received the letter solemnly informing me that I had been admitted to membership in the Bar of the State of New York, a call from New York City threw me right back to where I had stood at the end of the long path around the reservoir two years before. The call was from Seymour ("Sy") Linfield, a young lawyer for whom I had done research while at Columbia. He was assistant general counsel to the United Electrical, Radio and Machine Workers of America, then one of the largest industrial trade unions in the country. He asked me whether I would be interested in a job with the UE working with him and David Scribner, the general counsel. This was one of the shortest phone conversations I have ever had. My answer consisted of one word: "Yes." Linfield laughed and asked if I would not like to know the salary. I recovered enough to get into such details, and also to find out that they wanted me to start the next week.

Walking into Shea's office, I wondered how to tell him that I was leaving a top firm, with its prospects of partnerships, high salaries, and everything else, to go to work for a labor union which was engaged at that moment in bitter fights with some of the firm's most important clients. As a matter of fact, after I broke the news to Shea, he pointed out to me with a smile that the firm was representing General Electric in a number of battles then going on with UE, the union that had organized most of the General Electric plants throughout the country.

When I started to explain that I had to be on the other side of the fence in those fights, he interrupted and, again with his friendly smile, said: "I'll make a confession. I didn't think that you were going to last here anyway. Your life would have been miserable here. Call it an experience." And as he shook my hand, he said, "Maybe we'll meet across the fence."

I left his office thinking much about his words. Shea was a very human person, and I have often had occasion to remember him in the course of bitter struggles with corporate lawyers. To forget that they too are human beings, subject to all of the weaknesses and strengths of human beings, is to lose sight of a fact that may be helpful in the struggles that must be conducted. No one, not even one's opponent, is a one-dimensional caricature of evil or good. And sometimes, as that day in Washington twenty-five years later was to prove, a corporate lawyer like Bill Gossett may, if only for a moment, be on your side.

Back in New York, I was ready for my first day of work at my second job. The office of the UE was then, as it is now, on Fifty-first Street between Fifth and Madison Avenues. My first impression of the building was total disbelief. *This* was the headquarters of the third largest union of industrial workers in the Congress of Industrial Organizations? It was an elegant, five-story building with a mid-nineteenth century aristocratic flavor, and it was once the Vanderbilt mansion. When I later asked a UE organizer about the building, the half-cynical, half-honest response, which I was to hear from so many members of the labor movement in so many different situations in the future, was, "Nothing's too good for the working class." Slightly overawed by the mirrored foyer and the marble steps sweeping up to the second floor, much grander than the Wall Street law office I had just left, I made my way up to the fifth floor office of David Scribner to report for work.

It was quite an introduction to the active practice of law. I, like so many of us who had grown up in the student radical movement of the thirties, had of course heard a great deal about David Scribner. He had a reputation for being one of the most brilliant lawyers in the labor movement. As I walked into his office that morning, I wondered how in the world I—four months out of law school and barely admitted to the bar—could be of any help here. The question was answered rapidly. After the briefest possible conventional greeting, Scribner leaned over the desk, picked up an envelope, and handed it to me. "Here are the train tickets," he said. I stared at him. "Train tickets? What train tickets? What for?" He shot back, "Oh, didn't Sy reach you last night to tell you? You've got reservations here for the sleeper for tonight. You're going out to Cleveland. There's a hearing before a hearing officer of the National Labor Relations Board, and you're going to handle it tomorrow."

I was thunderstruck. I felt as though I was stammering when I said, "What do you mean, handle a hearing? I've never been in a courtroom before. I don't know what to do. I can't possibly do it."

He looked at me across his desk for a moment, then smiled and said, "Look, I've got a theory about learning, about education, about how you learn to be a lawyer." As he paused, I sighed to myself, expecting to hear another of those philosophical renditions about legal education one gets so used to at law school. He continued, "Yes, I've got a real theory about learning how to be a lawyer. Go do it."

Actually what was happening was pretty much due to the force of circumstances. The UE was intensely involved in the first major round of national and local strikes that had broken out in the electrical industry after the end of World War II, demanding wage increases and improvements in working conditions. As a result, hundreds of legal proceedings of the most varied nature, arising from the efforts of the companies to break the strikes, were taking place all over the country, and Scribner and Linfield desperately needed another body, another lawyer, to help cover the exploding situation. Neither of them had any time to take me by the hand and patiently teach me the practice of labor law. The pressures of the situation, combined with Dave Scribner's deep, instinctive confidence in people's ability to learn from experience, set up what developed into, for me, an extraordinary training school. Within a year I had been thrown into every conceivable form of legal struggle: administrative proceedings like the one I was heading to on my first day of work, courtroom battles from criminal courts to appellate arguments, arbitrations, grievance negotiations. And although I generally worked alone as a lawyer, I was never alone in the most fundamental sense of the word. The teaching was constant and steady—from the union organizers, from the people in the shops, from Dave Scribner, Sy Linfield, and the national union staff. It was during this learning experience that the seeds were sown of that approach to law teaching which, years later, I would experiment with in the first legal clinics in the country at Rutgers Law School. These clinics would challenge head-on the centuries-old separation between theory and practice in legal education—the very issue that Professor Cheatham and I had discussed so intensely just before I graduated from Columbia.

In this sense Dave Scribner was one of the finest teachers of law

I have ever met. That first day in his office, after telling me simply, "do it," he gave me a transcript of an NLRB hearing he had handled a few weeks before and told me to skim through it on the train and pick up the flavor of what a hearing was like. Then he gave me the most important guidance of all. "Listen closely," he said, "to the people in the shop. They will fill you in and tell you what they need out of the hearing."

I stewed most of the night on the train to Cleveland, reading and rereading the transcript. More than anything else, I dreaded the prospect of sitting alone, the only lawyer in the courtroom during the company's presentation of evidence, and not being able to identify in time the theoretical grounds for objecting to testimony going into the record that I sensed was harmful to the union's case. At Columbia I had been very impressed by Professor Jerome Michael's course on the esoteric philosophical underpinnings of the law of evidence. What panicked me now was the realization that I would not have hours and hours patiently to uncover the philosophical roots of each sentence of testimony, so as to determine the basis for a legal objection, but would have to decide the grounds for objection on the spot.

Suddenly I hit upon a bold plan. I would pull six or seven of Dave Scribner's most convincing objections out of the transcript, write down their key words on a little piece of paper, hold it tight in my hand, and then, as evidence was introduced that my gut told me was damaging, look down at the slip and pick out the objection which best fit the bill. This was not exactly an intellectually sound solution for the underlying theoretical problems in the law of evidence, but it proved to be a wonderful security blanket. I have often thought how startled Professor Michael would have been had he known how one of his top students planned to face his first test on the law of evidence in the real world. At least I was able to sleep a little as the train headed for Cleveland.

When I was met at the station by the UE field representative, I received the happy news that the hearing had been put off until the next morning. Twenty-four more hours to figure out what to do. In those hours I began to learn a critical lesson for a people's lawyer. The most important preparation is not the careful analysis of the argument of the opposition, as necessary as that is. What is decisive in preparation is knowing your own people and, out of your relationship with them, coming to understand their thinking, their analysis of the problems facing them, and their perception of the solution, of what must be done.

That morning in Cleveland, as I sat in the local union headquarters with the UE staff representative and three or four of the local union officers, of necessity I was in a situation in which I had to listen, to ask questions, and to hear what they were saying. I had no alternative. I had not the foggiest idea what to do. Long after that first experience, I realized that in a sense this was the best thing that could have happened to me. Through no ability of my own, but because of the circumstances, I avoided the pitfalls that so many young lawyers fall into in similar situations. They feel that the problems involved are legal and, because they know the law, they have the answers to the problems and know what to do. Consequently, they do not listen to the people involved. And time after time, by focusing so strongly on the legal issues, they miss the actual problems and fail to develop the approaches really required.

This was not my problem. I had no conception at all of what the questions in the next day's hearing were going to be. I had only one possible approach. As I sat with the UE field organizer, the shop stewards, and the local union officers from the plant, I had to listen to them tell me what the problems really were, and what they needed from me.

The hearing was to be on an unfair labor practice charge, which had been filed by the union local against the company after the conclusion, a few months before, of a national strike. They explained to me what the strike had been all about and what the problems now were. The national phase of the struggle had ended when the national strike was settled with a contract. Now it was a question of negotiating a local supplement to the national agreement. But the union was in a complicated bargaining relationship with the local management. The plant managers refused to negotiate honestly on certain key local issues, including working conditions that were important to the workers in the plant. Things were going badly in the negotiations, and the union bargainers needed some leverage with the local management. This was why the union had decided to press the unfair labor charges against the company which were the basis of the next day's hearing.

After listening to all this, I finally put to them the central question, "Tell me, what do you want? What do you really need? What are you trying to get out of tomorrow's proceeding?" This opened the flood gates. They were really not interested at all in whether they ultimately won an order from the NLRB that the company had been guilty of unfair practices. They needed two things. First, they needed time. They needed time to organize better their own union base in the plant in order to strengthen their bargaining position and to prepare, if necessary, for local stoppages. Second, to help this organizing process, they needed to take some initiative in the bargaining, to show both their own members and the other workers in the plant that they did not always have to sit back and take it from the company. There was a serious morale problem in the plant, because the union had not won much in the national agreement. Under these conditions, it was hard to organize a continued struggle around the local supplement. The NLRB charges were part of an effort both to gain time and to retake the initiative.

As the local union people explained the situation to me, I realized something which over the years was to become an essential ingredient in the building of a meaningful relationship between me as a people's lawyer and the people in struggle. The union members were being very patient with me. Maybe I was a lawyer, and maybe I knew a lot about the law, but I certainly did not know very much about them, or about the plant, or about their real problems. And they were patient in teaching me about these matters because of two things: they really needed my help, and I was really listening. That day in Cleveland I sensed, as I was to sense at so many other moments throughout the years, that to the degree that I honestly listened and did not arrogantly wave around an intellectual skill I was supposed to have as an instant solution to all problems, the people involved were more than willing to take the initiative in explaining problems and searching out answers along with me.

What finally emerged was a clear answer to what they really

wanted from me the next day in the hearing. Deep down, they wanted me to put up a good fight. They planned to pack the hearing room with workers from the plant. They particularly wanted me to take on the company vice president who was handling the bargaining negotiations. I was to call him as a witness, grill him, cross-examine him, and make clear to everyone in the room that just because he wore the mantle of the company he could not ride roughshod over everyone else. This was an important opportunity to challenge the company and the aura of absolute authority with which this vice president paraded around the plant, and it would give the workers an opportunity to see one of their own representatives, the union lawyer, taking the offensive against the company's representative.

We worked together all that day and late into the evening as the local union people supplied me with stories, episodes, material of all sorts to use in confronting the company's refusal to bargain in good faith. Knowing what was really needed, I concentrated on this factual preparation to expose the vice president's arrogance and refusal to bargain fairly with the local union representatives. While I intended to present the legal arguments as effectively as possible, I now understood the crucial objective to be the impact upon the workers themselves of the physical challenge to the company representative.

In the course of this very first experience as a UE lawyer, I began to learn what is often so difficult for many young lawyers just out of school to come to grips with, the fact that the test of success for a people's lawyer is not always the technical winning or losing of the formal proceeding. Again and again, the real test was the impact of the legal activities on the morale and understanding of the people involved in the struggle. To the degree that the legal work helped to develop a sense of strength, an ability to fight back, it was successful. This could even be achieved without reaching the objective of formal victory. Winning was often critically important, but over and over again the essential question would be the same as on that day in Cleveland: not whether the union was going to win or lose the NLRB proceeding, but whether the hearing was going to affect the strength of the workers in the plant. Did the legal struggle help to strengthen the

57

union? Or did it, as I would sometimes learn over the years, weaken the union? These were the central questions by which success could be tested, for in the long run, the struggles of the union with the company would be decided not by the labor board but by the strength of the union itself. Victory or defeat that day in Cleveland would be measured not by the ultimate ruling of the NLRB but by the immediate impact of the legal proceeding upon the organization of workers at the plant.

Yet another lesson for the functioning of a people's lawyer was driven home to me during that experience in Cleveland. After the hearing was over, something totally unexpected happened. By then I was worn out. The confrontation with management had seemed to go very well. I had sensed an excitement in the packed room when I took my courage in my hands and lit into the company representative, questioning him extensively about his refusal to bargain fairly with the local union. But I had summoned up every ounce of energy to carry off this first full-scale hearing, and I was ready to collapse. As I started to leave, the union field representative said, "OK, let's go to the meeting." I gasped, "What meeting? The hearing's over." He replied, "You don't understand. We're going to the local meeting. We always have a meeting of the local after an important hearing so that we can report back to the people."

Tired as I was, I now had to get up before three or four hundred people jammed into the local hall. After being introduced as the union lawyer and receiving a round of applause that felt very good after the long day's work, I was asked to tell what had happened at the hearing. This meant that I had to explain the developments in terms that everyone could understand, and answer the many questions which were then put to me. This was my first experience with the intense efforts of the leadership of the UE to build a union that was democratically controlled by the rank-and-file membership. As an essential first step toward that democratic control, the membership had to be made fully aware of every development that affected their lives. And this insistence upon rank-and-file knowledge was now being applied to the activities of the union lawyers. No elitism, no professionalism, could stand as a barrier between the lawyers of the union and the people they represented. As the labor struggles intensified in the years to come, this insistence by the union's leaders upon a responsibility to report to the rank and file had a fundamental impact on my developing understanding of the role and function of a people's lawyer. It marked the beginning of my realization that no matter how experienced, clever, and resourceful that lawyer may be, the most important element is still the informed support and active participation of the people involved. Without this, a legal victory has very little meaning indeed.

3

Union Busting
and Red Baiting

From my experience at the Cleveland hearing in early 1948 and at dozens of other such occurrences all over the country during the next few months, I began to get an insight into the role of a people's lawyer, an insight that would shape my thinking in diverse situations over the years. Increasingly I realized that people's lawyers must never forget their underlying purpose: to utilize their skills in order to assist people already in motion to carry forward their own struggles. What was becoming clear was that the lawyer's activity is rarely, if ever, the primary means of winning the struggle. Victory has to be achieved by the people themselves, through their own organizational strength and activity, and the legal work of a people's lawyer must be directed primarily toward helping to create an atmosphere in which the people can more readily function, organize, and move forward. Sometimes this is accomplished defensively, by holding off attacks by the establishment, and sometimes, as I was to learn the next fall in Evansville, Indiana, by using one's legal skills and knowledge to turn the tables and attack.

Evansville in September 1948 brought sharply into focus all the tensions that had been mounting in the labor movement since the end of the war. Shortly after the end of the fighting, workers in the major industries, strengthened by the returning veterans who had had quite enough of the sacrifices of Army life, began to press for wages that would provide a decent living standard for themselves and their families. While the major corporations had raked in profits of over $120 billion during the five years from 1940 to 1945, the cost of living had shot up 45 percent and wages, under the rigid war controls, had risen only 15 percent. The answer seemed simple, and in November and December of 1945 the industrial unions in the auto, electrical, and steel industries went out on national strikes against the major corporations. These strikes received enormous support in the cities and towns where plants were located, and substantial wage increases were won.

Not two months after this demonstration of strength and unity by the industrial workers, something happened in Fulton, Missouri, which signaled the opening of a concerted attack on organized labor such as the country had not seen in many years. On March 5, 1946, Winston Churchill, with the approval of the new President, Harry Truman, announced to the world the policy that would become known as the Cold War. Less than a year after the defeat of German fascism and Japanese imperialism by the Allied armies, Churchill sounded the call for a total military and political build-up by the "English-speaking nations" to contain and defeat the new danger which threatened their sacred traditions, the threat of world communism led by their wartime ally, the Soviet Union. This not only ensured a continuation of the companies' enormous profits from military contracts, now to be justified by the Cold War, but also provided a golden opportunity for big business to mount an all-out attack on the heart of the "red menace" at home—the militant labor movement. As James Matles, UE's director of organization, used to point out, big business' perspective on the Cold War was perfectly characterized in the 1946 remark of Charles Wilson, the president of General Electric, "The problems of the United States can be summed up in two words: Russia abroad, labor at home."

The National Association of Manufacturers, assisted by the new southern Democrat-Republican alliance which took over in the post-New Deal atmosphere, programed the campaign skillfully. Only a year later, in June 1947, the so-called Taft-Hartley

Act swept through Congress, undermining one of the great accomplishments of the 1930s, the organization of workers into industrial unions. The act legalized dozens of union-busting devices, including the use of massive injunctions against strikes and wholesale damage actions against unions. Most serious of all, Taft-Hartley wrote the use of red-baiting into law as a primary means of isolating and ousting militant unionists. This was accomplished by mandating that all union officers in the country, local and national, sign an affidavit declaring that they were not Communists. Refusal meant that their unions could not appear on ballots in NLRB representation elections and, most critical, could not be certified as the collective bargaining representative at a plant.

To a great degree, militancy soon became identified in the public mind with communism. The affidavit thus became a principal tool for accomplishing big business' main objective: to paralyze the labor movement and to split the unity of the CIO. If you were too militant, you were assumed to be a Communist. If you were a Communist, you could not be a union officer. Worse still, if you signed the affidavit, you were subject to jail sentences for perjury, "proved" by the manufactured testimony of paid government informers. The effect was to smother militancy and isolate activists. As people's lawyers, we were to live with the horror and paralyzing impact of the Taft-Hartley affidavit for much of the next decade.

With the help of this Taft-Hartley formula, Congress set up a mammoth red-baiting operation. Congressional committees began to tour the country, using the full weight of their authority to stamp as "subversive," a word that became increasingly frightening as the Cold War progressed, any union militant working in the plants. Wherever there was a closely contested NLRB election on union representation or a bitterly fought strike situation, the House Un-American Activities Committee or a subcommittee of the House Education and Labor Committee would suddenly appear on the scene. The local newspapers would be filled with scare stories that a committee of Congress was in town for the purpose of uncovering dangerous subversive agents in the community factories. As a crucial union election or a strike crisis drew closer, the House committee would open public hearings to expose these subversives. Time and again the story was the same. United States marshals would appear at a worker's home, always, it seemed, late at night. There would be a banging on the door. The worker, already asleep, would wake up and stumble to the door. Three or four stern-looking men, in those dark gray suits they all seemed to wear, would thrust upon him a piece of paper stamped with the Great Seal of the United States. No one could read or understand the tiny print, but the half-asleep worker would be brusquely told, "You are subpoenaed to appear before a committee of the House of Representatives," next week, or in two days, or even tomorrow morning. Terror would set in. Even the strongest people became frightened.

The pattern of the hearings soon became familiar. Some "friendly witness," either a terrified fellow-worker or, as was often discovered years later, a well-paid informer on a secret government payroll, would name as "Communist" all the militants in the local union. The sitting congressmen would thunderously denounce them, and the local newspapers would publicize the exposure of the "subversives" in flaming headlines. The next day, the company would fire these workers as security risks or, as hysteria mounted, organized goon squads of workers within the plants would drive the workers off the assembly line and out of the factory.

This was the pattern developing throughout the country when Dave Scribner called me into his office one morning in early September 1948, a little less than a year after I had started working with him. He wanted to discuss an urgent situation in Evansville. "Looks like Dayton all over again," Scribner said, "only worse."

He and I had just lived through a really tough time in Dayton, Ohio, where the UE workers at Univis Lens had gone on strike and stayed out for almost ninety days. The governor of the state had called out over 1500 National Guard troops to try to break the strike. Despite beatings by troopers and police, the workers stood firm. Then a conservative, strike-breaking union from the American Federation of Labor intervened with the NLRB and petitioned for an election to replace the UE. Shortly after a date for the election had been set by the NLRB, the Hartley subcommittee of the Education and Labor Committee of the House of Representatives subpoenaed all five leaders of the UE local to hearings in Washington. Pre-election hysteria mounted. The UE was already under an enormous handicap in the election because of its officers' refusal to sign the Taft-Hartley affidavits, a position that had originally been agreed upon by the entire CIO leadership and then abandoned by a number of the conservative unions within the CIO. As a "noncomplying" union, the UE could not appear on the ballot, and workers had to vote for "Neither" in order to choose to retain the UE as their union. In this atmosphere of fear and confusion, the election was lost by a very narrow margin on September 8, just a few days before my meeting with Scribner about Evansville.

Scribner handed me some materials he had just received from Matles. One was a letter to Matles from the UE field representative in Evansville, which laid out a desperate situation. Evansville was a city of heavy industrial concentration. The UE had successfully organized the workers in the major plants—Servel, Seeger, Faultless Caster, International Harvester. The UE local had also been certified by the NLRB as the collective bargaining agent for the workers at Bucyrus-Erie, but the president of the company had publicly announced in May that Bucyrus would not deal with the local because it was "Communist dominated." A strike was called on July 30, 1948, to force the company to recognize the union and negotiate a contract. After the employer secured sweeping Taft-Hartley injunctions against the strike and the state police repeatedly tried to break up the picket line, an AFL craft union moved in, as in Dayton, to raid the plant and try to oust the UE. An election was set for the end of September. In the meantime, under enormous pressure, the UE was forced to call off the strike and retrench organizationally within the plant.

At that moment, the local press headlined an announcement that a subcommittee of the House Education and Labor Committee had subpoenaed over thirty UE leaders in Evansville in order to investigate "Communist control" of the local union. The hearings were to take place in Evansville itself just before the election. Up to this point, these hysteria-producing hearings had generally been held in Washington. Now they were moving directly into the local communities. After the second day of the hearings, another headline blared: "Purge of Workers Accused as Reds Spreads Locally." The UE leaders were driven out of the plants by groups of workers who were apparently working with either a rival union or the plant management. The hearings were now scheduled to resume in a week, and a number of new subpoenas were expected.

The letter from the field representative was direct and blunt. It was clear to him that this was an all-out attempt to smash the Evansville local, because contract negotiations were coming up soon at Faultless Caster, Servel, and Seeger. Almost the entire local leadership had been subpoenaed and fingered as "Communist" and "subversive," putting everyone in the local on the defensive. Morale in the union was low, and hysteria was spreading in the plants. "We've got to do something to stop the panic," he wrote, "or we'll never be able to hold things organizationally."

A little note from Matles, addressed to Scribner and me, came clipped to this grim report from the field. In the few months I had been working with the UE, I had already begun to sense why John L. Lewis, that legendary figure of the labor movement, had once said that Matles was one of the most brilliant labor organizers he had ever met. Matles had an incredibly keen insight into possible solutions for the most complicated organizational problems. So when Scribner handed me his note, I expected some carefully worked out directive to us as union lawyers in this complex and difficult situation. The memo, however, was simple: "Do something."

Scribner and I sat there. What were we to do? The congressional subcommittee had moved in, and the pattern was set. We knew that the hearings would create more terror, and the panic would spread. Most serious of all, this would give the initiative to the companies. Our people were wholly on the defensive. What could we, as lawyers, do to help change the situation? What legal strategy would meet the needs of our clients, the union members, the working people of Evansville? The congressional subcommittee was backing its attack on the local with the full weight of the government of the United States. How could we lawyers alter that atmosphere of unquestioned legitimacy? How could we seize the initiative, even temporarily? How could we turn the tables and put the committee and the companies on the defensive in the eyes of the people of Evansville?

These were the questions we struggled with all that day, and out of our discussions emerged an experiment in the utilization of legal techniques which was to have a profound effect on my understanding of the role of a people's lawyer. Our plan would probably have been characterized as impossible or insane by most members of the legal profession. We decided literally to seize the initiative. We proposed to go into federal court and sue the subcommittee and the companies on behalf of the union and the workers of Evansville. We would demand an injunction to stop them from violating the Constitution of the United States.

The First Amendment to the Constitution guarantees the right of the people peaceably to assemble, and years before, at the height of the New Deal, the Supreme Court had declared that the right to assemble, to freely associate, is a means of protecting the right of working people to form unions. But in Evansville there was a conspiracy, plain and simple, between the companies and the congressional committee to violate this fundamental right of the working people who wished to form unions and elect union leadership of their own choice. We jumped to the audacious conclusion that, if there was indeed a conspiracy against the exercise of people's basic rights, there must also be a legal remedy against such a conspiracy. But Scribner and I also knew well that no one had dared to bring such an action against a congressional committee in recent years, and certainly not in those opening days of the Cold War.

We ploughed through the annotated federal statutes, searching for some authority, some legal basis, for demanding this injunction. And we found it in the seventy-five-year-old statutes enacted by the radical Reconstruction Congresses after the Civil War to protect the newly granted constitutional rights of Black people against the conspiracies of the former slaveholders. These statutes mandated that a federal court has power to grant an injunction and provide for damages when complaints charge the existence of conspiracies to keep people from exercising their basic constitutional rights. True, these statutes had lain buried

67

and nearly forgotten since the great betrayal of Radical Reconstruction in 1877. They had not even been mentioned, except for a minute or two, in all the courses I had taken at Columbia Law School. Yet there they were, still on the books. Then Scribner and I both remembered that they had once been used very effectively in the 1930s, when creative lawyers for the CIO had secured an injunction against a conspiracy by the notorious Mayor Frank Hague of Jersey City to prevent union organizing in his city.

That evening we drafted a rough complaint to take to Evansville the next day, which in effect resurrected the buried Civil War statutes. We charged that there was a conspiracy against the union and the union members, led by the congressional subcommittee, the congressmen involved, and the companies. We asked for an injunction restraining the defendants from violating the constitutional rights of the union members and compelling the companies to return the ousted workers to their jobs. And we asked for $100,000 in damages for the widespread injury already done. When we finished drafting the complaint late that night, we looked at each other and smiled. We knew that we probably had no real chance of winning in court, but we nevertheless had a feeling that this was the move required in Evansville. At that moment we had no way of knowing what a truly powerful effect it would have.

The first indication of the significance of our action came the next day during a meeting of the executive board of the Evansville local, where I went to discuss the complaint. Sydney Berger, the local lawyer who handled the UE legal work throughout Indiana with great courage, had met me at the station, and I first went over the draft complaint with him. His enthusiastic response reflected an underlying desire to take the offensive, stemming in part, he said, from the fact that his wife was one of the UE members subpoenaed by the subcommittee. Then we hurried to the hall where the local board was meeting.

The atmosphere as we walked in was glum. A mixture of panic and yet determination somehow to continue the fight was in the air. Everyone knew that the subcommittee was coming back next week, and no one was sure who else would be subpoenaed. One of the shop stewards asked me hesitantly, "Is there anything at all you lawyers can do to help?"

68

I took the rough draft of the complaint out of my briefcase and passed it around. The reaction was instantaneous. One of the board members who had been subpoenaed read the heading of the complaint, listing the congressmen and companies as defendants, and asked incredulously, "You mean we're going to make *them* defendants?" From that point on, there was a different atmosphere. We talked at length about what the suit really meant and how to use it. Certainly no one had any illusions. They knew their town much better than I did, and they knew that the chances of winning in the company-dominated federal district court were almost nil. But that was not important. What was important was what they could do with this. They could take the offensive. They could go to their members and talk about the complaint. They could show it around the shops. They could call meetings to explain what the real conspiracy was. They did not have to act as if all law, all right, was on the side of the subcommittee and the companies. They told Syd Berger and me to move ahead. When the suit was filed the day before the committee was to return to town, the local newspaper ran the headline: "Congressmen and 3 Plants Sued by Union. UE asks $100,000 in Ousting of Factory Workers."

After the suit was filed, I returned to New York, and we got daily reports from Evansville telling us how the atmosphere was changing. Everyone felt that the most important thing we had done was to turn the conspiracy question on its head. Yes, there was a conspiracy in Evansville, but it was not the "Communist" conspiracy everyone had been talking about up to that minute. It was a conspiracy between the companies and the congressmen to destroy the union and the gains that the working people of Evansville had won through hard struggle. It was the kind of conspiracy that some eighty years before Congress itself had said was unlawful and must be stopped. In a very real way, the complaint legitimized and assisted the educational and organizational work that the union had to do to resist the effect of the subcommittee's and the companies' propaganda in the plants.

The filing of the action brought immediate reverberations throughout the city. When the local newspapers reported that the UE was suing the congressmen and the plant owners, the recovery of morale in the Evansville local was impressive. Both union leaders and rank-and-file members could now take the offensive as they conducted their critical organizational work in the plants and community. At local union meetings, at plant gates, informally in the factories and in workers' homes, the legal action became a center of discussion. As the real issues emerged, the underlying strength of the working people in Evansville reasserted itself. The momentary hysteria, which after the first hearings had permitted the goon squads to operate inside the factories, died down. The union began to reconsolidate its organizational base in the plants. The complaint was distributed almost like a leaflet. It gave workers a good feeling to read the heading: "UE Against the Congressmen and the Companies." The *UE News* was able to report that the workers in Evansville had begun to "repudiate the Evansville formula." One after another the raiding attempts of rival unions were turned back, and the new contract negotiations were conducted in an atmosphere of renewed strength, the local winning a number of their demands from the companies.

Early in November, another victory was won. One of the most belligerent of the congressmen at the hearings had been Edward Mitchell, the local representative from Evansville. He had sat in on the subcommittee hearings, believing that this was a perfect way to pick up support for reelection. Mitchell was a Republican who normally won, counting on the farm vote of the areas outside of Evansville to offset the support for the Democrats within the city. It was Mitchell who, with a great show of moral authority, kept asking subpoenaed workers, "Are you a Communist?" "Do you believe in God?" "What church do you belong to?" In early September this behavior had appeared likely to guarantee a landslide reelection in November. But by the end of the month the UE local, reconsolidating its work in the spirit of the new counteroffensive, was urging the Evansville workers to "express their opposition at the polls in November" to the congressional conspirators, in particular to Congressman Mitchell. On the day after the election we got an excited phone call from Evansville. Mitchell had been defeated! I will never forget the organizer's gleeful comment, "That's one way of winning a lawsuit!"

And of course it was. I did not fully grasp the implications of the Evansville experience for the role of a people's lawyer until years later, in the midst of the massive uprisings of the Black people in the South in the 1960s. But even in those early days of the Cold War, certain questions were coming into focus. The ultimate test of the appropriateness of a given legal strategy could not be solely the likelihood of success within the court structure. The wisdom of bringing a lawsuit, of opening up a certain line of legal strategy, had to be judged in a wholly different way. The crucial question was what role it would play at that moment in protecting or advancing the people's struggle. If it helped the fight, then it was done, even if the chances of immediate legal success were virtually nonexistent.

We well knew the likelihood was that the federal district judge would throw the Evansville complaint out of court for "total lack of jurisdiction"—the professional, judicial way of saying, "What the hell do you think you're doing?" And three or four months later he did just that. But we also knew how important it was to say, loud and clear at that critical moment in Evansville in September 1948, that the House subcommittee, the congressmen, and the companies had entered into a conspiracy to undermine the constitutional rights of the workers of the city and that the shrill cries of "subversive" and "Communist" were only covers for a plan to steal from the workers the hard-won gains of their union. By having us file the complaint, the UE was using the court to tell the workers of Evansville, "We don't have to be afraid of the congressmen and the companies. What they are doing is wrong, is unconstitutional, and violates our rights. Stand firm. Don't be frightened by them."

There was no question in my mind that it was terribly important for the union to be able to take this action. Yet I felt a lurking uneasiness, stemming from the notion of "professional responsibility" implanted so thoroughly in every law student. Since we knew there was little likelihood of success in the courts, was this really an honest, responsible use of legal techniques? As I mulled over this question, the answer gradually took shape. At certain moments, bringing a lawsuit can be a form of political expression for people in struggle. The court system, like all other branches of government, is an arena in which the rights of people can be asserted. That is what we were doing in Evansville in the federal court. That is what the First Amendment is supposed to be about. To argue as we did in that lawsuit was in the deepest sense a political expression of the UE workers of Evansville, and it was protected and sanctioned by the Constitution, which we lawyers were supposed to be defending. But to have suggested this to most other lawyers or law professors at the time would have evoked derision or worse.

Not until almost fifteen years later, at an entirely different moment in American history, did the Supreme Court, in a case involving the use of the courts of Virginia by lawyers for the National Association for the Advancement of Colored People, approach this perception in an opinion which even today is not fully understood by most lawyers or law teachers. In *NAACP v. Button* the Supreme Court, rejecting massive efforts by the Virginia authorities to harass lawyers who were using the court to seek protection of the constitutional rights of Black people, openly stated for the first time that the act of instituting a lawsuit to vindicate the fundamental constitutional rights of the people is itself a political expression, an activity protected by the First Amendment to the Constitution—the guarantor of freedom of speech, assembly, and association.

In Evansville in 1948, and in the difficult years of the Cold War that followed, we did not have the comforting words of the *Button* opinion to encourage us. But in Evansville I gained a deeper insight into the fundamental reality that people's lawyers are part of the movements of struggle and that there is no contradiction between this commitment and their obligations as members of the bar. This was a concept I would have to grapple with over and over through the years. There would be many moments of doubt and confusion, but that morning in New York, after we heard the results of the congressional election in Evansville, I had no question at all about the propriety and effectiveness of our role as lawyers in the ongoing fight.

This fight was about to branch out to a wholly new front. The constant attempts of the press, the National Association of Manufacturers, and the congressional committees to play upon the fears of a supposedly pervasive Communist conspiracy to justify the all-out campaign against militant trade unionism no longer rested solely on the new international perspectives of Churchill's "iron curtain" speech two years before in Fulton, Missouri. The words "Communist conspiracy" had become very real in most people's thinking on July 21, 1948, when newspapers all over the country announced in banner headlines the arrest and indictment the day before of the twelve members of the national board of the Communist Party. They were charged with conspiring to violate the so-called Smith Act, the federal antisedition statute which made it criminal to organize a "society, group or assembly of persons" who "teach and advocate the overthrow and destruction of the Government of the United States by force and violence." The act also made it criminal to be members of such a society or group.

These very vague and general provisions were to generate in coming years thousands of pages of legal briefs, court opinions, and learned law review articles, none of them quite sure what a charge under the Smith Act really meant. However, in that summer and fall of 1948 there was no such erudite confusion in the public mind. The headline in the *New York Times* the day after the arrests clearly announced across four columns that the twelve Communists had been "indicted in an anti-government plot." The lead paragraph informed everyone that they had been arrested on charges of "conspiring to overthrow the United States Government." The Justice Department planned to expose the "anti-government plot" in a federal courtroom that winter in Foley Square in New York City, in the case that became known as *Dennis v. United States.*

The implications of this move were sweeping. If the government could make this charge stick, then all the plans to isolate and destroy the militant labor movement that were beginning to unfold, as in Dayton and Evansville, actions justified under the umbrella of protecting the nation from the "Communist conspiracy," might well succeed. As Dave Scribner and I rushed around that summer and fall, heading to the latest crisis points all over the country, we knew that whatever happened in the Smith Act trial was bound to have a profound effect upon all our work.

It was therefore with a great deal of excitement that I listened to a surprising suggestion made to me on the phone one evening late in September by Frank Donner. Donner had been an assistant general counsel for the CIO, working in Washington with Lee Pressman, the CIO general counsel. I had met him a few times while I was at law school and later during my first year at the UE, but he, like Lee Pressman and Gene Cotton, the other CIO assistant general counsel, was still classified in my mind in that unapproachable category of "experienced labor lawyer," clothed in the golden mystique of all the sweeping victories of the 1930s during the building of the CIO and the mass industrial unions. Donner had already begun to achieve that level of recognition throughout the people's movements which to this day has marked him as one of the most creative and brilliant legal thinkers in the practice of people's law, and he had just been asked by the defendants in the impending Smith Act prosecution to come to New York to work full-time on the case, helping the team of trial lawyers develop their legal arguments. I was understandably overwhelmed when he asked me if I would help him in fashioning the legal approaches for the coming trial.

For many reasons, this was an irresistible offer for someone just starting out in the difficult field of people's law. The trial loomed as one of the most threatening moves in the campaign of fear now underway, providing an opportunity to see from within the dynamics of a political trial of the first magnitude. It was also a great opportunity for a young person to watch at first hand and perhaps get to know some of the best-known progressive lawyers in the country who had come together as the defense team: Harry Sacher and Abe Isserman of New York, Richard Gladstein of California, George Crockett of Detroit, and Louis McCabe of Philadelphia. And for me personally, the trial was important because I had close ties to some of the defendants, having come to know Gil Green, John Gates, and Henry Winston when they were leaders of the Communist youth organization during the days of my participation in the radical student movement at both Harvard and Columbia.

So I agreed to work with Donner, without thinking about what it would mean in terms of adding to the complexity of my life. The work would just have to be jammed into evenings, weekends, and hours stolen from an already jammed schedule. The effects of the additional workload would be felt most strongly in my personal life. Susan Knopf and I had been married shortly after my discharge from the Army. From the earliest days of our relationship, my round-the-clock activities, first at law school and then at the UE, along with her social work education and participation in one of the first campaigns to organize social workers and then bank workers into a union, created a situation that often reduced the time so necessary for our personal life. At the moment, our son Peter was barely six months old, and Susan was assuming an entirely unfair and often overwhelming share of the new family responsibilities. As was the case with so many men in those years before the new consciousness raised by the women's movement of the sixties and seventies, I was too often oblivious to the burdens that this way of life thrust on Susan. This was one of my first experiences with the continuing problem of a people's lawyer, which I would make some progress on but would never fully solve for myself—how to find enough hours in the day to do what has to be done and have any time left over to share the joys and the burdens of a personal life, in particular to share equally the responsibilities of parenthood, which in those days, and too often even today, the men of our society refuse to face.

But no matter the time and energy drain, my work with Donner in the preparation of pretrial motions challenging the indictment and my participation in some of the basic strategy discussions which shape a trial of that importance proved to be an invaluable experience for a young lawyer barely out of law school. For at the heart of the agitated discussions before the trial were central questions which, even to this day, are critical for people's lawyers. What kind of trial was it to be? How does one conduct a political defense in a trial of this magnitude? How does one use the courtroom to take the political offensive?

This was to be a trial like those in the days of the Palmer raids at the close of World War I, when from one end of the country to the other the Department of Justice made wholesale attacks on labor organizers and radical people as "foreign agitators." Once again, people would stand trial for the "crime" of forming a political organization. There was never any doubt that it would be a political trial. The underlying, often unformulated question was *whose* politics were going to be expressed at this political trial, the government's or the defendants'?

The Department of Justice had set up a skillfully constructed trap. It was based on the fact that at the end of the war the defendants had reconstituted the Communist Party as part of their rejection of the policies of their former general secretary, Earl Browder, who during the war had dissolved the party as one of his acts of accommodation to the war policies of the United States government. The government now charged that this reconstitution of the Communist Party was in fact the organization of a conspiracy to overthrow the United States government by force and violence. The conspiracy, therefore, was the party itself, and everyone who either was a member of the party or had worked with it in any way was a "conspirator." This would provide the justification for isolating from critical sections of American life every militant and effective organizer. The formula was simple. Just label people "Communists," and they automatically become "conspirators." Big business would thus have a powerful weapon. All it had to do was tag people as Communists or as associated with Communists to drive them out of the labor movement, the plants, the universities and schools, out of Hollywood and the theater and every public forum.

By the fall of 1948 this formula was being tested by members of Congress in the plants and the communities. I myself had seen the beginning attempts in Dayton and Evansville. The Smith Act trial was designed to write this formula firmly into the law of the land.

The government's political strategy for the trial, as revealed in the pretrial activities, could not have been clearer. All it had to do, it thought, was to demonstrate the obvious. First, it would try to establish that Communists did indeed believe in the overthrow of capitalist government by force and violence. That would be easily done by throwing in some books on Marxism-Leninism. Marxist books taught the advocacy of force and violence to overthrow capitalist government; Communists read these books; the Communist Party advocated what was said in these books. The conclusion was inescapable: the Communist Party advocated the overthrow of the government by force and violence, and since

76

the defendants had conspired to reorganize the Communist party, the conspiracy was one to overthrow the government by force and violence. Presto, the case was made! The formula was now ready for use all over the country. The task would then be simple: identify the "conspirators," and get,rid of them. Here in the courtroom in Foley Square was to be fashioned the ultimate weapon to undermine every potential movement of popular opposition and dissent for years to come.

The government's strategy was simple and clear, but what was not so obvious was how the defendants should respond to this strategy. How could the defendants, the entire national leadership of a political party openly committed to the principles of revolutionary socialism, avoid the trap set for them by the prosecution and, in effect, force the politics of this trial to be their politics rather than the government's? In a sense, the problem here was similar to the one in Evansville, though on a much larger scale. The question was how to turn the tables, how to take the offensive, how to expose within the courtroom the real conspiracy, while not falling into the prosecution's trap by confining the defense to the four corners of a response to the government's charges.

One evening that fall, I sat stewing over the preliminary results of the government's strategy in the pretrial maneuverings. Increasingly the energies of both the defendants and those who were participating in preparing their defense were being expended on complex and abstruse analyses of this or that quotation from a Marxist writer and this or that theoretical formulation from the past, designed to show that it did not really mean what it appeared to mean on first reading. The trial promised to become what the government had in mind. A trial of books, a trial of ideas. All my instincts warned me that this was a dead end.

Then something began to click. Why accept the government's premises at all? There was one question the Department of Justice never talked about—the First Amendment to the Constitution. People were not supposed to be sent to jail in this country for anything they taught or advocated, no matter what it was, unless, in the words of that most revered and respected Supreme Court Justice, Oliver Wendell Holmes, what they taught or advocated presented "a clear and present danger of a serious substantive evil which the legislature had the power to prevent."

The issue in the trial was not at all whether the Marxist books the defendants were reading and teaching meant what the prosecution said they meant, or even what the defense said they meant. The issue was whether the Constitution of the United States was to be ignored or enforced. The real question boiled down to whether the acts with which the defendants were charged presented "a clear and present danger of a serious substantive evil" with which the legislature had the power to deal. Otherwise the government had no power even to place them on trial.

Everything turned on the nature of the political party that the defendants were charged with conspiring to organize. The defendants were not charged with organizing a party to teach or advocate murder, or arson, or any criminal act obviously within the power of the legislature to prohibit. They were a political party that openly advocated a revolutionary seizure of power and the creation of a new classless society. Was this a "substantive evil which the legislature had the power to prevent," or was it a right guaranteed to the American people in a Constitution that rests upon a document, the Declaration of Independence, which proclaims the inalienable right of all people to revolution? Was Abraham Lincoln merely being rhetorical when he reminded the nation at his inaugural in 1861 that, "whenever the people shall grow weary of the existing government they can exercise their constitutional right to amend it, or their revolutionary right to overthrow or dismember it." If, in the words of Lincoln, the right of the people to revolution is a fundamental right rather than a "substantive evil within legislative power to prohibit," then the First Amendment to the Constitution deprived the government of any power to proceed with this trial.

As these questions emerged, the potential for a counteroffensive within the courtroom took shape. Once again, the real conspiracy was not the one charged. The real conspiracy was the conspiracy to undermine and set aside the protections of the First Amendment. And the target of this conspiracy was not just the political party led by the defendants but all militant trade unionists and organizers. The real target of the conspiracy was thus the living standards and working conditions of millions of Americans and the peace and security of all the people of the world. The real challenge of the Smith Act trial was to turn everything upside down: to show that the Constitution itself prohibited the trial of the defendants, and that the defense of the Constitution and the needs and interests of millions of Americans required a repudiation of these criminal charges. This kind of attack would enable the political defendants to expose what was the real "clear and present danger" to the country—the underlying conspiracy of the rulers of the country against the Constitution itself, against the elementary rights of the people.

As this perspective began to unfold, a wild thought overwhelmed me. This kind of political counteroffensive might best be developed in the courtroom not by the lawyers, as skillful as they were, but by the political leaders of the party under attack. Why not have them represent themselves? All of us in the student movement of the thirties had heard of the heroic act of self-defense in 1935 in Leipsig, Germany, of Georgi Dimitroff, the Communist leader, before the German high tribunal during the Reichstag fire trial. In this trial, staged by the Nazis in the early days of the Hitler takeover, leaders of the German and Bulgarian Communist parties were charged with having burned the Reichstag building as a signal for an uprising against the Nazis. Dimitroff defended himself by questioning on the stand the Nazi leaders Hermann Goering and Paul Goebbels, which not only resulted in a political confrontation that rallied millions of people throughout the world to the antifascist cause, but also, and amazingly, led to Dimitroff's acquittal. And so I prepared a memorandum to the lawyers and the defendants proposing such an approach. Using the Dimitroff example, I suggested that the Smith Act defendants, the political leaders of the party under attack, should consider defending themselves and opening up a full-scale legal and political counteroffensive.

Whether the memorandum was ever seriously considered, by either the trial lawyers or the defendants as a group, I never knew. Looking back on it years later, I began to understand that the proposal was a brash move by a young and inexperienced person in a complex situation of such staggering dimensions that it was difficult to comprehend them at the time. Here I was, hardly two years out of law school, suggesting an approach which, regardless of its merits as a fundamental strategy, might seem to threaten, if not undermine, the central role of the more experienced lawyers in the public arena of the trial to come. In those hectic days preceding the trial, I found it increasingly difficult even to discuss such questions with anyone, much less participate in any attempt at resolution. Almost from the first moment of my contact with the defense, I experienced certain of the problems that continue to this day to be serious obstacles to the healthy functioning of a people's lawyer. The team of trial lawyers assembled for the defense included some of the most brilliant and dedicated progressive lawyers in the country. Few could match their ability and courage. They were among the best of the generation of lawyers who had been trained and toughened in the labor struggles of the thirties. Yet it was their very experience and well-deserved credentials that, in a strange and complicated way, made the solution of this underlying question of trial strategy so difficult during those tense days as the opening of the Smith Act trial approached.

At the root of their apparent hesitancy to come to grips with the dilemma of how to try this case may have been questions concerning their own role. Perhaps I had unwittingly thrown myself into conflict with a quality of lawyers in general that people's lawyers rarely acknowledge or face—the inner drive to obtain ego satisfaction, to dominate the scene, which often shapes their legal, tactical, and strategic decisions. Many times in the years to come I would look back at decisions of my own and wonder in retrospect to what degree I too had been influenced by this drive to hold center stage.

This natural impulse of experienced lawyers to assume for themselves the protagonist role in the courtroom struggle was reinforced by a certain reluctance on the part of the political defendants, surrounded by the tensions of the Cold War, to think in terms of a political counteroffensive within the courtroom itself. Only one of the defendants ever discussed the proposal with me personally. It was a moment of extreme excitement for me when Ben Davis, the first Black Communist to be elected to the New

York City Council and a leader whose courage I had admired from afar during my student days, told me that my proposal seemed to him to make a great deal of sense and that he wanted to explore it. He must have had a little impact upon the situation because shortly before the trial opened in January 1949, an announcement was made that he and Eugene Dennis, then the secretary-general of the party, would defend themselves. However, no other defendant actively supported my approach. And its effectiveness was never really tested, since the constant, active presence of the five trial lawyers as the central figures in the proceedings completely overshadowed the two defendants who were technically defending themselves. I never knew whether the underlying hesitation to develop a political counterattack within that courtroom flowed primarily from the adherence of the lawyers to their traditional role as the principal figures in a trial, or from a political hesitation on the part of the defendants to transform the proceeding into an attack upon the Cold War conspiracies of the Truman administration. In any event, the opportunity to use that courtroom at that moment to take the offensive was lost.

As the pretrial legal work wound to a close, and the central strategy of the defense emerged as an intense effort to find plausible explanations for the statements torn by the prosecution out of Marxist-Leninist writings to try to prove the case, my own direct contact with the defense team diminished. Raids on the UE by rival unions were exploding all over the country, and I found myself spending most of my time traveling from crisis to crisis. The rising tensions of the Cold War, and the increasing responsibilities of the struggle to meet the enormously intensifying attack from every quarter on the embattled UE, left little or no time to reflect on the developments in the courtroom in Foley Square and their inevitable impact for years to come on the course of people's struggles throughout the country.

In a fundamental sense, the strategy of the government succeeded. The formula was established in the trial that the Communist Party was the "conspiracy" and everyone associated with it was a "conspirator" who had to be driven from active life. Thus, when the trial ended on September 23 with a sweeping guilty

81

verdict of all the defendants, followed by sudden and unexpected contempt of court sentences for each of the defense lawyers, the Cold War instrument was fashioned and ready for use from one end of the country to the other.

Perhaps of equal seriousness, but not so easily perceived by any of us at the time, was the long-term effect of the defendants' failure to take the offensive in that courtroom, setting a tone for the struggles to come as the Cold War grew more intense. There is no question that each of the lawyers and defendants in the long-drawn-out trial had personally and courageously resisted the government's strategy. But unlike Dimitroff facing the Nazi court, they remained mainly on the defensive. Unable to convert the trial into a political exposure of the government's real purpose, the defense fell back into the trap that had been so cleverly laid. Instead of openly championing the nation's democratic and indeed revolutionary traditions, which the government's strategy was in effect burying, the radical defendants and their lawyers began, imperceptibly at first, to reshape their own political doctrines to meet the prosecution's asserted standards of what was permissible to believe. Instead of finding ways to utilize the deep-seated contradiction within the prosecution's own case—that the advocacy of a right to revolution was at the very base of the building of our constitutional system—the defendants sought out ways to soften their own theories of society and social change, in effect accepting the government's assumptions as to the illegality of certain beliefs. The failure to solve the problem of how to develop a political counteroffensive in the midst of a serious repressive attack led not only to an inability to reach out beyond the courtroom to the millions of working people who in the last analysis would have to be moved if the government's strategy was to be checked. It also began a process of discrediting the integrity of radical thought, as the Smith Act defendants in effect responded to the attacks on them by reformulating their theories to meet the government's Cold War standards of propriety.

Over the years which have followed, I have often thought back to the experience of having been dipped, even momentarily, as a young lawyer, into the seething cauldron which was the Foley Square Smith Act trial. Many of the problems which to this day haunt the functioning of a people's lawyer were fed and shaped in that arena. Many times I have felt within myself the conflicting pressures that the role of lawyer generates, which can lead to a failure to meet the basic challenge of how to turn the tables, how to launch the counterattack. The Smith Act trial illustrated a problem that would emerge again and again: the demoralizing and sometimes devastating effect of the inability of political defendants and their lawyers to take the offensive, to turn the trial itself into a trial of those in power the way Dimitroff did before the Nazi court in the 1930s.

The immediate consequences of the defeat in the Smith Act trial were no less than we had feared. Within a few months after the guilty verdict came in, the Department of Justice, encouraged by the results of the trial, was moving against people's organizations on a hundred different fronts.

The growing atmosphere of fear lay heavily around us as Frank Donner and I sat talking one afternoon late in November 1949 on a bench just outside the federal courthouse in Foley Square. I had not seen much of him in the last hectic days of the Smith Act trial, and when he called me at the UE office that morning to ask if I could meet him downtown, I expected him to want to talk about where we should go with the appeals. I was not prepared in the slightest for what he actually threw at me that afternoon. "What would you think of going into general law practice with me," he said, "opening a law office together, starting a new firm?"

Without waiting for me to recover from my surprise, Donner spelled out an exciting prospect. There were going to be all kinds of work for lawyers who were ready to step into the fight. The lines were drawn. We as lawyers had to be prepared to go wherever the battle called, and the calls were coming from all over. The purge of radicals and left-wingers was taking place in every area of life. The Evansville formula of driving out militant workers from the factories was being applied to government workers, teachers, doctors, writers, and actors. More people were certain to be rounded up in Smith Act arrests. Others would be knocked off by the Truman loyalty order of November 1947, known as the Attorney General's list, which listed hundreds of people's organizations as subversive and was already being used as the basis for firing federal employees charged with membership in the proscribed organizations. Still other people would receive House Un-American Activities Committee subpoenas to testify about their alleged "subversive activities." In New York City alone, hundreds of such people would need lawyers to stand by them. Now was the time, Donner said, to take the leap, to build a new law firm prepared to play this role.

Something deep inside me wanted to do this. The frustrations of the Smith Act trial had led me to conclude that in the battles ahead young lawyers should speak out more boldly and play a more independent role in the shaping of tactics and strategy. But except for the special area of my UE work this would be impossible without becoming a practicing lawyer in my own firm. No one really listened to lawyers unless they made this jump. Here was the chance! Yet it also seemed foolhardy for me, still only two years out of law school, to undertake the tremendous challenge of helping to build an independent law firm. Donner, however, was optimistic. Between us, he said, we knew loads of people all over the country. What could we lose by trying?

I continued the discussion with Donner over the next weeks, exploring, hesitating, edging to a decision. What shoved me over the edge was a meeting we had with Dave Scribner and the three UE officers: Albert Fitzgerald, the president, Julius Emspak, the secretary-treasurer, and James Matles, the director of organization. I had been very uneasy about opening up the question of an independent practice at the national office. This was an extremely tense time for the UE. Less than two weeks before, together with ten other militant and progressive industrial unions, the UE had been summarily expelled from the CIO because of its aggressive anti-Cold War policies. Philip Murray, the CIO president, and the rest of the CIO leadership then chartered a rival union, the International Union of Electrical Workers. Led by James Carey, a renegade from the UE who had been its first president, the new union had the declared mission of raiding and destroying the UE. Then only a few days before the meeting, House Un-American Activities Committee subpoenaes had arrived at the UE office for Emspak, Matles, and Thomas Quinn, the UE representative from

Pittsburgh, requiring them to appear before the committee in Washington. The Evansville formula was in full flower. This was not the moment, I felt uneasily, to be discussing a change in relationship with the union which might suggest a lessening of commitment to the legal battles that loomed ahead.

I was wrong in my apprehensions. The UE officers and Dave Scribner were enthusiastic about the plan to start a firm. They were excited about the prospect of Donner, whose work with the CIO national legal staff they deeply respected, throwing in with Scribner and me in the ongoing UE work. In the rough days ahead, they said, the people's movements, within and beyond the labor movement, would need lawyers whose independence from the establishment and whose integrity were unquestioned. They were afraid of what might develop throughout the country, even among lawyers who had heretofore considered themselves committed "labor lawyers," as the pressure mounted to isolate and destroy the militant sectors of the labor movement. There was going to be an increasing need for lawyers who were not afraid to take their stand with those attacked as "subversive." So they viewed our tentative plan as a positive move in the right direction. And then, in the practical spirit of realistic organizers, they went out of their way to say that once we had set up the new firm, we could negotiate with them a financial retainer to pay for the UE work we would continue to do.

I was overwhelmed by this warmth and show of support. Any doubts or questions I had about the contemplated move vanished. Within a month, Donner and I had set up our new offices. One of our first moves was to call Marshall (Mike) Perlin, the local lawyer for the UE in Schenectady, and propose that he join us in New York in the venture, since it was already clear after the first days that Donner and I could not possibly handle the work to be done alone. Perlin, an old and close friend from my student days at Columbia Law School, agreed to join us after tying up his work in Schenectady. The firm of Donner, Kinoy, and Perlin was underway.

The first year of work together more than bore out Donner's prediction that lack of work would not be a problem. In June 1950, the Korean war exploded in full force, intensifying the atmosphere of the Cold War. In July, monster headlines in the newspapers announced the arrest in New York City of "Red Atom Spies," the young couple Julius and Ethel Rosenberg, and in August the papers trumpeted the news of a third arrest in the same case, of a young New Yorker, Morton Sobell.

In September 1950 the federal court of appeals delivered an opinion in the Smith Act case. Written by the person whom we had all been taught in law school to regard as the paragon of civil liberties, Judge Learned Hand, it upheld the constitutionality of the Smith Act and of the convictions of the Communist leaders. With deep uneasiness and growing pessimism, we helped to draft a petition for certiorari, the formal paper for an appeal to the Supreme Court. The case was argued in Washington that winter, and we all waited tensely, few expectations still alive within us, for the decision to come down. At the same time Donner was preparing the final appeals for the embattled Smith Act lawyers, each facing his own contempt of court conviction, and I was giving him a hand in between trips all over the country responding to raiding situations against UE local unions. There was little time that winter to speculate on what form the Cold War attacks would take next. Day after day the phone would ring with another subpoena, another firing. All our fears that the government's target went far beyond the Smith Act defendants were coming to life.

In early 1951, the full sweep of the government's drive against political opposition became clear in a very personal way. One afternoon Donner called me into his office and introduced me to an older man who was sitting there with an overflowing folder of papers and looking particularly grim. He was Peter Shipka, one of the national officers of the International Workers Order (IWO), a highly successful cultural fraternal benefit society, built primarily by groups of immigrant working people to provide inexpensive insurance and other medical benefits for people whom the commercial insurance companies would not touch. I could not imagine what Peter Shipka would want from us.

Shipka, it developed, wanted to know if we would represent the IWO officers. He pulled out of his folder a legal-looking bunch of papers and handed it to us, saying, "They want to liquidate us." The petition was from the New York State Superintendent of Insurance, asking the New York courts for an order "liquidating" and "dissolving" the IWO.

We did not know what to think. Was the IWO in financial trouble? Shipka laughed. The IWO, he proudly informed us, was the most financially solvent and sound mutual benefit society in the country, with over 130,000 members, assets of $6 million, insurance policies totaling $110 million, and $13 million in benefits paid out over the years. On what grounds then, we asked, were they trying to "liquidate" the organization? "They say we're 'hazardous,'" he replied, explaining that the insurance law of New York allowed a petition for liquidation of a company or benefit society where its operations were found to be "hazards." "But how on earth can you be hazardous," we asked, "with such a solid financial record?" "You don't understand," he replied, "we're *politically* hazardous."

There it was. The IWO, though financially sound and successful, was a "danger" to New York state because of the political opinions and affiliations of its leadership. Over three years earlier, in November 1947, the Truman loyalty order had listed the IWO as a subversive organization under Communist Party domination and control, membership in which could be a basis for firing from federal employment. Together with several other organizations fingered in the original order, the IWO had gone to federal court to challenge the entire device of labeling as unconstitutional. Without waiting for the outcome of this federal challenge, New York State, in a classic partnership of assault, moved in to wipe out the organization. Because the leadership of the Communist Party had just been convicted of violations of the Smith Act, the New York Superintendent of Insurance asserted that there was a "danger" the leaders of the IWO might also be charged with violation of the Smith Act, and they might at some time in the future also be found guilty. This potential danger was said to present a "hazardous" condition within the meaning of the insurance law.

Here was a new twist to the Cold War formula. This was not just a question of moving against the leadership of a people's organization, the technique devised in the Smith Act trial. It was a move to dissolve the entire organization. We had never dreamed they would move so far.

Shipka explained that there was going to be a hearing before a

New York state judge on the petition to liquidate. The IWO leadership had already asked an experienced trial lawyer in Brooklyn, Ray Weisman, to represent the IWO. Would we help him to prepare for the hearing and take on a share of the responsibility for developing the constitutional defense?

In a few days we were plunged into a morass of legal research into the meaning of the words in the insurance statute, dredging out support for the position, which seemed crystal clear to us, that the use of the term "hazardous" obviously must be restricted to *financial* hazards. Anything else would be an open assault on the elementary protections of the First Amendment. We became so convinced of the power of our argument that it seemed inevitable that Henry Clay Greenburg, the New York state judge who had signed the original order to show cause, would throw out the petition. Known as a good "law" judge, one who placed a great deal of emphasis on scholarship and learning, he was bound to dismiss the entire proceeding after hearing our arguments. For the moment I was swept away by the force of our legal arguments and could not believe that the proposed liquidation of the society might actually be tolerated by the courts.

In a sense, it was still too soon after the Smith Act trial to foresee the full consequences of what was happening. Not until a number of years later did I begin to develop an insight into an underlying misconception that inevitably affects those of us seeking to integrate legal skills with political struggles. We sometimes fall into an attitude of overreliance upon the stated premises of justice and fairness built into the constitutional system, which from time to time overwhelms the recognition of political reality. As a result, while we were preparing the motions to dismiss the petition for the liquidation of the IWO as wholly unlawful, without a shred of statutory support, and totally in violation of the state and federal constitutions, we became filled with a feeling of utter disbelief that the proposed dissolution of the society would ever be tolerated by the courts.

In a way, the attitude of the IWO officers themselves served to feed this sense of unspoken reliance on the legal structure. Unlike the attitude within the UE, which always responded to new legal attacks within the context of discussing how to mobilize support and develop a fighting resistance among the workers in the plants involved, the IWO appeared to have no discussions at this critical moment as to how the legal response could stimulate the involvement of its 130,000 members in some sort of massive defense activity, to say nothing of a political counteroffensive. A committee of individual policyholders and members was later organized to intervene in the proceedings, but this remained wholly a technical legal move, designed to raise in the proceedings certain issues which the lawyers representing the organization felt they could not bring forward themselves. The Cold War strategy of fear, fed by the recent Smith Act trial and inflamed by the intensifying moves of the Justice Department, the congressional committees, the press, and now the government machinery, was having its effect in subduing the responses of the people's organizations under attack.

With some exceptions, the UE being one, the powerful people's movements of the thirties and forties were on the defensive, and no political strategy of counterattack was even being considered. One of the results was an almost total dependence upon the formal legal defense put up by lawyers to each new attack. This in turn encouraged an overreliance upon the legal structure itself and, as we were experiencing in the IWO case, inevitably affected both the people under attack and the lawyers.

As the Cold War went on, these expectations, both of the system and of the performance of lawyers, instilled deep feelings of hopelessness, sometimes resulting in personal disasters and tragedies. Several of these were to touch us personally. The frustrations piled up on even the strongest and most courageous people's lawyers, ones like Harry Sacher of the Smith Act trial, who was to share office space with us before his death in the early 1960s. Time and again in his last years, in the intimacy of his office, Harry would talk to us younger people about the loneliness and unhappiness that had flowed from the defeats and abandonments of the period.

And so when Judge Greenberg blandly disregarded what had seemed to me to be our unanswerable argument, so carefully documented, that the proposal to liquidate the IWO was wholly without legal authority and completely unconstitutional, and in-

89

stead ordered a full-scale hearing on the charges of the New York Superintendent of Insurance, I was filled with dismay. We were now faced with the prospect of a court hearing where the stakes would be the life or death of one of the most successful working people's organizations. The reality of the Cold War had moved even closer, and certain of the more troubling aspects of being a people's lawyer were beginning to surface.

One question was becoming especially insistent. How does one function as a lawyer for the people when there appears to be no immediate prospect of struggle other than in the arena of formal legal defense? If the driving motivation of a people's lawyer ought to be the use of skills and legal techniques to help create an atmosphere in which the people themselves can better organize, function, and move forward, how does one meet this responsibility when the people's movements seem to have lost their own sense of struggle and are wholly on the defensive? This became an increasingly pressing question, which sometimes seemed insoluble, as the work of the new firm took off during our first year together.

Another question quickly became apparent as we struggled to create a law firm that could function under the enormous tensions of the period. At the very center of the question of whether we could survive the demands of the work was the degree to which we could build healthy, honest, open relationships with the people on whose shoulders a great deal of the work of the firm would rest, the legal secretaries whose work around the clock was essential to fulfilling the responsibilities thrown on us all. In this respect the dedicated activity of Phyllis Lewis, Hannah Leichtman, Selma Trauber, and Myra Jordan Polan made a major contribution to our ability to keep going in those early years. Their extraordinary commitment to fight against the Cold War led these four workers to fulfill with great drive and accomplishment the frequently overwhelming tasks placed upon them by the volume and nature of the work.

One of the most serious problems we had to come to grips with from the start was how to overcome the elitist and often sexist attitudes that male lawyers then brought, and too often still bring, to their relationships with legal workers, who are almost always women. In grappling with this problem, I came to understand the tremendous importance of establishing an equal relationship with such co-workers. To the degree that we were able to share fully with legal workers the issues in a case and to the degree that they participated with us in the tactical and strategic decisions, to that degree did we begin to realize that we had real colleagues with us, able to share the roughest and most difficult decisions, as well as to provide the kind of support needed to continue functioning at a level that would keep our heads above water. For we were literally swamped with work.

The UE work continued at a hectic pace, brought on by the government's decision to focus its strength on attempting to isolate and then destroy this remaining powerful center of working people's militancy. Emspak, Matles, and Quinn, who during the past summer had refused to cooperate with the House Un-American Activities Committee political witch hunt by asserting their constitutional rights and privileges not to respond to the committee's questioning, were brought to trial for contempt of Congress. To our amazement, Jim Matles was acquitted by the trial judge on technical grounds, but Julius Emspak and Tom Quinn were found guilty. The convictions of Emspak and Quinn were serious. Not only were jail sentences hanging over their heads, but the UE would be devastated if the government and the companies knocked out Emspak for any period of time. And Quinn was critically needed in the Pittsburgh area where the raiding of UE plants was intense. Most damaging was the way the convictions could be used in the propaganda blasts now developing against the UE. "Contempt of Congress" would have an ominous ring on leaflets handed out at plant gates by raiding unions in this time of mounting Cold War hysteria.

That hysteria was now reaching a new peak. On March 8, 1951, the trial of Julius and Ethel Rosenberg and Morton Sobell for atomic espionage on behalf of the Russians opened in New York City. The Smith Act trial had bluntly propounded the theory that those who associated with Communists were part of a conspiracy to overthrow the government. Now the Rosenberg-Sobell trial sought to establish in the public mind that "reds" were in addition the most dangerous and despised of traitors—spies—deserving no less than the ultimate penalty. The trial was a quick job as these things go, and two weeks later, on March 29, the jury found

91

the trio guilty as spies. Within a week, the Cold War formula received its ultimate embellishment. On April 5, the headlines blared, "A-Spy and Wife Sentenced to Die." Morton Sobell was sentenced to thirty years. The sentencing judge, Irving Kaufman, remarked with contempt, "By your betrayal you have altered the course of history. I consider your crime worse than murder." Almost twenty-five years would pass before the shocking fact emerged, in papers released from secret FBI files in the aftermath of Watergate, that this sentence of death had actually been discussed as politically "necessary" in secret talks between the trial judge and the government prosecutors before the trial even opened!

The Rosenberg death sentence was the finishing touch to the machinery for the repression of all popular dissent that the administration had been carefully constructing from the first days of the Cold War. Now everything was set. The Evansville formula was expanded to national proportions. Anyone actively organizing opposition to the policies of the government or the industrial power structure, whether individually or in organizations, was subject to a one-two punch: since all "Communists" or "Communist sympathizers" were part of a national conspiracy of spies and traitors, it was legitimate not just to drive them out of every aspect of life, fire them, isolate them, ban them, jail them, but even to kill them if necessary. To eliminate the troublemakers from a factory, school, union, office, or organization, it was necessary only to identify them as "Communists" or "Communist sympathizers." Then the ax would fall with the sanction of legality.

The identification itself was comparatively easy. After all, when the Rosenbergs were arrested, cans to collect money for loyalist Spain were found in their closet. And the Communists had backed Henry Wallace in 1948 as the Progressive Party candidate for President. There was a good chance the person to be eliminated had supported either loyalist Spain or the Progressive Party. And there were plenty of other identifying marks to spot Cold War "subversives." Participation in one form or another in any of the hundreds of popular causes that the Communists had supported throughout the thirties and the forties became the touchstone for identifying subversives.

The application of the Cold War formula was in full swing by the spring of 1951. We had barely begun to be known as a firm of young lawyers willing to get into these situations when we were almost drowned with work. As we worked on the full IWO hearing before Judge Greenberg and drafted the Emspak and Quinn appeals briefs, in between dashing around the country whenever Dave Scribner alerted us to the next UE crisis spot, we found ourselves drawn into another situation that drove home the extraordinary dimensions of the Cold War offensive. It involved us in an arena of legal struggle that we would never have dreamed of, the Administrative Tribunal of the United Nations.

Late in March, five UN employees, including Benedict Alper, the president of the United Nations Staff Association, were summarily discharged by Trygvie Lie, the Secretary-General of the UN, after he had received what were termed "confidential" reports from the FBI as to their "reliability and trustworthiness." We were called in to represent these employees, all United States citizens. They were losing their employment as a result of what looked like a direct attempt by the United States government to inject the Cold War formula into the United Nations itself. Not until later were these firings admitted by UN officials to have been the result of United States insistence upon the elimination of what was characterized as the "subversive influence" of certain American citizens within the UN. At the time, we had no conception of this actual extent of United States intervention into the supposedly neutral operations of the UN structure, but as we proceeded to arguments before the Administrative Tribunal of the UN, its highest judicial body, it became clear that although there was not the slightest justification for the firing of these admittedly capable and devoted employees, the power of the United States within the world organization in those days was such that the final outcome of the Tribunal hearings was inevitable. Its members reached the embarrassed conclusion that there was nothing they could do to remedy the actions of the Secretary-General. It was becoming strikingly apparent that no limits would be set on the extent to which the Cold War formula would be applied in every arena of life.

This was driven home to me in a particularly ironic way. Don-

ner, Perlin, and I had agreed among ourselves that in order to
meet the more mundane responsibilities of paying the rent, the
salaries for legal workers, and some money for us to live on, each
of us had to develop at least one area of private practice, plain ordinary legal cases without political implications, which would
bring in sufficient fees to carry our other work. We recognized the
harsh reality that as the Cold War intensified, more and more
people lost their jobs, and resources dwindled, the financial ability of organizations and individuals to defend themselves would
drastically diminish. I assumed the responsibility for developing
what became known as the area of "theatrical law." In college
and law school I had come to know a number of people who were
beginning careers in writing, acting, and directing in the rapidly
expanding television industry. Many of these people I had met as
friends of my younger brother Ernest, who was on the way to becoming a successful radio and television writer. Some of these
people were doing very well, and their credits were beginning to
appear in popular programs. In the normal course of events they
had a good deal of legal work which had to be done, mainly negotiating and writing up contracts. Some of them were willing to
let me try my hand at this work, so I found myself increasingly
involved in at least one area of nonpolitical, comparatively well-
paid legal activity.

Or so I thought. One day in that spring of 1951, one of our most
successful theatrical clients, Arnold Perl, the senior writer for a
popular television show called "The Big Story," came into the office to see me. I could tell by the tone of his voice that this was no
minor matter. He explained that he was going to be fired. All of
his contracts with the producer, Prockter Productions, were about
to be torn up. "Why?" I asked in amazement. His reviews had
been fabulous, and he was acknowledged to be one of the best
writers in television. "Simple," he said, "I've been blacklisted.
Some joker in Syracuse, New York, name of Johnson, who runs a
supermarket, called up the sponsors of the show, American To-
bacco, and said if they didn't have me thrown off the show, he'd
start a boycott of their products!" Being blacklisted meant Perl
would be not only fired by Prockter Productions but excluded
from writing jobs anywhere in the industry.

Why, I asked, was this Johnson insisting that he be blacklisted?

Some "superpatriotic," right-wing outfit, which published a magazine called *Red Channels,* had listed Perl as a "Communist sympathizer" because during the war he had written a script for a fund raiser for Russian war relief in Madison Square Garden and in 1947 he had attended a peace conference at the Waldorf Astoria. Now the producer and the sponsor were telling him, no contract, no work, unless he "cleared" himself. And how did they suggest he should "clear" himself? No problem, just appear as a friendly witness before the House Un-American Activities Committee and tell them the names of all the "subversives" he knew who were writing for television. There was the plan, simple and clear. If he talked, he wrote; if he refused to play the game and finger his colleagues, he was finished.

Perl then threw out the hardest question yet, "What the hell do we do now? I told them to go to hell." With that question, the area of "theatrical law" was turned upside down. We were facing a particularly insidious example of the Cold War formula, and as the blacklist apparatus spread its net, attacking one after another of the most creative writers, actors, and directors in the country, our search for a meaningful answer to the challenging question of "what do we do" led to a dead end.

Then in June 1951, the Supreme Court, over the powerful dissents of Justices Black and Douglas, upheld the constitutionality of the Smith Act and affirmed the convictions of the leaders of the Communist Party. When the word reached us, we were jamming out the last pages of a brief to Judge Greenberg in the New York Supreme Court, arguing that the evidence presented in the hearing before him, which had ended in April, did not justify liquidating the IWO. We frantically tried to rewrite our brief, arguing that the news out of Washington did not affect the IWO case, because not even the Superintendent of Insurance had ever charged that the IWO officers or the society itself had violated the Smith Act. But we knew what was going to happen. The decision in Washington was the final signal. The Supreme Court, highest symbol of legality in the country, had placed its stamp of approval on the wholesale application of the Cold War formula. "Communists" and "Communist sympathizers" were now fair game.

Within a month, Judge Greenberg entered an order dissolving

95

the IWO. I remember bitterly comparing what we called the two "execution speeches," Judge Kaufman's statement the day of the sentencing to death of the Rosenbergs, and Judge Greenberg's order of dissolution of the IWO. Greenberg admitted reluctantly that the organization was in excellent financial shape and had done a beautiful job of protecting the security and needs of its thousands of members. However, the IWO constituted "an enormous danger" to the people of New York, because sometime in the future it "might" be convicted of a violation of the Smith Act. The "Communist influence" within the society was too strong. After all, the evidence showed that IWO had supported the Scottsboro defendants in the 1930s and had participated in raising funds to support the defense of the republican government of Spain. It was dangerous to permit such an organization to continue to exist. The IWO officers and the New York Superintendent of Insurance were ordered to prepare for the society's final dissolution.

With the Smith Act decision, the Cold War machinery took a giant step forward. During the summer of 1951 over hundred Communist activists were rounded up in New York City, Pittsburgh, Los Angeles, San Francisco, Maryland, and Hawaii, in what became known as the second-string Smith Act arrests. Under the shadow of the Rosenberg death sentences and the Supreme Court vindication of the Smith Act formula, a full-scale operation was underway to put the brand of traitor on the entire people's movement. Every day brought new phone calls to our office. Workers in plants who faced security clearances under the loyalty order, writers and actors hit with the exploding blacklist, UN employees facing the growing purge, foreign-born IWO members suddenly hit with deportation proceedings because of membership in a "subversive" organization—on and on it went. And underneath it all, an unanswered question haunted us—how were we to fight as people's lawyers in this atmosphere of retreat, defeat, and disarray among the people's movements?

4

Grand Juries
and the Rosenbergs

It was no accident that the work with the UE continually provided insight into the pressing question of how a lawyer for the people's movements can function effectively in the midst of frustrating attacks. Even when the government attack was most intense, the question of how to fight back was always on the UE agenda. This was one of the reasons that big business and its friends in Washington were so determined to use every resource at their command to eliminate this vital center of trade union militancy. No matter what the nature of the attack, one thing never changed: the UE people would not run. Often they did not win, but always the question was how to stand and fight—how to reach out to the working people in the plants and factories. This attitude of the UE to meeting the Cold War attacks affected our own responses and thinking as people's lawyers, shaping approaches that would not have emerged so sharply in other situations where the atmosphere was more defensive and less tied to the central UE question of how to move the people.

There was just this fighting tone in Dave Scribner's voice when he called me one November morning in 1952 and said urgently, "You'd better come up here as soon as possible. Your friend Cohn is up to it again." As I walked over to the UE office, all sorts of questions rushed through my head. What was Roy Cohn up to now? Scribner had sounded tense.

Scribner's phrase "your friend" had been ironic, for Cohn was hardly my friend. He had been in my class at Columbia Law School, where our contact was pretty much limited to an episode toward the end of our last year, when he suddenly became very friendly and even expressed interest in joining the student chapter of the Lawyer's Guild, which I had helped organize. This was merely a prelude to borrowing from me what at the law school in those days was very precious: my collection of "purples," the invaluable class notes that the *Law Review* collected and produced on a purple-inked mimeograph machine for the use of its members in preparing for exams. I lent him the purples and never heard from him again. But he obviously got through the exams, because the next time I ran into him was at the federal courthouse in Foley Square in 1951. He was then a special "confidential" assistant to the United States Attorney, Irving Saypol, with whom he was working on the Rosenberg-Sobell trial.

Several months later I had my first direct conflict with Cohn. It was during a carefully orchestrated CIO-company-government raid on the UE local at the General Electric plant in Schenectady, New York. Just a few days before the NLRB representation election was scheduled to take place, by strange coincidence two federal grand jury subpoenaes arrived in New York for Emspak and Matles. Cohn showed up as the representative of the United States Attorney who was in charge of that grand jury, and the news that he planned to question the UE national officers about the "truthfulness" of the Taft-Hartley non-Communist affidavits that they had signed a year before was perfectly timed to produce scare headlines in the Schenectady papers a few days before the election. But Emspak and Matles blasted Cohn before the jury, and his efforts to discredit them in advance of the NLRB vote fell flat. Cohn's legal arguments before the sitting federal judge, Sylvester Ryan, were too extreme even in the tense atmosphere of those days, and Judge Ryan threw out the contempt charges.

When I responded to Scribner's call in November 1952, I wondered what clever scheme Cohn, who was still with the United States Attorney's office in New York, was involved in now. After ten minutes in Dave Scribner's office, I understood. Cohn had come up with the Taft-Hartley affidavits again, but this time with a brilliant new twist.

Originally the UE and other unions, including the fur, office, and communication workers, had refused to go along with the non-Communist affidavit requirement, but in the face of sweeping raids on their membership by the auto worker and steelworker unions, they had reluctantly decided in September 1949 to comply with the provisions of the act. The organizational reasons for this decision seemed compelling. A union like the UE, although representing a majority of the workers at a plant and having a contract with the company, was barred from NLRB elections if it did not file the non-Communist affidavits. Only the raiding union could appear on the ballot, with disastrous results. So the UE decided to file the non-Communist affidavits, which up to that point it had opposed as a matter of principle. Afterward the union began to hold its own against the massive attacks, as in Evansville and Schenectady, and to everyone's amazement started winning labor board elections.

This was too much for the companies and the raiding unions. The whole purpose of the Taft-Hartley affidavit requirement was to isolate and then eliminate militant unions like the UE. But the device was not working. This is where Cohn came in again. He met secretly with General Electric and Westinghouse management representatives, and together they worked out what seemed to be a perfect gambit. Accordingly Cohn used his position in the United States Attorney's office to call the national UE officers once again before federal grand jury, where he repeated the questions about the "truthfulness" of the non-Communist affidavits they had signed. This was, of course, what he had done a year before in New York, and it had gotten nowhere. The federal court itself had held that the UE officers had a right to refuse to participate in Cohn's fishing expedition, and when they did so again, he obviously did not have sufficient evidence to get the grand jury to indict them for perjury. But this time a new wrinkle was added when Cohn filed in the name of the federal grand jury a written statement called a "presentment."

I was mystified when Scribner told me about this development, thinking that I had missed something at law school in the course on elementary criminal procedure. "I thought grand juries were supposed to indict people rather than issue statements," I said to him. He smiled wryly and replied, "So did I," as he handed me the copy of the presentment that he had just gotten from the courthouse.

It was a beautiful scheme that Cohn and the companies had worked out. The presentment reported that the grand jury, after questioning the UE officers and several other union leaders, including the officers of the fur workers, the office workers, and the communication workers, had concluded that the affidavits filed were "not worth the paper they are written on" and were really "a subterfuge." Based on this sweeping conclusion, the grand jury formally recommended that NLRB "revoke the certification" of the unions involved. There it was, a formula for instant destruction. As I sat there increasingly stunned, Scribner explained the final twist. The Washington papers that afternoon had printed a story that came directly from the office of the general counsel of the NLRB. Based upon Cohn's presentment and paying "due deference" to a federal grand jury, the NLRB was considering ordering the UE officers to "affirm" and "demonstrate" the truth of the non-Communist affidavits they had filed. Failure to "affirm" would result in a declaration by the NLRB that the union was not "in compliance" with the act. This would mean that these unions could not appear on any election ballots and that companies did not have to enter into labor contracts with them.

This was a crisis situation in every sense of the word. If the presentment was not undone quickly, the companies, the raiding unions, and the government had an effective technique to wipe out unions like the UE. As we stewed over the situation, one of the union organizers rushed into the room and threw down a copy of the afternoon *World-Telegram.* The headline put the problem bluntly, "Jury Would Outlaw Four Leftist Unions." Cohn's technique eliminated all necessity of the government's actually proving any charges that these unions were "subversive" or that their officers were "Communists" and had thus "perjured" themselves in the Taft-Hartley affidavits. The plan was a tour de force, and its implications were awesome. We could all visualize the impact of the headlines to come, in one election situation after another: "Federal Grand Jury Finds UE Officers Red, Union To Be Outlawed." It was like writing the "trial" in *Alice's Adventures in Wonderland* right into the heart of our legal structure.

The reaction of the UE officers was direct and to the point. There had to be an all-out organizational response to this new threat, and at the heart of the response must be an attack on the legitimacy of the grand jury action. As in Evansville, once again the UE officers' direction to the lawyers was simple. "Do something, and do it fast." Our work as lawyers was to take some action that would assist the union organizers as they went into the factories and meeting halls to challenge the presentment and which would simultaneously say to the NLRB and the companies, "Don't think you can get away with moving so fast down the road to illegalization. We're going to fight you every step of the way." The question was how to attack the presentment without falling into the defensive trap of accepting its assumptions— how to take the legal offensive and block Cohn's maneuver.

That night, as we started digging into cases in the law library involving grand juries, we quickly discovered that this was not going to be easy. The inescapable conclusion seemed to be that there was no way to keep a grand jury from performing its functions. One thing that was sacrosanct was the right of a grand jury to move ahead and carry out its operations. Nothing had proved more futile in the past than the few attempts made by people to get an injunction against the functioning of a grand jury. If mounting a legal counterattack had seemed difficult in Evansville and Schenectady, here it looked totally impossible.

And then, as I hopelessly read and reread the few old court decisions peremptorily brushing aside any effort to interfere with the functioning of a grand jury, something clicked. These cases always used one phrase: no court was permitted to stop a grand jury "from its lawful functioning." This was the opening I needed. For the next two days I threw myself into it. What was the "lawful functioning" of the grand jury? And was Cohn's manipulation of the jury to produce the presentment part of its lawful functioning and thus protected absolutely from court interference?

These questions forced me to undertake an intensive explora-

101

tion into history, which I would never before have dreamed could have the slightest relevance to the work of a people's lawyer involved in the life-and-death struggle of a modern labor union. The search for an understanding of the perimeters of the lawful functioning of a grand jury took me back to the earliest days of English law, and it produced an insight which over the years has proved invaluable in forging new legal weapons to help turn retreat, and sometimes rout, into counterattack and advance. Probing the historical origins of a legal institution such as the grand jury opened up an approach with almost unbelievable potential.

The grand jury as an institution was born out of bitter popular struggle against the oppression of the British Crown. It was specifically designed to protect people against harassment by prosecution officers of the Crown, who frequently instituted criminal proceedings for improper purposes, without cause or justification, in order to obtain results far beyond the scope of the criminal law itself. As a result, the demand grew for a structure to give representatives of the community an opportunity to consider in advance whether prosecutors should be allowed to proceed with serious criminal charges. People otherwise had no protection against groundless accusations, which could result in the enormous inconvenience of a trial with the risk of possible conviction.

According to the old cases drawn from the cobwebs of English history, the institution of the grand jury was thus created to be "a shield against the oppression of the Crown." Its function was solely to protect against unfounded accusations by requiring that a cross-section of the community pass upon criminal accusations before individuals could be forced to stand trial. The last thing in the world a grand jury was supposed to be was a tool of the prosecutor for the Crown, manipulated in whatever way the prosecutor devised. To protect against any weakening of the role of the grand jury as "a shield" for the people, the courts were required to prevent abuses or distortions of its single critical function, which was to vote on indictments after due consideration of the adequacy or inadequacy of the prosecutor's evidence. This alone was the meaning of the "lawful functioning" of a grand jury as embedded in the federal Constitution and the Bill of Rights. It was to be a shield against the oppression of the prosecutors, the representatives of the executive arm of government.

102

This historic function of the grand jury conflicted sharply with the modern reality of the institution. Roy Cohn was acting with the federal grand jury exactly as every other contemporary prosecutor acted with a grand jury—as if they owned it. The shield of the people had become the tool of the prosecutor.

But as we thought about this reversal of roles, a startling fact slipped into place. In one way Cohn was acting a little differently from other prosecutors. He had crossed the line here. Whereas the ordinary functioning of the indictment process kept the prosecutor's role hidden, the use of the presentment, a published report, reversed the historical role of the grand jury, openly turning it upside down. Instead of protecting the people accused by examining whether or not there was any evidence that warranted criminal proceedings against them, this jury had condemned them by issuing a report which, because it was *not* an indictment, foreclosed any opportunity for a fair hearing and any chance to refute the charges. This was wholly beyond the lawful functioning of a grand jury.

With this new understanding of the legal institution, the pieces of the counterattack suddenly fell into place. Since courts had traditionally refused even to consider interfering with the lawful functioning of grand juries, why not file a complaint in federal court charging that the role of this grand jury had been totally distorted by the United States Attorney and that the presentment issued was wholly beyond the lawful functioning of the grand jury and should therefore be, in the classic words of such cases, "expunged and stricken"? Here was an approach, flowing from the historical origins of the legal institution itself, which provided a counterattack against the presentment.

After drafting an application for an order expunging the presentment, Scribner and I talked the matter over with the UE officers. They urged us to move ahead. They saw the organizational advantage of taking the initiative in this dangerous situation and of challenging the Cohn-company-rival union plan before it drove ahead. No one had any illusions about the outcome. Every branch of government, every major company, and the entire CIO structure were now openly attacking the union. No one expected simple solutions in the courts. But the now familiar creed of the UE leadership was: if we do not run, the workers in the shops will stand with us. The proposed legal attack on the presentment was part of not running.

So we filed the motion to expunge in the district court. It created a sensation when it was called on the regular motion calendar. The judge acted as if he could not quite believe what he was reading. He repeated quizzically several times, "Expunge? You want to expunge this presentment?" I sensed his relief when, in the middle of Scribner's presentation of our argument, one of the clerks handed the judge a note. He stopped Scribner short and snapped, "This is not for me. Take it to Judge Weinfeld. He was the judge in charge of that grand jury."

When we went to Judge Weinfeld's chambers to discuss with his clerk a date for the argument, no one seemed to be in much of a hurry. Christmas season was almost upon us, and the clerk blandly said that he would call us after the first of the year for an argument date. We had mixed feelings about the delay. On the one hand, the rumblings we had heard of possible NLRB action based on the presentment made the delay seem serious. On the other hand, we were still alive. The precipitous, out-of-hand dismissal which we had expected was put off. This might give us time to dig more deeply into the ancient English yearbooks and dredge out further background on the popular origins of the grand jury. Word had it that Weinfeld was a "law" judge, who thus might be more responsive if our unorthodox approach were backed by strong authority and not just spun out of fantasy or wishful thinking.

But when we got back to the UE office that afternoon, it was clear that we would have no time that holiday season for a leisurely academic preparation for the coming argument. The news awaiting us was grim. Federal marshals had arrived earlier in the day with papers announcing that the Department of Justice was filing a suit to revoke the citizenship of Jim Matles, who had come to the United States as a youngster from Rumania. The Department of Justice charged that years before, at the time that he had become a citizen, he was secretly a Communist.

"Denaturalization" proceedings, as they were technically called, were flaring up all over the country, as one of the major Cold War assaults on foreign-born citizens who had taken an active role in progressive causes during the 1930s and 1940s, particularly in the building of the industrial union movement. But there was a special meaning in the timing of this particular proceeding. While a major scheme was underway virtually to outlaw the UE, the Department of Justice coincidently decided that this was the very moment to knock out Matles, the union's director of organization.

The concerted attack on the union and its leadership became even more obvious three days later, only a few hours after word had come through from Washington of the federal appeals court affirming Emspak's conviction and jail sentence for contempt of the House Un-American Activities Committee. Then the ax fell. Russell Nixon, the Washington legislative representative of the UE, called with the news that the NLRB had just issued the order for which Cohn's clever ploy had paved the way. Using the grand jury's presentment as an excuse, the NLRB abruptly declared that unless the UE officers conceded the invalidity of all the non-Communist affidavits they had filed over the last two years and immediately signed new affidavits within seven days, the national UE would be out of compliance with the Taft-Hartley Act, with all of the dire consequences that would entail for the future existence of the union.

Everything was happening at once. As Donner, Perlin, and I tried to take stock of what was going on and what we had to do, we felt almost overwhelmed. We had to think simultaneously of how to proceed with Matles' defense in the denaturalization proceeding, how to prepare the appeal to the Supreme Court in Emspak's case, how to handle the presentment hearing before Judge Weinfeld, and what to do about the NLRB order. It was a relief when the telephone cut into our discussions with a message from Scribner that an emergency meeting of the entire UE leadership had been called to discuss the developments, and we were invited to attend.

Representatives came to that meeting of December 28, 1952, from every local union throughout the country. An atmosphere of grim reality pervaded the discussions. Everyone knew that this was no routine union gathering to consider proposals from the leadership; it was an extraordinary session to save the very life of the union. As the UE officers discussed this new stage in the Taft-Hartley assault, a central theme emerged which was to have a profound effect on our thinking and activity as lawyers in the people's movements in the years to come. Their overriding concern was that in this situation the union should not be sidetracked into a defensive, apologetic posture. Although the individual defense of union officers was important and no officer or member would ever be abandoned under company or government attack, the union itself must not be diverted from its central role of championing the everyday needs of working people. We faced, as Albert Fitzgerald, the UE President, stressed, a campaign to destroy the UE, the symbol of militant unionism, and ultimately to destroy free collective bargaining in America. The key to resisting this campaign was the mobilization of the entire UE membership to protect the union's collective bargaining status. Critical to this mobilization was the UE members' understanding that the NLRB had changed drastically from the days of the New Deal, when it supported the unions, and that it was now a tool of the employers and the antilabor forces in control of Washington. A plan was drawn up for a major campaign of organizational protest by the union members, including local protest meetings, delegations to Congress, and petitions and telegrams to the NLRB demanding that it rescind its order. This plan also included the direction, which was most important for us as lawyers, to undertake a "full-scale legal fight" against the NLRB's action.

When we met with Dave Scribner at the end of the first day of the two-day meeting, our legal direction seemed momentarily clear. Although sooner or later we would have to face up to the serious problems of the pending Matles denaturalization action and the Supreme Court appeal from Emspak's contempt conviction, our immediate concern had to be how to attack and, in the course of the attack, to expose the NLRB's threat to the continued life of the union. What we must do was obvious: attack the NLRB directive in the federal courts. Any effort to convince the NLRB bureaucracy itself to change its strategy would have been futile, given the current atmosphere in Washington. General Dwight Eisenhower had just been elected President in a Republican sweep, overwhelming the cautious liberalism of Adlai Stevenson, the Democratic candidate. The conservative establishment was riding high as the Republicans prepared to restock the federal agencies with their own people. This was no moment to expect anything from the NLRB, which had edged into a position openly allied with big business, particularly as the tune in Washington was being increasingly called by that watchdog of the Cold War, Senator Joseph McCarthy. The obvious way to proceed, therefore, was to launch an immediate attack on the NLRB directive in the federal courts.

Although our mandate as union lawyers was clear, when we started to translate it into action that evening by framing a federal injunction against the NLRB order, we suddenly stopped short. "Impossible," said Scribner, as the weight of years of experience as a labor lawyer pressed down on him. Instantly I knew what had hit him. We faced what seemed to be an insuperable roadblock.

During the 1930s and the 1940s a whole body of law had developed which held that no one could go into a federal court and get an injunction to interfere with or stop the functioning of a government agency like the NLRB. The technical words were that one had to "exhaust" all remedies, go through every level of appeal, before the agency itself before a federal court would consider the case. Yet we had not even begun to exhaust our remedies before the NLRB. That would require months, maybe years, while the crucial order decertifying UE remained effective. The only thing exhausted, someone bitterly pointed out, would be the union, and it would be exhausted because it would be dead.

It was then that the full irony of the situation hit us. This entire body of law had been built up in the past mainly by the progressive labor lawyers who were fighting the efforts of employers to go into federal courts to get injunctions to stop the NLRB from performing its function, as mandated in the Wagner Act, the original New Deal statute, of assisting workers to form trade unions and bargain collectively with employers. It was the lawyers representing the CIO unions who in the early days of industrial organizing successfully developed the legal concept that a legitimacy attached to the actions of government agencies such as the NLRB, which meant that companies could not interfere with an organizing drive protected by the NLRB by immediately going into a federal court to stop it. Under this principle the company was required first to exhaust all avenues of appeal within the NLRB, and only after a final decision by the NLRB could the company take an appeal to a federal court. This requirement usually gave the workers time to complete their organizing and the process of bargaining before the company could get an injunction from a friendly antiunion federal judge to stop the assistance that the NLRB was giving to the workers, even though that assistance was part of the original congressional mandate.

We faced a really mixed-up situation. Life had totally changed since the 1930s and 1940s. The NLRB, which in the early years had been an important source of strength and assistance to unions, had turned into its opposite. Its present role in the Roy Cohn-big business maneuver was clearly to help to destroy the independent militant trade unions. And the body of law which progressive labor lawyers had themselves constructed in order to protect the NLRB's original role now became a barrier to challenging that role's reversal.

The conventional solution for us as lawyers would have been to go back to the union meeting the next day and tell them frankly that there was no way to launch a legal counterattack on the NLRB and that the union would just have to take its chances and accept the inevitability of an order of decertification. We could then exhaust our remedies inside the NLRB and take an appeal to the federal courts, maybe two or three years later. But this was an alternative which we refused even to think about that evening. Within the context of the situation, we had only one choice, to do what we had done in Evansville, in Schenectady, and two weeks earlier in New York when attacking the grand jury's presentment. We would concentrate on the reality of the situation and search, in the body of conceptual law, for a key to taking the offensive.

And once again we found it. As we struggled with the case law which had developed during the 1930s and 1940s to protect the NLRB from company interference, one simple fact suddenly opened the door for us. The refusal to permit federal court interference with actions of the NLRB prior to the exhaustion of all other remedies within the agency itself rested upon a fundamental assumption that the NLRB was functioning within the boundaries of its mandate from Congress to protect and implement the constitutional right of working people to organize freely into trade unions and to bargain collectively with their employers without interference or restraint. As long as the NLRB was operating within this mandate, it was to be protected from any court interference, because these ends—the right to organize into unions and bargain collectively—were constitutional objectives of profound importance to all people. But when the NLRB acted outside of these objectives, it in effect acted without power or constitutional sanction, and thus the entire body of law that had grown up around it did not apply. At such a moment a federal court was duty bound to intervene and stop the unauthorized action without requiring the exhaustion of remedies within the NLRB.

This was it. We agreed among ourselves that we could develop a strong basis for a legal counterattack against the NLRB order, and the next day we told the UE officers that we were set to move. Our decision was announced at the meeting as a part of, but by no means the major part of, the counterattack to be opened immediately. The main attention of the UE leadership was on the intensive organizational work to be done when they returned to their home locals throughout the country, where the emphasis would be placed on large delegations of workers pressing local Congress people to protest to the NLRB against its illegal action.

Scribner and I immediately headed for Washington to file our complaint for an injunction against the NLRB in federal court. Since we were asking for emergency temporary relief as well as for a permanent injunction, we were granted a hearing in open court. I was a little surprised to discover in court how seriously the government was taking us. Four lawyers showed up to represent the NLRB. The federal judge, R. Dickinson Letts, pressed them hard on where, in the basic law setting up the NLRB, they found any authority at all to challenge the legitimacy of the non-Communist affidavits that the UE officers had already signed and filed. Then one of the NLRB lawyers blurted out, "We're just following that presentment from the grand jury in New York." "Presentment?" asked Judge Letts quizzically. "Did they hand down indictments?"

This gave Scribner the opportunity he needed to get in a fast word about our attack on the legality of the presentment, which was awaiting decision before Judge Weinfeld in New York. Scribner also threw in a powerful piece of information learned from Russ Nixon that morning. Testimony by a representative of the Department of Justice before a Senate subcommittee had just been released which revealed that repeated investigations of these affidavits by the department had found nothing to challenge. This highlighted the underhanded nature of the Roy Cohn-NLRB maneuver. So when Judge Letts ended the hearing that afternoon by stating from the bench that since many important issues were involved requiring serious consideration, he would expect no action from the NLRB on its challenged order until after his decision, for the first time I sensed the possibility of an extraordinary turn of events—that the judge was taking our legal position seriously.

Later that day, though, we ran into a problem of some complexity. Scribner and I were spending the evening with a group of his friends, labor lawyers who included some of the most experienced veterans of the historic battles in the early days of the CIO. One of them had been a top lawyer for the NLRB itself in the New Deal period. When we casually talked about the approach we had developed that afternoon in court to justify our request for an immediate federal court injunction against the NLRB, their reaction was one of horror. In effect, they said, "Look here, we spent years constructing this theory of the exhaustion of remedies and ultimately getting the Supreme Court to accept it. We agree with you that the NLRB has changed its role and is no longer doing what it was set up for—to support the basic right of working people to organize. We agree it is acting as an agent of the big employers. Who can disagree with that?" Then they touched on the sensitive point. "But what you're doing is just for today. Some day, maybe soon, this will change. Some day the NLRB will once again play the role it was supposed to play, that of protecting the unions and the working people. And if you are successful now in breaking down the conceptual barrier that we built in the courts to protect the NLRB from interference from corporations, where will we all be then? You may help at this moment, but you will irreparably damage the future."

On certain levels, this was a disturbing argument. In a way, it

110

may have been more upsetting for Dave Scribner than for me, because he was very much a part of that generation of progressive labor lawyers who had carefully, brick by brick, constructed the wall of theory which had insulated the NLRB, and then all other New Deal government agencies, from corporate attack through the courts. So it was with deep respect that I listened to him later that night on the train as we headed back for New York and thought out loud together about the earlier conversation. In challenging moments in the years ahead, when I would be faced with the seemingly insuperable barrier of a legal concept developed in the past, I would remember some of the ideas Scribner put to me on that train. "Don't be trapped," he said, "by the impression that concepts, particularly legal concepts, last forever. Ideas, approaches, especially in the law, which are built and developed to play a certain role in one period of history, very often turn into their opposite in a different period." Then he issued a warning that has proved invaluable at other times of crisis in the people's movements: "Don't be paralyzed by the notion of the eternal life of an idea or of a body of legal concepts. After all, the only thing which is 'eternal' to a lawyer for working people is the struggle of those people for a better life."

As we talked, I felt easier. True, the needs of that struggle shift and change. And as they do, the legal concepts required to protect that struggle also shift and change. The one immutable element is the necessity of searching out ways to make the law and the legal processes meet the fundamental needs of the overwhelming majority of the people. This was always supposed to be the objective of law in a democratic society, even if in reality, throughout the history of the country, this idea has often turned into its opposite, and the law and the legal system have frequently been used to meet the needs of the corporations and the establishment. So the answer to the question raised by the older labor lawyers became clearer. The protection for the future was hardly to be found in preserving inviolate the body of law developed in the 1930s to protect the NLRB from corporate intervention. Our responsibility to the future lay rather in the preservation of an independent union of working people exercising their fundamental right to organize. If the NLRB was today threatening the existence of such

111

a union, then the very reasons which in the 1930s impelled the development of a body of law restraining court intervention with their actions today required such intervention. Scribner summed it all up with a laugh and the wry comment, "If ten years from now there's a New Deal and the NLRB is back in the business of protecting workers, we'll be the first ones in there figuring out arguments to keep General Electric and Westinghouse from interfering with injunctions."

Back in New York, we found the national office of the union buzzing with activity. Organizers were throwing their energies into the national campaign against the NLRB. The news that the federal judge had even temporarily held up the decertification order was a shot in the arm. Delegations of workers all over the country began meeting with their representatives in Congress, demanding repeal of the Taft-Hartley legislation. Things were moving. Morale in the plants was good. We were fighting back. And then the impossible happened.

One day at the end of January 1953 while I was working in the firm office, Scribner called from the UE. I had never heard him so excited. "You won't believe this," he shouted. "Letts has entered a permanent injunction against the NLRB. We won!"

This sensational outcome had a powerful effect. As the lead story in the union newspaper stated, "A victory of far-reaching importance, not only to the UE but to all organized labor, has been won by the Union against a conspiracy between forces within the National Labor Relations Board and the U.S. Department of Justice." All over the country the morale of UE organizers shot sky high. Victory meetings were held in every local. The words of the injunction "restraining" the NLRB and "all others conspiring with them" were made to order for leaflets and plant gate meetings. UE President Fitzgerald summarized the organizational response when he stated, "By issuing a permanent injunction against the illegal action of the NLRB against our union, the federal court action has emphasized the extreme danger that lies in current schemes and intrigues of anti-labor forces. UE will continue the demand for full repeal of the evil Taft-Hartley law . . . and will work with all other unions toward that necessary end."

Then something else unexpected happened. We had been

waiting and waiting for word from Judge Weinfeld's office as to the disposition of our application to expunge the presentment. The judge had asked us for supplementary briefs, in which we laid out the origins of the grand jury itself. We even found some old English cases that limited statements from a grand jury, other than indictments, to charges of prosecutorial misconduct, based once again on those lovely old words expressing the grand jury's sole reason for existence: to be "a shield against the oppressions of the Crown."

One April morning in 1953, the phone rang with a call from the judge's chambers. An opinion had been filed that day in our case. We had won! Judge Weinfeld ordered the presentment "expunged." His opinion was tremendous. As I read it that afternoon, I was filled with that warm feeling of excitement which comes over a lawyer when discovering that a court's opinion has entirely adopted points or approaches submitted in the brief. Judge Weinfeld wholly agreed that it was his duty as a federal judge to strike the presentment as being totally beyond the power of the grand jury and indeed as violating the historical purpose of the institution of the grand jury itself, which was the protection of citizens from unfounded accusations of crime by public officials.

The reverberations of this victory, not three months after winning the injunction against the NLRB, were enormous. True, the slap in the face it represented to Roy Cohn, who a few months before had publicly bragged about having written the presentment himself and told the jury to issue it, had no immediate effect upon his personal role in fanning the Cold War hysteria. In December 1952 he had been rewarded for his repressive activities in the United States Attorney's office by receiving an appointment as staff counsel to Senator Joe McCarthy's investigating committee. Thus Judge Weinfeld's decision did not moderate Cohn's capability for devising schemes to harass the UE and other centers of popular struggle. Nor did these victories in court blunt for long the efforts of the companies and the government, aided by the CIO unions, to search out new forms of attack on the UE. But what could not be lightly brushed aside was the powerful effect of these two victories in momentarily halting the combined effort to eliminate this center of working people's strength. Even more significant than the derailing of the conspiracy to destroy the union was the boost it gave to the fighting spirit of the UE workers and organizers all over the country. The word was out: the UE was not going to be crushed, and although rough days might lie ahead, the union had survived the worst attacks so far.

As a result, a key element indelibly impressed itself upon our work as lawyers in the people's movements. No matter the intensity of the Cold War attacks or the hysteria of the period, it was possible at moments to win. We could never give up the prospect of winning—perhaps limited victories, perhaps only momentary, but still victories. And because winning was possible, we had to fight, despite the odds, as if we really believed we could win. This deep conviction would be critically important in the days to come. We realized that a mind-set of total frustration leading to cynicism, even if hidden by a sophisticated veneer of "understanding" how the legal system was really "owned" by the establishment, could only result in lessening the work put into the struggle and diminishing the energy available for solving the immediate legal challenge. In contrast, a recognition that victory was possible in even the roughest moments, particularly when the legal battle was an integral part of the rest of the people's struggles, served to heighten our level of performance. For all of us, there was a growing realization that even the most limited victory could build morale tremendously for the organizational struggle that must remain at the core of all resistance to repressive activity.

One of the most remarkable aspects of David Scribner's leadership in this period of exploding attacks and counterattacks was his creation of a UE legal network stretching from one end of the country to the other—a network that helped to solve one of the most devastating problems of people's lawyers, their isolation and lack of resources. At the center of the network was Scribner himself and those of us working with him in the UE national office, first Sy Linfield and myself, then an old friend of mine from Harvard student days, Basil Pollitt, whose determination and ingenuity kept the network functioning day and night during these hectic times. Whenever a new problem developed in one part of the country, all of the lawyers in the network were fully briefed and received copies of all necessary papers in order to be ready when the same crisis hit them.

The development of this network gave me an insight into one of the most important aspects of the functioning of people's lawyers: the need for new forms of organization to provide the basis for collective ways of work, overcoming the traditional professional isolation of lawyers who have taken a stand against the corporate and governmental establishments. This understanding would lead us in the years ahead to search for other forms to meet the same pressing need—forms such as the National Lawyers Guild's massive mobilization of lawyers and legal resources to support the civil rights struggles of the 1960s, and the organization of the Center for Constitutional Rights, which continues to this day to provide this support for people's lawyers.

But there was always the other world we lived in, the world of frustration and agony, of defeat and isolation, generating our ever-present feeling that still another disaster lay ahead. This feeling, as we well knew from our own experiences, was no general paranoia of the left but a reaction to the complex reality of the Cold War. In that summer of 1953, something happened which drove home with brutal directness the fact that the life of a people's lawyer would always be filled with tragedy and despair.

Mike Perlin, Frank Donner, and I were working late on a Thursday evening in June in the small rooms of the converted New York apartment that served as our office when the telephone rang. The call was to have an effect upon us from which, in a sense, we never recovered. When I picked up the phone, Emanuel Bloch, the chief counsel for Julius and Ethel Rosenberg, was on the line from Washington. I had never heard anyone quite so distraught and upset as Manny Bloch sounded. He stuttered, then blurted out, "They may vacate Douglas' stay. The execution may go ahead tomorrow night!"

As he talked on, what had happened became clear. All the Rosenbergs' formal appeals had previously been exhausted and their executions had been set when, two days before the scheduled executions, in an act of judicial heroism, Supreme Court Justice William Douglas had granted them a stay of execution until new issues just raised by their lawyers could be briefed and argued in the lower courts. All of us had breathed a sigh of relief when Justice Douglas signed the stay, because a week before that the Supreme Court had adjourned for vacation and would not be back for business until the new term opened in September. All was safe through the summer! Since the trial almost two years before, huge movements of support had developed for the Rosenbergs, demanding a halt to their executions. People had demonstrated in major cities throughout the world, insisting that the barbarism of the executions be stopped. Even the Pope had pleaded for the Rosenbergs' lives. The relief just granted by Justice Douglas seemed to be the answer to the world's demands.

Now this new development that Manny Bloch was explaining to me threatened their lives again. The Chief Justice, Fred Vinson, had convened an emergency session of the entire court, calling them all back from their vacations, to consider overruling the stay of execution granted by Justice Douglas. Stunned, I could think of no other time that such a thing had happened in the history of the Court. Manny went on, in the words I shall never forget, "The Court sits again at noon tomorrow. Looks like they're definitely going to vacate Douglas' stay. Execution tomorrow. Do something. Figure something out. Get back to the Court of Appeals. Do something."

I hung up the phone and repeated everything to Donner and Perlin. The enormity of the development began to dawn on us. We had not been officially involved in the case up to that point, providing only occasional help with research and errands for Manny Bloch and Gloria Agrin, another dedicated and courageous lawyer working on the trial. Yet tonight Bloch had turned to us, young lawyers in only our third year of practice as a firm, with a cry for help in one of the most critical situations we could dream of facing. There was no time even to speculate, "Why us?" The reason may have been partly that the three of us were becoming known as fighters who had little or no respect for the barriers of established law and precedent and who never seemed to quit, and partly that, unhappily, there were so few older, more experienced progressive lawyers who in the rough years of the trial had shown any real willingness to become closely involved in it.

Manny Bloch's call to us that evening symbolized one of the most difficult problems of the Rosenberg-Sobell case. In a sad way, Manny Bloch, Gloria Agrin, and the handful of defense lawyers with them at the trial had stood alone, although this was probably the most bitterly prosecuted political trial that the country had experienced in many years, and much rested on its outcome—far beyond the lives and liberty of the three defendants, Julius and Ethel Rosenberg and Morton Sobell. Today, over a quarter of a century later, impartial historians of the period are beginning to understand that the trial was the cornerstone of a plan, of which Joe McCarthy was only one of the prime architects, to develop a national mood of hysteria that would allow suppression of all political opposition to the unfolding strategy of the Cold War. The blueprint called for developing a national scare around the specter of atomic spies stealing the country's most precious secrets and jeopardizing national security. These "atomic spies" would then be clearly identified as radicals, as members of the Communist Party, driving into the minds of the public the overall political identification that the establishment wanted to make. This is the classic technique of reactionaries: brand the opposition with a caricature that the reactionaries themselves have fashioned. Radicals, people who opposed the Cold War policies of the government, were illegitimate, because they were spies, agents of a foreign power, Russia. They were selling out their country and should be treated accordingly. The very survival of the country demanded extreme measures. So drive the radicals out of the factories, the schools, the professions, and even kill them if necessary. The stakes are indeed high when such a caricature is being fashioned, be it at the Reichstag fire trial in Leipsig in 1933 or at the Rosenberg-Sobell trial in New York City in 1951. Sadly, understanding this technique is much easier from the hindsight of history.

The tragedy in 1951 was that when this crucial trial started, the handful of lawyers who came forward to defend the Rosenbergs and Sobell stood practically alone. Many progressive lawyers of the New Deal period had become expert in representing the new industrial unions and social agencies as well as in handling every phase of the practice of law. But almost without exception, these lawyers held back from participating or assisting in the defense of the Rosenbergs or Sobell. It was not so much that they were intimidated by the difficulties of the case; many of them had successfully fought harder fights. And it certainly was not that they accepted the government's charges against the defendants. Something else was involved, something that those of us who were just starting out as young lawyers, just entering the field of political law, began to sense, but could scarcely bring ourselves to accept.

We felt that these lawyers of the older generation of progressives were hesitant to participate in the defense of the Rosenbergs and Sobell because they were afraid that by doing so, they would fall into the government's trap. If they participated in the defense of people charged with being atomic spies, they might unwittingly injure the progressive movements that they had openly represented all of their lives. They feared that by a kind of algebraic magic, an equal sign would be created in the minds of the public between their own progressive, left, and radical activities and the so-called atomic espionage involved in the Rosenberg-Sobell case. Out of this fear of becoming identified with the charge developed a reluctance on the part of almost the entire progressive bar to participate in any way in the defense of the Rosenbergs and Sobell at the trial level.

What we did not fully realize at the time was that this fear of involvement in the government's creation of the atomic spy stereotype did not originate with the progressive lawyers. It lay deep in the reactions of most of the American left. Few of the leaders of people's organizations who had been so active in the years of the New Deal and World War II participated in organizing a mass defense for the Rosenbergs and Sobell at the trial level. It was almost as if the most influential leaders of the left had made a conscious decision that participation in this defense, either legally or in the public arena, would jeopardize their organizations. This was the height of the Cold War at home, when the left was under attack in every area of life and was falling back in disorganized retreat. If the left became identified in the public mind with atom spies, it believed it was finished.

This kind of reaction has recurred throughout American labor history. In the 1920s there were those who were afraid to help organize the defense in the frameup prosecution of Tom Mooney, the trade union organizer, because of the accusation that he had thrown a fatal bomb in a strike situation. There were those in the same period of history who pulled away from the defense of Sacco and Vanzetti because of fear of public revulsion at the charges of robbery and murder brought against the two immigrant radicals. But what was most tragic about the reaction to the trial of the Rosenbergs and Sobell was the failure of the left to understand that the very purpose of the case was to destroy the effectiveness of any opposition to the Cold War policies. The left seemed to believe that by immunizing itself from the charges, by separating itself from the case, it would protect itself and the people's movements. But the dynamics of the government's plans worked in precisely the opposite direction. By not rallying a mass movement of support to the victims of the government attack, the left, in the mind of the public, virtually accepted the prosecution's charges. By its passivity, it lost a chance to fight back, to begin exposing and undermining the carefully constructed design to implant in the minds of Americans the idea that being a dissident, a radical, or a Communist was the same as being a traitor and a spy.

So the tiny handful of lawyers who were willing to participate in the defense stood virtually alone, except for what little help some of us were able to offer them. But the assistance of a few lawyers could not meet the real need in that embattled courtroom. When you are involved in a case of such intensity, you need something more fundamental than technical help and assistance. You need emotional support. You need companionship, comradeship, a feeling that other people and other lawyers support you and identify with you in the struggle. No matter how well you may understand, intellectually and politically, what is happening in the courtroom, you cannot avoid feeling the impact of the prosecution's attack. You need, just as much as do the political defendants, the strength which flows from the knowledge that others are standing with you in the inevitable moments of crisis.

Manny Bloch and Gloria Agrin did not have that. And so, when Bloch's telephone call came that Thursday night, it was no surprise to us, if still a shock. We stayed up all night, talking, pulling out books, and poring over the appeals papers that were in the office. By three in the morning we came up with an ap-

119

proach, a way to "do something." We even got excited about it. It was a last resort plan of action. When the full Court vacated Justice Douglas' stay the next morning, we would ask for another federal stay of execution by developing a variation on the approach that had captured Douglas' attention a week before. The act under which the Rosenbergs had been sentenced permitted the death penalty only in time of war. But there was no declared war at the time of their alleged acts of espionage. Applying the death penalty at a time when the country was not actually at war might thus be challenged as unconstitutional and without statutory authority.

By five in the morning we had jammed out a set of federal habeas corpus papers which put forth the theory that the courts had no power under the statute to sentence the Rosenbergs to death. Then we started working out a plan of action to obtain a last-minute stay of execution that same day, pending full consideration of the new habeas corpus papers. The only way we could do so was by going back to the trial judge in the case, Irving Kaufman, and starting all over again. There was no hope of getting Kaufman to grant any relief, particularly if the Supreme Court vacated Douglas' stay, for Kaufman's own reputation as a judge depended upon a full vindication of the propriety of the death penalty he himself had mandated. But all we needed to get from Kaufman that morning was the one word "denied" on the petition for a stay of execution, so that we could present an emergency appeal to the Court of Appeals for the Second Circuit.

We worked out the logistics carefully. Robert Lewis, a young lawyer and close friend from my student movement days, and Frank Scheiner, an older labor lawyer, would take the papers to Judge Kaufman's chambers in Foley Square the first thing in the morning and, without bothering to argue for a stay, would attempt to get the critically needed word "denied" on the papers. Perlin and I meanwhile would drive up to New Haven, where Chief Judge Thomas Swan of the Court of Appeals had his office. Samuel Gruber, the lawyer who handled all the UE work in Connecticut, would meet us there to help out. We would stand by until we could call Bob Lewis in New York after he had returned to our office from Kaufman's chambers. We would then attempt to persuade Judge Swan to see us and allow us to go through our argument that there was sufficient legal validity in the papers we were presenting to hold off the executions, at least until we had had time to present the petition to a full panel of the Court of Appeals.

This plan was riddled with long shots. If Judge Kaufman held off denying the application, we were through. If Judge Swan was tied up or not in his office, we were also through. But Manny Bloch had said, "Do something," and we had to try.

Bob Lewis and Frank Scheiner left early in the morning for Kaufman's chambers, while Mike Perlin and I drove up to New Haven. We waited in the corridor of the federal courthouse until the time we had agreed to try to reach Lewis in New York. We called him at about 12:30, time enough for him to have seen Kaufman. Sure enough, Lewis' excited voice came through at the other end. He sounded as if he had just won a million dollar verdict from a jury. He practically shouted over the phone, "I got it. I got it." That precious word "denied" was written on the petition.

So now it was up to us. With fear and trepidation, Gruber, Perlin, and I walked down the corridor to the office of the chief judge of the circuit, the highly respected, conservative Judge Swan. To our surprise, we won the first important battle, getting past the bailiff in the outer office and then the secretary, by insisting that we had a critically important paper to present to the chief judge. While we waited for the judge, Perlin put in a call to Washington. The news, as expected, was that at noon the full Supreme Court had vacated Douglas' stay, and the execution was now set for 8:00 that very evening.

After what seemed like an hour of sitting in the reception room, looking at our watches every minute in the knowledge that eight o'clock was the outer limit, we were shown into Judge Swan's office. We quickly told him why we were there, and to our astonishment, he did not throw us out as we had expected. He looked at us and said, "All right, tell me what your theory is. Why should I grant a stay of these executions?" Then with a faint smile, he added, "You've got a mighty heavy burden to carry. After all, the full Supreme Court has vacated Douglas' stay."

So Perlin, Gruber, and I sat there and laid out our theory, developing every point. As we talked, Judge Swan picked up our papers. We had mentioned several cases on which we were relying. He called in his clerk and asked for the volumes we had mentioned. He opened them up and leafed through them. And then it happened. He looked up at us and said, "You've got a point there. It makes some sense. I'll tell you what I'll do. I can't grant a stay by myself after the High Court has vacated Douglas' stay. But what I can do is convene a panel of this court this afternoon, two judges of the court and myself to hear your application, and I'll vote for the stay. I'll convene a panel if you can get one other member of our court to agree to sit on the panel and consider granting the stay."

This was beyond our wildest expectations. We blurted out, "Judge Swan, what other members of the court are around? Who can we get to see? Who is in New Haven?" He thought for a moment and then said, "Judge Frank is here, at his home."

We sat stunned for a moment. He was sending us to Jerome Frank, the leading liberal judge on the court; Jerome Frank, the intellectual leader of the New Deal and architect of its most progressive legislation; Jerome Frank, the idol of young progressive law students and leader of the liberals when he taught law at Yale, who had led the fight against the conservatism of the old-guard faculty by championing, long before its actual victory years later, the cause of clinical education in law school—we were going to see Jerome Frank!

As we stood up, half-dazed at this turn of events, and scooped up our papers, one of us turned to Judge Swan and asked, "What's Judge Frank's address?" The judge looked at his watch. It was about two o'clock. He said, "You don't have very much time." Then he picked up his telephone and called for the car assigned to him as chief judge to be brought around and gave instructions that we be taken immediately to Frank's home. Things were moving in a way we had never dreamed of. For the first time since Manny Bloch's phone call, the possibility of stopping the Rosenberg executions became real.

We grabbed our briefcases and rushed downstairs. The judge's car was waiting. As we sat in the back seat of that huge limousine, with a chauffeur driving us through the streets of New Haven to meet Judge Frank, I could not help but think, "What an odd way for radical lawyers to argue a matter in the court of appeals."

Judge Frank was at his door to meet us. Swan evidently had alerted him that we were coming. He welcomed us in a friendly way, escorted us into his living room, and as we sat down in comfortable easy chairs and nervously opened our briefcases to take out our papers, he smiled at us and looked for ways to put us at our ease.

The first thing he told us was that Judge Swan had called to say that an open telephone line had been established between the clerk's office in New Haven and Sing Sing, the New York state prison where the Rosenbergs were being held because the federal authorities were borrowing its electric chair for that evening. We looked hastily at our watches. It was about 2:30 in the afternoon. As Judge Frank saw us glance at the time, he said, "All right. Present your case."

We argued as we had never argued in our lives. We put forward all the arguments. When we tried to cut short any point, worrying about the time, Judge Frank would interrupt, saying, "No, develop that point. Lay it all out." Afterward he would say, "Fine. Develop the next point." And we did.

At last we were finished. We had been talking and arguing for more than an hour. We looked up at him, and he looked at us and was quiet for a moment. Then he said something that I shall never forget. He said to us in soft, slow words, "If I were as young as you are, I would be sitting where you are now and saying and arguing what you are arguing. You are right to do so. But when you are as old as I am, you will understand why I"—and he paused, and repeated—"why I cannot do what you ask. I cannot do it."

We sat there stunned. This was Jerome Frank the liberal, Jerome Frank the progressive. Something deep inside me voiced the agonizing statement: "He knows we're right, and he cannot, he will not, stand up against the powerful forces gathering in the country who are demanding the blood of the Rosenbergs. Why?"

We left without saying more than a formal goodbye to Judge

Frank. Time was pressing furiously upon us, and we had only a few hours left to find another judge of the circuit. Everything in Judge Frank's words and tone made it abundantly clear that he could not be moved from his position. He said nothing to us and would not look at us as we left. His back was turned; he just stood there in the door, motionless.

After picking up our own car at the courthouse, we drove frantically to the home of Judge Charles Clark, whose address Judge Swan's clerk had given us. No one was there. We drove to a nearby gas station, and Perlin rushed out to the pay phone to call Clark's office. "He's at a golf course," Perlin called to us from the phone booth. "I'm going to try him there." After an intense exchange with someone on the other end, Perlin told us that they would get a message to Clark on the course, asking him to call us back. We waited for almost fifteen minutes, and then the phone rang. Perlin grabbed it and sat listening. When he hung up and walked slowly over to Gruber and me in the car, we could tell from the expression on his face how the land lay. Judge Clark had said that he had not been involved in the case, he did not want to get involved, he had talked to other members of the circuit, and an emergency panel would not be convened. That was that.

We got into our car and drove down the Merritt Parkway back to New York. Over the car radio we listened to the news bulletin: "At eight o'clock this evening Julius and Ethel Rosenberg will be electrocuted." Then it all welled up inside us. Jerome Frank could have stopped that. He knew we were right. He could not look us straight in the eye and say we were wrong. Swan, the conservative, could say we were right, but Frank, the liberal, could not do it. He had made the determination deep in his heart that it would jeopardize his role as a liberal, as a progressive— even, I thought, as a progressive Jew in an increasingly conservative society—if he were to follow what his conscience, his innermost sense of right and wrong, was telling him. And when it came to the crisis point, Jerome Frank, the liberal of liberals, could not do what Swan, the conservative, was prepared to do.

We were shaken to our roots. I suppose we should have known better; we should have understood the dynamics at play. But it was a blow which shook the entire structure of the world we lived in. Back in New York that evening, as the news of the electrocution came in, Mike Perlin and I looked at each other. The same thought was in our minds, and the same words were on our lips: "What's the point of it all? Let's chuck it. What's the point of being a lawyer? It's a farce." Yet we knew that for us to stop, to give up, to abandon the fight, would in its own way be giving in to the same pressures that had overwhelmed Jerome Frank. The words of Sam Gruber upon leaving the car at his office in Stamford came to mind reassuringly. Sam had said to us, with that beautiful directness which over the years typified his role as both teacher and emotional support to younger lawyers, "No matter what, we'll keep fighting."

How many times have I thought back to that moment in Jerome Frank's living room. How many times, in the days and months which followed the executions, in the depths of the Cold War years, have I said to myself, "Is it true? Will we all be like that when we're his age? Does it happen to everyone? Is it inevitable that there will be a betrayal—that concepts of morality, of justice, of honesty, are at a certain point meaningless?"

Jerome Frank might, in a profound sense, have changed the course of American history that afternoon. He could not do it. He was a prisoner of the system he served. As a liberal, as a progressive, he had risen to a position of leadership in society. He would jeopardize the usefulness of those labels and, accordingly, the position they afforded him if he participated in the act of courage that Judge Swan, the conservative, was prepared to take. The labels themselves, Frank's "liberal" past, imprisoned him— kept him from the course he would have taken if he were "as young as" we were. When we were "as old as" he was, he was telling us, we would understand that to preserve our position in society, we must compromise with those in control.

In the months to follow, I remembered with bitterness the words he had used as he fingered the opinions of the Court vacating the Douglas stay—opinions which, we learned years later, the FBI had arranged to have taken to New Haven by special messenger when they became aware, through their omnipresent surveillance, of our last-minute plans to go there. Holding Vinson's opinion in his hands, Frank had said to us, in what we thought at the moment was an attempt at humor, "How can I overrule my bosses?" In actuality, Frank was deadly serious. He was afraid—afraid of threatening the already shaky position of himself, of all the liberals, of the progressives, and even of the Jews—although that was a thought which I, as a young Jewish person, was most reluctant to face. It simply was not prudent for a "liberal Jew" to be the one to save the two "Jewish atom spies." This was what we would understand only when we were "as old as" he.

Shortly after the execution, Mike Perlin, Frank Donner, and I became the lawyers for Morton Sobell, who had been sentenced to thirty years in prison. When Helen, his wife, asked us if we would take what seemed to be a hopeless case, there was no question in our minds. After that Friday afternoon it was a necessity. But we could not bring ourselves to talk about that afternoon with anyone. It all poured out of me only years later when I was talking to a freshman class of law students at Columbia University about the role of a radical lawyer in American society. Someone asked me to define the difference between a "radical" and a "liberal" lawyer. I realized that for me the difference was contained in that afternoon experience with Jerome Frank. His basic commitment was to his position in the existing system, and at that moment of crisis the ultimate ideas of justice, or right and wrong, became submerged, while survival within the system became paramount. So as they listened intently, I told them the story of that difficult and painful day.

There are deep personal reasons why, over the years, it has been so hard to talk—or even to think—about that Friday afternoon. I ask myself how much of it was our fault? How much was our youth and our inexperience to blame? What could we have done which we did not do to move Frank? Even though we know objectively that there was little more that anyone could have done under the circumstances, it still cuts deep. The experience taught us one of the deepest agonies of being people's lawyers: of necessity, you become so personally involved and identified with the struggles you are involved in that you find yourself assuming responsibilities for events which are objectively beyond your control. And then living with these responsibilities becomes extremely difficult. Living with the failure to prevent the Rosenberg's executions was very painful for us. However, Mike

Perlin and I came through the experience with the inner hope that at least never in our lives would we become "as old" as Jerome Frank was that afternoon.

But the real failure in the Rosenberg case was not our futile last-minute attempt to hold off their executions. The failure of the organized people's movements—of the militant trade unionists, the liberals, the socialists, the Communists—of any of us, to respond to the original indictments and arrest with the organization of a massive political and legal counteroffensive, or even with any manifestation of a mass opposition to the government's strategy, is a question that has rarely been faced by anyone. Yet it goes to the heart of the issue: the survival of democratic movements at moments of establishment attack. When people's movements implicitly accept the enemy's position by failing to rally in defense of individuals or organizations charged with frightening accusations and, out of fear of being identified with the victims, hesitate to launch an essential counteroffensive exposing the real conspiracy of the power structure, then they have little or no hope of victory. Over and over again through the years, as the government and the companies have launched new attacks on the people's movements through new frameups, I have thought back to that sad day in June 1953 and wondered whether we would fall once more into the well-laid trap or whether, with courage and foresight, we would stand firm and find ways, no matter how hard, of launching a popular counteroffensive, the only real guarantee of victory.

5

Surviving McCarthy and the Dirty Decade

There was little time during the next months to think about the bitter, pointed words of Jerome Frank that Friday afternoon in New Haven, or to relive the frustrations and agonies of the futile last-minute attempt to hold off the deaths of Julius and Ethel Rosenberg. There was too much to do. It soon became clear that the victories we had just won in stemming the NLRB and grand jury attacks on the UE were only momentary. The destruction of this seemingly irrepressible group of militant trade unionists remained high on the agenda of those who were calling the shots in the escalation of the Cold War.

Late in the fall of 1953, we heard news from Massachusetts which boded no good for the union and, for us personally, raised warnings of a very busy winter. Back in 1950 at the General Electric plant in Lynn, the IUE, the rival union set up by Murray and the CIO, had succeeded, by a plurality of only several hundred votes in the ten thousand ballots cast by the workers, in ousting the UE as bargaining agent. Over the next three years a considerable amount of rethinking went on among the Lynn workers. Then in the middle of 1953, following the end of the open fighting in Korea, the company instituted a wholesale program of layoffs and speed-ups on the assembly line. At this point a large group of workers asked the UE to petition for a board election. The IUE used every legal trick in the book to hold off an election, but signed cards and testimony from workers in the plant were overwhelming evidence that the UE had tremendous support. The NLRB, frustrated by our injunction against its plans to bar the UE from all labor elections, on November 17 reluctantly agreed to a new election, to be held within thirty days. From what we were hearing from the organizers in Boston, the UE sentiment in the plant was growing fast.

Then the new attack hit. On the very same day that the NLRB released news of its agreement to a new election at the Lynn plant, Senator McCarthy announced that on the next day his Internal Security Committee planned to hold a closed hearing in Boston on security policies and alleged Communist infiltration at General Electric's Lynn and Everett plants. But the hearing the next morning was not closed; it was televised. During the hearing a self-styled "undercover agent for the FBI" informed the senator and the viewing public that he knew at least thirty "Communist agents" at the Lynn plant. He conveniently named two workers who happened to be leading UE supporters in the forthcoming election. Less than an hour later, a representative of the company announced publicly that these two workers were being promptly suspended from employment. And less than a day later, twenty-eight other General Electric workers from plants throughout the country were suspended, as the result, McCarthy proudly announced to the press, of testimony given in secret session by the same undercover agent.

When a few days later this so-called undercover agent was exposed by the police chief of his home town, Fitchburg, Massachusetts, as an inveterate liar with a 34-year police record of arrests and convictions, even the local FBI office denied responsibility for him, claiming with some embarrassment that he was a "volunteer" witness and not an agent of theirs. But when this damaging bit of information came out, it received barely an inch of coverage in the local papers. McCarthy was riding high, at the height of his popularity and with massive public support.

At this point, Dave Scribner asked us to sit in on a discussion of the situation with the UE officers. Jim Matles, who was handling the Lynn campaign, brought us up to date. Something was changing. Cohn and McCarthy, by concentrating their attack on rank-and-file workers and local organizers this time, sidestepping what had been their previous emphasis on the national union officers, seemed to be preparing for some new move. Matles, Emspak, and Fitzgerald all stressed that it must be basically a company move. The firings came too quickly. As Fitzgerald said, looking at the list of the thirty suspended workers, if General Electric had singled out thirty of the most obstinate fighters against the speed-up that the company was pushing in the plants, they could not have done a better job. It was necessary for the union to begin quickly exposing the McCarthy attacks as covers for a company move against the most effective union leaders in the plants. It was also necessary to make it dramatically and personally clear to the rank-and-file leadership—those subpoenaed and those waiting, a little scared, to be subpoenaed—that the UE national officers were right beside them in the fight.

How to do that? One of the officers half-longingly said, "Hell, if they had only subpoenaed *us* this time, we could really tell them off. They can't fire *us* from their plants." All at once everyone got excited. Why not call McCarthy and Cohn's bluff? Why not demand that they subpoena a UE officer? Why not? We had to find every possible way within the growing atmosphere of fear and terror to say loud and clear that this was no high-level government effort to eliminate a dangerous foreign conspiracy but rather a simple union-busting, company-directed move which working people in this country had experienced time and again.

A sensitive question then arose, as it often would for people's lawyers at vastly different moments of struggle. By demanding the right to appear before McCarthy in order to expose his underlying role as a company tool, were we in any way legitimizing his opposition? At that moment it seemed clear that there was no simple, one-dimensional answer which held true at all times under all circumstances. As one UE officer pointed out sharply, "It all depends on what we do there. Just let us get at him, and no one will think we are legitimizing anything." So once again it appeared that, for a people's lawyer, the key to testing the validity of a given approach was to recognize that what was sound and

131

helpful at one moment might not be so useful at another moment. The test, as in our first experiences in Evansville, was still valid: how will it help to advance the fighting ability of the people?

Later that afternoon it was decided that Matles, being directly involved in the Lynn campaign, should be the one to take on McCarthy head on. After the meeting we gathered in Scribner's office and drafted a telegram to Cohn that must have bowled him over when he received it the next morning. It was probably the only time anyone had ever demanded receiving a subpoena from the McCarthy committee.

After waiting two days without an answer, Scribner decided to flush out Cohn. He used the one approach we knew Cohn and McCarthy could not take. Scribner called up Cohn and said simply, "Either give Matles a subpoena immediately, or we will call a press conference in Lynn and announce that you are scared to hear what Matles has to say." That did it. The next day the subpoena arrived at the office. Matles was to appear two days later, on November 25, in New York, not Lynn, and the hearing was to be a closed "executive session." Only one lawyer would be allowed to appear with the witness. As we did not want to give them any excuse to hold up the hearing, Scribner alone went with Matles to the hearing in the federal courtroom.

The report of the hearing made to us late that evening by Scribner was very exciting. The hearing, he told us, had been amazing. From the moment that Matles was called to testify, he had grabbed the initiative. The tone of the hearing was set by his first response to McCarthy. When McCarthy opened up his conventional political attack, Matles replied—as headlined in the next issue of the *UE News* two days later—"You're a liar, Senator." From then on, the proceeding was a debacle for Cohn and McCarthy, with Matles accusing McCarthy directly of playing General Electric's game and of giving the company "lawless and indecent aid."

At the end an incredible thing happened. McCarthy, who had been banging away with a gavel to stop Matles' testimony, jumped up, rushed down to where the witness sat, and stood glaring as Matles said right to his face, "You are doing a dirty thing, Senator, going to Lynn and Schenectady for the General

Electric Company, terrorizing and browbeating decent working people. I tell you to stop it."

McCarthy literally screamed at Matles, "I want to set you straight on the purpose of this executive session. We've got a lot on you." To which Matles shot back, "You've got nothing on me, not a damned thing. You've been trying to frame me on my non-Communist affidavits for three years, the pair of you, and you haven't done it. Let me ask you a question. Are you a spy for the General Electric Company? That question is as good coming from me to you as coming from you to me."

At that point McCarthy blew up in a way he rarely ever had. He spun around and yelled at Cohn, "Come on, we are wasting our time. Let's get the immigration authorities in here and get this man deported." And at that moment he revealed the real stimulus behind the long drawn-out denaturalization proceedings against Matles that would take place over the next four years.

The hearing ended abruptly on one last abrasive note, the full significance of which none of us could grasp at the time. Matles lashed back at Cohn and McCarthy with a question that was to contribute, six months later, to the Senate resolution of censure against McCarthy and to Cohn's firing as committee counsel. As Matles got up to leave, he turned to Cohn and put the question to him, "What are you doing around here, Cohn? I see you lost Schine. What about you?" David Schine, another young "special assistant" to McCarthy, had just been drafted into the army, amid rumors that McCarthy had pulled every trick and brought every pressure to bear on the army high command to keep Schine from being drafted. Now the same stories were circulating about Cohn, who so far had managed to avoid the draft. Matles pressed his question, "I put in my time in the armed services, Cohn. What are you doing here?"

This hit a raw nerve, and Cohn shot back, "Do you want me to tell you?" Then McCarthy, probably for the first time in his career as a Cold War investigator, found himself in the strange position of advising one of his own staff virtually to "plead the Fifth," blurting out to Cohn, "You don't have to answer that, Roy."

This confrontation between Matles and Cohn and McCarthy

became a powerful instrument in the protracted struggle over the next years. Time and again in the roughest days it helped to illustrate the counteroffensive that had to be developed if the Cold War strategy of big business was to be withstood. On the night of the hearing, the workers were given a blow-by-blow report on it at a large public meeting in Lynn. By the end of the year, few UE members did not know the story of the "You're a liar, Senator" confrontation. That showdown helped more than anything else to raise morale when fighting spirits were low. It drove home to all of us the critical need, in periods of long and frustrating struggle, of seeking out opportunities in the legal arena to provide sharp examples of courage and steadfastness to counterbalance the seeming invincibility of the establishment.

We needed such reminders in the months to come. On December 8, one day before the scheduled NLRB election at Lynn, General Electric dropped a bombshell which finally placed the Cohn-McCarthy moves during the entire preelection period in focus. The front pages of every plant newspaper trumpeted a new company policy, to go into effect immediately. The company announced that "it would suspend employees who refused to testify under oath when questioned in public hearings conducted by competent government officials." This policy came to be known throughout General Electric plants as Policy No. 20.4, or the "General Electric Fifth Amendment firing policy." Anyone named as a "subversive" before the McCarthy committee who failed to "cooperate fully" was to be fired by the company. It was widely known that McCarthy had said repeatedly that all UE supporters were "subversives." The inference was inescapable. Anyone who became too closely identified with the UE was subversive. If they were subversive, the McCarthy committee would finger them. If they were fingered and did not play the company's game, they were fired.

Under a camouflage of pompous, patriotic reasons put forward by Ralph Cordiner, the General Electric president, this was the first unabashed public blacklist of union militants since the open shop days of the early 1930s. What no one knew at that time was that the whole approach—the committee subpoenaes, the fingering of UE militants, and the General Electric blacklisting—

134

had been carefully worked out late in October at a secret meeting at the Mohawk Club in Schenectady between company representatives and McCarthy's aides Roy Cohn and George Anastos. This fact would not come out until over a year later during depositions made by company officers in the course of pressing our legal counterattack against Policy 20.4.

The company's blacklisting policy had an immediate effect on the Lynn election. The IUE retained representation rights at the plant by only a few hundred votes. This was a defeat for the UE, no question, but considering the general atmosphere of the times, it was a surprise that so many thousands of working people at the home plant of one of the largest and most powerful corporations had held out against the terror and hysteria and stood fast by the UE. Two or three days after the Lynn results, the UE officers urged that as part of a stand-and-fight policy against the wholesale layoffs and speed-ups taking place in major electrical plants throughout the country, we figure out some kind of legal attack against the Cordiner-Cohn-McCarthy scheme. They were looking for an approach that would cut through the phony patriotism of the company and expose the union-busting essence of the "cooperate with the committee or be fired" scheme.

It was while working out such an approach that we came face to face with a new and, for us, wholly unexpected attack on the UE, which was in certain ways the most difficult and complicated to face. The legal counteroffensive that we began putting together was one of our most ambitious experiments to date. It took the form of a major federal legal action against General Electric, demanding damages for the illegal suspension of UE members from employment and an injunction against the company's conspiracy to destroy both the constitutional rights of union members and the protections of the national collective bargaining contract with UE. The complaint was to be brought by Fitzgerald as a representative of all UE members, by virtue of his being the national president and a former member of the Lynn local. Another plaintiff who was made to order for the suit on behalf of all UE workers at General Electric was John Nelson, president of UE Local 506, who represented the workers at the Erie, Pennsylvania, plant, one of the most important shops in the company's chain.

Nelson, an active young UE leader, had been one of the first people suspended by the company under the blacklist policy for refusal to cooperate with the McCarthy committee. His Erie local was one of the three main centers of UE militancy, along with the Lynn and Schenectady locals, and thus a natural target for the company-McCarthy attack.

By March 1954, as we sat in Dave Scribner's office going over the final draft of the complaint, only one problem remained. One piece was missing: representation of the Schenectady UE leadership among the plaintiffs. It should have been there. Only a few weeks before, on February 19, McCarthy had duplicated the Lynn performance at the Schenectady General Electric plant, where seven rank-and-file UE workers, after refusing to cooperate with the committee, had been promptly suspended by the company. But there was something strange about that situation, which had made us hesitate about including Schenectady representation in the lawsuit. Several of the most experienced leaders of the local, including the business agent, Leo Jandreau, a founding member of the UE, had also received McCarthy subpoenaes for those hearings, but they had never actually been called to testify.

When someone at our March meeting again raised the question of including Schenectady leaders as plaintiffs in the complaint against General Electric, Scribner, obviously disturbed, said somewhat bitterly, "I've got to fill you in on the developments of the last few days. We'll probably be writing a federal complaint tomorrow with Jandreau as a defendant. He's leading a secession move trying to pull Local 301 into IUE." This was a bombshell for us, particularly for Mike Perlin, who had been the Local 301 lawyer in Schenectady before coming down to join the new firm in New York.

When the dust cleared, the enormity of the situation impressed itself on us. Jandreau, one of the original organizers of the Schenectady local, who over the years had withstood one blast after another as a "Communist" and a "subversive," was now running for cover. In the face of the McCarthy attack, he and other leaders of the local had met privately with James Carey, president of the rival IUE union, to arrange what had all the appearances of being a three-way deal between the bitterly anti-Communist, pro-Cold War IUE, the company, and the Senate committee, which would get rid of the UE once and for all at the Schenectady plant. The committee would let the subpoenaes lapse, Jandreau and the local UE leadership who were with him would engineer a secession vote in the local and affiliate with the IUE, and the company would join them in calling for an immediate NLRB election to knock out the UE as the collective bargaining representative at the Schenectady plant.

This agreement went into effect with lightning speed. Jandreau succeeded in holding tightly controlled secession meetings of the UE local. The NLRB, in record time, ordered a new election. By June 1954, Jandreau and his followers had accomplished what seven years of Cold War attacks had not been able to do—eliminate the UE as a militant center of rank-and-file trade unionism at the Schenectady General Electric plant. We quickly discovered that what had happened in Schenectady was no isolated phenomenon and that the UE was just beginning the period of its most intense struggle for survival, a period the UE officers would for years afterward refer to as the "dirty decade."

All around us UE organizers—district and local leaders with solid reputations won over the years as militant union fighters—were being strongly influenced by a theory put forth by a number of radicals in the country in response to the Cold War developments. This approach came to be called the "mainstream theory." In essence, it said that militant workers of the left were being systematically isolated from the so-called "mainstream" of the working people, namely the AFL and CIO unions, as a result of the Cold War attacks and propaganda, and that unions like the UE, led by militants and those who openly fought against the Cold War politics, could not survive the massive onslaught. Therefore, the militants had to find ways to rejoin this "mainstream" of the working people, even if it meant disbanding or giving up the independence of the left-led militant unions.

The seriousness of this strategy was underscored by the fact that it was put forward by a number of experienced militant labor organizers, including some of the leadership of the Communist Party. Throughout the 1930s and 1940s, the Communists had

137

grown into one of the largest, most effective groups of organizers and union members dedicated to building and maintaining mass industrial unions in every section of the country. What they had to say on major questions of strategy would undoubtedly have a significant impact on the course of events.

This mainstream strategy added a heartbreaking new component to the conventional lineup of Cold War warriors who had always led the onslaughts against the UE—the congressional committees, the companies, the reactionary press, elements in the religious community, and the raiding AFL and CIO union hierarchy. Now a substantial number of UE leaders, including four district presidents and almost thirty staff organizers and local union business agents—people who had been among the most dedicated and skillful organizers of the union—began in one way or another to act out the logical conclusions of the mainstream theory. They expressed increasingly blunt opinions that the UE was "finished" as a union and that, since it was impossible to stem the Cold War tide, the union members should, no matter the sacrifices, rejoin the "mainstream of labor," the AFL and CIO unions.

We had been aware of some of these discussions in left union circles, but we were frankly thrown by the drastic consequences we were experiencing. The majority of the UE leadership, including the three national officers, were in firm disagreement with the mainstream analysis. They refused to accept its underlying assumption that the UE could not survive as an effective fighting force. Every experience of the last years had proven otherwise. The lessons of Evansville, Dayton, and Schenectady itself all showed the contrary.

But the rejection by the UE leadership of the defeatist mainstream approach did not rest solely on the pragmatic experiences of the struggles, important as they were. I remember vividly Jim Matles' reaction to arguments advanced by mainstream advocates that the elimination of the UE as an independent force was required in the interests of the unity of working people, as symbolized by the AFL-CIO merger in 1955. Matles' response was sharp and to the point. He said that Emspak, Fitzgerald, and he were second to none in the progressive labor movement in their commitment to the need for unity among working people in the struggle against corporate power. But unity for what? Unity like that developed in the AFL-CIO merger to protect the profits of big business, to facilitate the work speed-ups, and to cover up the layoffs of so many workers—unity behind the Cold War policies of Truman and now Eisenhower and his new Secretary of State, John Foster Dulles? Or real workers' unity behind rank-and-file democratic trade unionism to build the political and economic power of working people? Matles' answer to the mainstream hypothesis was a slash to the jugular. Only the continued existence of powerful, independent, rank-and-file led unions like the UE, unafraid to fight for the needs and interests of working people, would ever insure real influence for militant policies within the so-called mainstream of American trade unionism. This was the only real guarantee of any meaningful unity. To eliminate such unions in the name of working people's unity was simply to surrender to corporate power, and the UE national leadership would have no part of it.

Mainstreaming caused inevitable confusion among the rank-and-file workers in the UE plants. At secession meetings, workers who had withstood the worst of the McCarthy attacks were told by formerly dedicated and devoted militant organizers of the UE, who had themselves been attacked as "Communists" and "subversives" more times than anyone could remember, that the union was "finished," that it now was necessary to leave the UE and join those unions who for years had led the worst attacks on the UE. On many occasions, these meetings were called suddenly, loyal UE members were excluded from attending, and the UE national officers were actually barred. I remember the horror, on the day before the Schenectady secession meetings, of rushing into federal court to get a temporary order from a district judge to restrain Leo Jandreau, the other local officers, and the IUE from barring UE members and national officers from attending those so-called UE meetings.

In many ways, mainstreaming was the most disheartening of the Cold War attacks. For over seven years, this militant union had withstood the worst combination of external forces. By the end of 1954, over 140,000 UE workers remained committed to their union. Despite defeats, as in the close election at the Lynn plant, by and large the policy of standing and fighting, of counterattack and offensive, had worked. The corporate power had not succeeded in eliminating one of the most militant centers of workers' strength in the heart of the electrical industry. But when this blow was dealt from within, in less than two years the organizers of the secession move succeeded in pulling away about 50,000 UE members, leaving an embattled 90,000 to stand and fight. What the combined forces of business and government had not succeeded in doing, union organizers committed to a radical objective had now momentarily accomplished: the overwhelming of certain local centers of militant trade unionism.

The irony of the situation came home to us in a sad way as, day after day, we heard of radical organizers who, having wiped out the UE at a given plant and delivered the workers over to an AFL or CIO union, were themselves expelled from that union and fired from their organizing jobs. Few of the "secessionists" who had dreamed of entering the "mainstream" survived. Those few who did were obliged to endorse the open Cold War policies of the AFL-CIO.

The real miracle of the dirty decade was that despite these blows, the UE remained very much alive as a center of militant activity. Over the years, as new forms of government repression have hit the people's movements, I have often had occasion to think back to those days and mull over the underlying lesson that the heroism of the 90,000 UE workers and their national leaders who remained committed to the struggle taught to us all, radical organizers and lawyers alike. At the heart of any program of survival in a period of intense conservative attack must be the determination to stand and fight, to refuse to abandon one's principles in the vain hope of securing protection from the right-wing onslaught. Above all, survival requires a confidence in the strength and ability of working people to see through the barrage of lies and propaganda and to join in a counteroffensive against the real adversary, the corporate power. For lawyers who would seek the path which that long walk around the reservoir way back in 1945 had set me on, this understanding is crucial. If their legal skills are put to work to aid in the development of such a program of resistance and counterattack, then they are moving forward, no

140

matter what defeats and setbacks are encountered along the way.

Perhaps the saddest aspect of the mainstream strategy was its timing. At the very moment that left forces were urging workers to abandon their militant unions for the supposed safety of the now united AFL and CIO, signs were appearing on the horizon that augured the beginning of a fundamental shift in the political atmosphere of the country. Matles' confrontation with McCarthy over Roy Cohn's draft status in the fall of 1953 had revealed a raw nerve in McCarthy's facade: his sensitivity to the reluctance of the military establishment to jump to his commands. The Pentagon's unwillingness to defer to his efforts to protect his assistants Schine and Cohn from military service may well have led to his decision, in the so-called "Army-McCarthy" hearings later that year, to attack the army itself as "soft on Communism." This was a blunder of historic dimensions. The attack on the military was too much for the power structure. After extensive hearings, a special Select Committee of the Senate concluded that McCarthy had "overstepped" his boundaries and was subject to a resolution of "condemnation." The Senate endorsed this action by a vote of 67 to 22 in early December 1954.

Something was happening which would slowly moderate the Cold War climate. Crevices were opening in the once seemingly unified repressive government-industry front, which would facilitate a new upsurge of people's movements. This potential shift away from the hysteria that had dominated the political climate was driven home to me by the sweeping results of a telephone call from Montreal late one night during the last week in 1954. On the line that night was a young television writer, Reuben Ship, who almost a year before had been deported from this country to his home in Canada on the grounds of having been a member of the Communist Party. When a mutual friend had called me then for advice on the actual deportation, I had been of little help to Ship. In those days there was not much one could do at the final moment of deportation. So when Ship called me now from Canada, my heart sank, as I thought, "Here we go again, another attack on him."

But the call could not have been more surprising. It appeared that in the previous spring, Ship had written a radio script for the Canadian Broadcasting System, which had been bootlegged by record producers in New York and was to be released the next day for public sale. The record, called "The Investigator," was a satire on Senator McCarthy in which the undaunted investigator replaced St. Peter as the gatekeeper at the entrance to Heaven and proceeded to conduct an investigation into the subversive backgrounds of such previous admissions to Heaven as Jefferson, Milton, Voltaire, Socrates, and Luther. A reporter had just called Ship from Washington to tell him that, according to a story floating around town, President Eisenhower had heard the record and "greatly enjoyed it." Major sales were expected the moment the record was released.

I asked Ship if he wanted us to obtain a court order to prevent release of the bootlegged product. He practically shouted, "Hell, no! Let them distribute it all over. It's the least I can do in the fight." What he actually wanted was help in insisting on royalty payments while permitting the distribution.

The next morning, Jack Gould of the *New York Times* called the record "the most hilarious and brilliant satire ever done on the controversial Senator from Wisconsin." We quickly worked out an agreement providing for payments to Ship as the author, and the record sold in the tens of thousands. Reuben Ship's accomplishment was spectacular at that particular moment of transition in our history. He had, in Gould's words, "projected laughter into the midst of a reigning political controversy in this country." "The Investigator" helped to shatter the aura of sanctity which surrounded the McCarthy Committee and its techniques. I myself learned a much needed lesson: people's lawyers must understand the power of humor and satire in even the most desperate struggles.

It was in this changing atmosphere that we prepared for the final Supreme Court arguments in the contempt of Congress cases of Julius Emspak and Tom Quinn. As I worked on the briefs with Dave Scribner and Frank Donner, I experienced for the first time the very special tension and pressure that Supreme Court cases have always generated in all of us over the years. These two cases were assuming increasing national importance as, on the one hand, the attacks on the UE from within accelerated and, on the other, the public distaste for the excesses of

McCarthyism grew. The stakes were high. In the case of Emspak, a UE national officer and a central target of attack for the anti-Communist forces in the labor movement, a High Court slap-down resulting in his jailing would be dramatic proof for those who said that the UE was dead, so bury it quickly. For Quinn, a jail sentence enforced against this committed activist would say to all other organizers, "Play it cool. Don't stand up against them." But a High Court vindication of their refusal to participate in the HUAC congressional investigation could go far to encourage the growing antipathy to McCarthyism and give renewed life to the UE struggles.

Out of the intense work on the briefs with Scribner and Donner, who had already gone through what to me was a new and awesome experience, I gathered certain insights which were to prove useful in later confrontations with the Supreme Court. "Act as if you're serious," Scribner said constantly. "Act as if you expect to win." This was not a casual expression of a simple maxim. To people's lawyers who faced a court which only three years before had upheld the Smith Act and which only a year before had allowed the execution of the Rosenbergs, it was an almost impossible challenge. But a startling development soon forced us to take the advice seriously.

A year before, Chief Justice Fred Vinson, the architect of the *Dennis* opinion upholding the convictions in the Smith Act case, had left the Supreme Court. Eisenhower had replaced him as Chief Justice with Earl Warren, a state prosecutor from California, whom none of us knew much about. During Warren's first term as Chief Justice he promptly helped to persuade the Justices to hand down on May 17, 1954, a unanimous decision in *Brown v. Board of Education,* holding that racial segregation in public schools was unconstitutional. At that time, while we were working on the Emspak and Quinn briefs, it was far too soon for us to begin to understand the complicated internal contradictions within the highest governing structures in the country which had led to this astounding decision by a court still functioning at the pinnacle of a Cold War conservative society. But one thing was clear. Scribner was right. We could take nothing for granted with this Court.

We needed an approach that could reach out and speak to the Court, in concepts that touched on its own perception of its duty as an institution, of the dangers lying in uncontrolled congressional investigations that ruthlessly shoved aside the elementary rights of citizens, which was what so many people watching the Army-McCarthy hearings were just beginning to feel. We could, of course, throw sophisticated technical arguments at the Court in the hope of a reversal of the convictions. But as we read and reread the record of the hearings at which both Emspak and Quinn had taken on the House Un-American Activities Committee, what came through loud and clear was that our argument had to center on what Emspak and Quinn had actually done. For they had challenged head on the idea that these congressional committees were all-powerful by finding, within the Constitution itself, a weapon to protect themselves, and everyone else, from this unbridled use of power. This weapon was the invocation of the Fifth Amendment as a barrier to the probing of the committee into their private beliefs, associations, and actions.

The problem here was that the McCarthy Committee and the House Un-American Committee had so successfully jammed the phrase "Fifth Amendment Commie" into everyone's head that to take the Fifth was viewed simply as an admission of guilt. Any concept of the Fifth Amendment as a barrier against governmental tyranny had been lost in the tumult of fear and defensiveness into which most people were thrown by the inquisitors. It was necessary to convince the Court that the use of the Fifth Amendment to cut off congressional probing was something that the Court, pursuant to its own basic responsibility as an institution, must protect, even if it meant breaking with the momentum of the McCarthy tide. Clearly no one on the Court was going to step out that way if they actually believed that the Fifth Amendment and its "privilege against self-incrimination" was really only a technical trick for criminals to evade rigorous exposure by honorable prosecutors.

At this point the lessons we had learned in the struggle against Roy Cohn's recent grand jury manipulations showed us the tack to take. We turned back to the buried history of the constitutional institutions themselves. This revealed that we, the radicals, the targets of the conservative attacks, were in fact defending the oldest traditional democratic institutions from destruction by the right, which was so bent upon power that it was trampling on the very historic concepts it was purporting to save.

This was the approach we took in our briefs. Out of the forgotten past we reminded the Court that, like the grand jury, the Fifth Amendment privilege not to testify was fashioned, in the earliest days of popular resistance to the oppressions of the British Crown, as "a sword to protect the innocent" from the unbridled power of government prosecutors. The Fifth Amendment privilege was an institution constructed for the very purpose for which Emspak and Quinn had invoked it—to protect citizens from inquisitorial power run amok. At a critical moment in the Court's history, we were saying to it—as sections of the ruling establishment itself had just said in the Senate vote condemning McCarthy—that the Cold War McCarthy hysteria had begun to undermine the very institutions which the Court itself was designed to protect: the elementary institutions of constitutional democracy, of which the Fifth Amendment was a fundamental part.

As we sat there at the counsel table, listening to Dave Scribner argue our position to the Court with the passion and eloquence that always characterized his courtroom activity, for the first time I experienced a potent feeling which was to return at future moments in this room when I was again facing those nine black-robed, awe-inspiring figures. We were not intruders here. We were not alien "outside agitators." We had a duty and a right to be here, indeed more right than our opposition, despite their comfortable title of "counsel for the United States." As we argued against the McCarthy-HUAC technique to this, the highest court in the land, in the deepest sense we were the real "counsel for the people of the United States." I felt this very strongly that morning as I listened to Dave Scribner put the questions we had wrestled with so vigorously in the weeks of preparation. This feeling, overwhelming in its impact, expressed in a fundamental way the essence of the role of people's lawyer, which in those days we were just barely beginning to sense—the realization that lawyers who help to defend movements of people in struggle against those in power are, at the very moment that they speak for those popular forces in society who are reaching for a better future, the real defenders of the oldest democratic institutions of the nation.

In a certain sense, we must have persuaded some members of the Court that this was a moment to reassert, even if in a hesitant way, the central role of the Supreme Court in protecting the fundamentals of the written Constitution. For when the decisions came down in May 1955, the opinions, written by the new Chief Justice himself, went even further than we had dared to dream. The Court reversed the convictions of both Emspak and Quinn for contempt of the House Un-American Activities Committee, holding that they had properly invoked the protection of the Fifth Amendment privilege and that the legislative power to investigate was, in fact, bound and restricted by the Constitution.

The *UE News* that week waxed understandably enthusiastic, hailing these "history making decisions" as a "sweeping reaffirmation of the right of the people to the protections of the Bill of Rights" and jubilantly reporting that the opinions of the Chief Justice "specifically declared that no stigma rightfully attaches to the use of the Fifth Amendment which it termed 'a precious right' that was 'hard earned by our forefathers.' " But most important of all to the union leadership was the conclusion expressed in the banner headline, "Tide Rises Against McCarthyism." The Court's opinions directly reflected the Senate vote of several months earlier. The Chief Justice went out of his way to say, with respect to the congressional committees, that "the power to investigate, broad as it may be, is also subject to recognized limitations. It cannot be used to inquire into private affairs unrelated to valid legislative purpose."

By June, other hopeful decisions came down suggesting a Court that was pulling back from the total Cold War commitment of the not so distant past. Clearly something was happening. We were not the only ones in the country to sense this. McCarthy, still reeling from the Senate vote of condemnation, issued a statement calling the Warren Court "completely irresponsible." Senator James Eastland from Mississippi, a conservative Democrat from whom we were to hear a lot more over the years, made the rather profound public comment that "we have politicians instead of lawyers on the Court." Eastland and the other southerners in

Washington were already furious beyond belief at the school segregation decision, handed down on what was now termed by
them the nation's "Black Monday." But what none of us fully
understood at the time was the interrelationship between the
school segregation decision and the pullback from McCarthyism
reflected in the Emspak and Quinn opinions. In a certain respect,
Eastland and McCarthy were much more sensitive than we were
to the long-range implications of these decisions and the intimate
connection between them.

Only years later did we appreciate the underlying divisions
within the power elite that had begun to develop in the mid-1950s
and which were to shape many of the events to come. For certain
of the long-range planners in the Pentagon, the State Department, the White House, and the new United States worldwide
multinational corporations, an embarrassing conflict was beginning to emerge. This was the contradiction between the United
States' assumed role as the "leader of the free world" and the
spectacular lack of freedom inside the United States, as evidenced
by the unchecked McCarthyism in every area of life and the total
segregation and enforced inferior status of Black people in the
South, affecting every other section of the country as well.

With this embarrassing situation at home, it was becoming difficult to parade as the champion of a "free world" in the international competition for leadership of the third world peoples. Yet
the century-old alliance between the entrenched white power
structure of the South and the northern and western leaders
of industry and their friends in government was far too comfortable to risk undermining the system of racial discrimination on
which the southern power structure rested. And the mechanisms
of McCarthyite repression were much too successful in derailing
popular opposition to establishment policies to risk totally dis-
mantling them. The question before the national leadership was
therefore how to resolve this dilemma, how to *seem* to be "the
leader of the free world" to millions of people abroad without in
reality changing the situation at home.

Only within the framework of this dilemma is it possible to understand the motivations of those in high positions in the mid-
1950s who encouraged precisely the developments that were tak-

ing place within the Warren Court. Decisions were shaped there which loudly announced to the world the reaffirmation of old concepts of freedom and liberty, but which did not in themselves dismantle the existing structures of repression. This gap between declarations of principle and actual results was most evident, as the next decade of agony and struggle was to show, in the school segregation decision, whose boldly stated commitment to the proposition that racially segregated schools violated the Constitution remained almost totally ineffectual, owing to the failure to provide any effective and immediate remedy to eliminate racially segregated schools. But the gap was equally true in respect to the Emspak and Quinn opinions and other opinions that year which began to reassert the democratic principles that had been submerged by the McCarthy onslaught. None of these decisions struck down any of the basic mechanisms of Cold War repression, such as the Smith Act, the criminal syndicalist laws, the Subversive Activities Control Board, the Loyalty Orders, the Taft-Hartley provisions, and the whole string of other orders, statutes, and provisions which had been trotted out at one time or another during the dirty decade of McCarthyism. All of these mechanisms remained operative and basically untouched, although occasionally restricted to some degree in their functioning by the new decisions.

One thing was all too clear. Whatever the change in the Court meant, it did not mean a total end to the Cold War attacks on any of the many fronts where we were engaged. The Subversive Activities Control Board, not five months after the Emspak and Quinn victories, was petitioned by the Attorney General to issue an order declaring the UE to be a "Communist-dominated union." For four long years we fought that proceeding in every legal arena, until it was finally dropped by the Department of Justice in 1959. The denaturalization proceedings against Matles, which McCarthy had demanded back in 1952, dragged on until 1958, when the Supreme Court finally reversed, as a violation of due process of law, a lower court's revocation of Matles' certificate of citizenship. Both the struggles against the Subversive Activities Control Board and those against the efforts to denaturalize Jim Matles continued to be occasions for the full-scale mobilization of UE members into activities of support to the legal moves. The loyalty purges of government workers proceeded unabated. The blacklisting of writers, actors, and directors continued, reaching its height in 1956 and 1957. Day and night we were involved in these struggles, and they seemed almost endless.

One of the most infuriating and frustrating experiences of our numberless encounters with the operation of the blacklist in the entertainment industry occurred at this time. For several years, we had represented a boundlessly energetic and progressive young theatrical producer, Richard Saunders, who was attempting to put together what struck us as exciting packages in film and television, some of them dealing with important social themes in challenging and creative ways. A few months before, he had come up with a natural winner. He had convinced one of America's most renowned playwrights, Arthur Miller, to write the script for a movie dealing with the impact of urban life upon young people, based on the pioneering work of the New York City Youth Board. The Youth Board had agreed to endorse the movie. United Artists, through its president, Robert Benjamin, had agreed to fund the film and distribute it. Arthur Miller had already written an outline for the film. It was going to be another great Miller artistic work.

But after I had drafted agreements and contracts and they were all ready to sign, the bottom dropped out of the plan. Benjamin himself called me with the news. Miller had been attacked as a subversive by McCarthy, the Youth Board had withdrawn its endorsement of the project because of the Mayor's fear of re-election problems, and so the film could not be made. I practically screamed at Benjamin on the phone, "But United Artists doesn't have to pull out. It's still just as exciting a film as you said it was." And then Benjamin, one of the most powerful figures in the movie industry and a senior partner in a major Wall Street law firm, said to me in words reminiscent of those of Judge Frank three years before on that fateful afternoon in New Haven, "You don't understand. We can't do anything. I'd like to myself, but it's bigger than all of us."

Dick Saunders and I later shared our feelings of anger, frustration, and hopelessness. Unless Benjamin could be turned around at once, the project was lost. Saunders had a long talk with Benjamin, who was very friendly. Benjamin stressed that he was a "liberal," but that these days one had to be "realistic." Even a writer of Arthur Miller's eminence could not be sold if he had the red smear on him. Benjamin had heard from someone in Congress that Miller would soon be subpoenaed by the House Un-American Activities Committee. If Miller "cleared" himself, Benjamin suggested, the movie might proceed.

At this point Saunders lost his temper and yelled, "Miller wouldn't finger other people." But Benjamin replied simply that life in the film business these days was tough. And that was the end of the Miller film.

There was little or nothing we could do about it. Lawsuits, as we had learned the hard way in the blacklist struggle, went on for years without immediate results. Unless a massive people's movement was prepared to take on the blacklisting apparatus, there was no real hope of quick change in this situation. And as for such a movement of opposition, at that moment none was anywhere around.

Firehoses used to rout civil rights demonstrators in Birmingham, Alabama, May 3, 1963.

Civil rights March on Washington culminating in rally at Washington Monument, August 28, 1963.

Mississippi Freedom Democratic Party Convention, August 1964.

Empty seats of disputed Mississippi delegation at Democratic National Convention in Atlantic City, August 24, 1964.

Martin Luther King addressing supporters of MFDP delegation outside Convention Hall in Atlantic City, August 24, 1964.

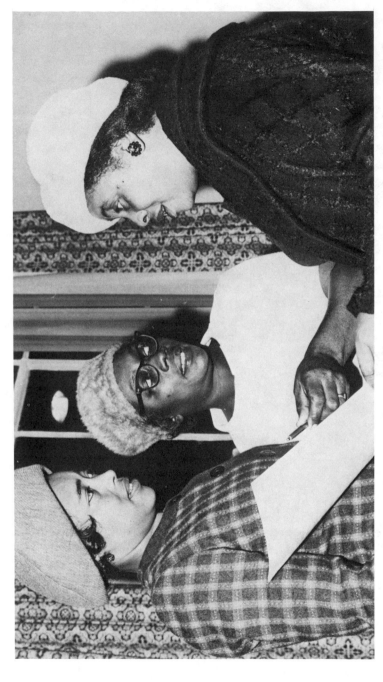

MFDP congressional contestants in the Mississippi Challenge, January 1965. From left: Victoria Gray, Annie Devine, Fannie Lou Hamer.

6

The Montgomery
Bus Boycott
and Willie Seals

In the months following the Emspak and Quinn victories, which followed closely on the earlier decision in the school desegregation case, *Brown v. Board of Education,* there was very little time to even think about the implications of the new shift within the Supreme Court and the long-range effect it might have on our work. But late one evening early in 1956, I received a phone call at home that was to open a window on developments which, in their own time, would stem the tide of McCarthyism in a way no court decision possibly could and launch us all into new forms of people's struggle during the years to come.

The call was from Ella Baker, who at that time was a southern field representative for the National Association for the Advancement of Colored People. We had met a year before at the home of mutual friends. Over the years, she was to influence deeply the lives of the many young people she led and taught in the course of social struggle. In a way, her phone call that evening reflected that impact. She had just returned from Montgomery, Alabama, and was anxious to talk to lawyers and other people who might help in pulling together some northern support for a bus boycott that the Black people of Montgomery had organized. When we got together the next evening, the story Ella Baker told opened up wholly new paths for people's lawyers, though none of us sitting there listening to her could have conceived at that time of the horizons that would stretch out from Montgomery.

Ella Baker told us about Rosa Parks, a courageous Black woman who had decided on her own, one day in December 1955, to take a seat in the front of a bus, from which Black people were barred by segregation laws and customs surviving from the slave society. She was forcibly removed from the bus and arrested. A group of leaders of the Black community then met with her and made the historic decision to take enforcement of the antisegregation commands of the Constitution into their own hands by organizing a mass action of the Black people of Montgomery. They proposed to boycott the buses until segregation in city transport was eliminated.

By early 1956, the boycott was underway. The Black people of Montgomery, responding to the leadership of E.O. Nixon, an experienced organizer of the Brotherhood of Sleeping Car Porters who lived in the city, formed the Montgomery Civic Improvement Association and persuaded an enthusiastic young minister by the name of Martin Luther King, Jr., to act as their spokesperson. This new movement of southern Black people was calling for the immediate enforcement of the fundamental guarantees of equality promised almost a hundred years earlier in the post-Civil War Amendments to the United States Constitution. Their demand was expressed eloquently in the simple words repeated to us that evening by Ella Baker, "Freedom now."

Ella Baker put a direct question to us. Could a support group of some kind be organized in the North, to help meet the urgent need for funds, publicity, and legal help if that became necessary? The few of us whom Ella Baker had called together talked it over. Several of us were lawyers who had been working together in the anti-McCarthy struggles, and several were organizers in various people's organizations still holding fast against the right-wing atmosphere. In the wave of excitement generated by her presentation, we decided to set up such an organization, to be called In Friendship. One of the most active participants in the establishment of this new support group was my wife, Susan Kinoy.

As we talked that evening, a variety of emotions surged

152

through me. I could not help but contrast the reactions of two people, worlds apart from each other, when brought face to face with the harsh facts of oppression. I thought of Rosa Parks in Montgomery, who had faced up to the full force of the southern power structure by sitting in the front of the bus, putting her body and her life on the line. And I thought of Bob Benjamin, who just two weeks before, in New York, had sat in his elegant office, surrounded by material comforts, and refused to lift a finger to oppose the open blacklisting of Arthur Miller. These two human beings, symbolizing wholly disparate forces of society, in a strange way highlighted the simple fact that without the willingness of people to stand up and fight, there can be no successful struggle to enforce the constitutional guarantees of equality and justice. I had felt this willingness throughout my work with the UE, as working people stood and fought against the most intimidating forms of Cold War pressure. And I had found it possible to live and function as a lawyer for these fighting people in such an atmosphere. Now I felt instinctively that Montgomery and the new path of struggle it seemed to open up might lead again to a similar way of life and work.

The most important personal impact of the work of In Friendship as a support organization, first for the Montgomery bus boycott and then for the growing southern Freedom Movement, was the way that it brought those of us who had been so immersed in the Cold War tensions into a close relationship with an exploding new social force. In its own way, this new movement would take hold of the role of people's lawyer and thrust it to new levels of creative activity we never dreamed of in the first days of the Cold War.

The white power structure throughout the South was responding to the decision in *Brown v. Board of Education* with the pre-civil War arrogance of total defiance, enshrined in such legalistic terms as "nullification" of unacceptable Supreme Court decisions and "interposition" of the authority of the "sovereign state." Both of these concepts concealed a blunt, go-to-hell response on the part of the southern states to the Court's banning of segregation. The flat refusal of the southern states to lift a finger to undo the system of segregation placed in center stage the failure of the Supreme Court in the original *Brown v. Board of Education* decision back in 1954 to provide for any effective remedies to enforce its decision. As we had sensed in those early days, the opinions in *Brown,* proudly proclaiming the illegality of racial segregation under the Constitution, had seemed a perfect solution to those in positions of power and control who sought to solve the international Cold War paradox of the United States claiming to be the champion of the "free world" abroad while its image at home remained tarnished by the spectacle of racial oppression and McCarthyism. The absence of any sweeping remedies within the opinion made it safe for the establishment. It was a beautiful, clear statement for all the world to hear, and with no enforcement to endanger the white power structure at home. The Supreme Court had announced "the law of the land," and yet no one was prepared to enforce it! The judicial system's only remedy was on a strictly individual case level, which could be stalled indefinitely by endless appeals, and the executive and legislative branches of the national government were both taking the easy way out by doing nothing. President Eisenhower had charted this course when he piously announced, shortly after the *Brown* opinion, "Great decision, but this is for the courts—not us."

Within this framework, however, the *Brown* decision began to have some totally unexpected results. No one had counted on what the first architects of our republican form of government, from Thomas Jefferson on down, had told Americans so eloquently was the *fourth* branch of government: the sovereign people. Beyond the first three branches—the executive, the legislative, and the judicial—the supreme power in the land was to rest in a fourth branch, the people of the nation. Over the years this proposition became reserved mainly for the most esoteric seminars in law schools, for fear of the incredible dangers posed to those in power if the people themselves ever heard about their real powers. In a way that would literally shake the foundations of the governing institutions, the Black people of the South, confronted with the arrogant posture of the southern states and the refusal of the three other branches of the national government to act, took the enforcement of the Supreme Court's decision into their own hands. Grasping the promise of freedom and equality, they began to say, loud and clear, "We will enforce this promise ourselves, now!" This was the message of Montgomery, understood and soon acted upon from one end of the South to the other.

It was a message that the new Black southern movement meant to impress swiftly upon the national consciousness. Early in 1957, those of us working with In Friendship received word from a newly formed, southwide organization, the Southern Christian Leadership Conference, headquartered in Montgomery, in which the young minister Martin Luther King played a leading role. The SCLC wanted to organize a national demonstration in Washington, D.C., on May 17, the third anniversary of the Supreme Court decision, calling upon the president and Congress to enforce that mandate by passing a national civil rights law. After a series of hurried discussions, in which Ella Baker played a key role in bringing people together, a relationship was worked out between the older Black leadership, represented by A. Philip Randolph, the deeply respected president of the Brotherhood of Sleeping Car Porters, who had organized the 1942 March on Washington demanding an end to segregation and racial discrimination in the armed forces, and the new younger southern Black leadership, centering around Dr. King in Montgomery. After much hesitation, Roy Wilkins, the executive secretary of the NAACP, agreed to join in a joint call for what was to be a "Prayer Pilgrimage for Freedom."

All of us involved with In Friendship threw ourselves into helping to organize what we hoped would be the first really massive demonstration in Washington to demand positive social action since the onslaught of McCarthyism in the early fifties. It was in this period of activity that I first met Bayard Rustin, that skillful organizer, creative advocate of nonviolent resistance, and close associate of Randolph who was to play a central role in the first years of organizing a national response to the new southern Black upsurge. It was such a refreshing experience to meet people all over whose response to the Montgomery boycott was one of excitement and commitment to the call for demonstrative action, rather than the cautious holding back so characteristic of the McCarthy period. We were just beginning to feel the long-range

155

effects that the southern movement would have in lifting the Cold War atmosphere of fear and discouragement.

But the work around the Prayer Pilgrimage also revealed certain underlying tensions that were to shape the events of the future. The first coming together of A. Philip Randolph with the new southern leadership that had formed around Dr. King and the Montgomery bus boycott reflected a beginning shift within the Black Movement which would have sweeping implications for the functioning of people's lawyers but which at the time very few of us outside the movement understood. For a number of years, ever since the founding of the NAACP in the early 1900s, there had been two distinct trends within the leadership of the Black Movement. One trend relied upon the development of legal test cases within the court system to accomplish the objective of overthrowing the legally sanctioned structure of Jim Crow segregation. The other trend, while not totally rejecting the utilization of legal challenges, emphasized the accomplishment of the objectives of the movement through mass action, mass pressure, and militant demands. Randolph had typified this trend when he organized the 1942 March on Washington. However, throughout the postwar period the test case approach dominated the work of the NAACP and most of the other Black Movements. The Supreme Court decision of 1954 was the triumph of the test case approach.

When the Black people of Montgomery and throughout the South began to take the enforcement of these legal victories into their own hands through mass activities, boycotts, marches, parades, and demonstrations, calling for "Freedom now," they found quick support in those national leaders like A. Philip Randolph who had always seen mass action as the most productive path to follow. But the leadership of the other trend, with its base primarily in the NAACP, was uneasy about the new alignments. Mass action, whether in the streets of Montgomery or in Washington itself, might well frighten off those forces within the judicial, legislative, and executive branches whom the NAACP leadership still counted on to enforce the policies enunciated in *Brown v. Board of Education*. This fear that militant popular action would fail to accelerate and might even derail the middle-of-the-road forces induced Roy Wilkins to issue an NAACP press statement shortly before the Prayer Pilgrimage, saying that this event "is not a March-on-Washington in the sense of the 1942 movement inasmuch as it is not designed to exert pressure on the executive branch of the government."

The serious implications of Wilkins' strange pronouncement were manifest not at the time of the demonstration but in the future. The Pilgrimage itself was beautifully attended, and it was important mainly for its inspirational effect. People came from all over the South, and they returned home inspired to take the message of Montgomery out to their own towns and cities. Dr. King, in his first speech to rock the nation, threw out the potent demand, "Give us the ballot." The real impact of the NAACP's attempt to disassociate the Prayer Pilgrimage from Randolph's March on Washington as a form of militant struggle would be felt in the days to come when the NAACP leadership, perhaps fearful of the effect of this exploding mass movement upon the government structure, increasingly pulled away from support of the growing militant movements.

Shortly after the Prayer Pilgrimage, I personally felt a little backwash from these developing tensions, when we were called into a pressing legal situation that had suddenly erupted in Montgomery. Charles Conley, a Black lawyer from Montgomery whom I would get to know very well in later years, came to New York to get help and advice concerning threats by the Alabama state authorities to harass Dr. King with absurd perjury charges arising out of statements that he was supposed to have made concerning the bus boycott. Chuck Conley made it quite clear to us that, as one of the few local lawyers willing to represent the Montgomery movement, he was not getting much help in handling the legal problems that arose, and he welcomed this chance to get together.

As we sat and talked over the situation, I sensed for the first time that the legal problems of the new Black Movement in the South were going to be very different from the carefully staged, delicately handled national test cases in which, in earlier years, a core of trained experts sought decisions from the highest courts challenging the old prosegregation rulings. Something very different was involved in what we were discussing with Chuck Conley. His was a problem that stemmed from the attempt of the power structure to use the machinery of the state to harass and interfere with the efforts of people to enforce their constitutional rights. In a fundamental way, the traditional role of the lawyer in the civil rights movement was changing in order to meet the new need. It was shifting away from the older, relatively independent role of seeking to attain the goals of the movement through developing key test cases, to a role of a very different character, that of defending the ability of the people themselves to attain the goals of their movement through their own strength and power.

This was a role with which I felt at home. It was the role of the people's lawyer I had learned in Evansville, in Schenectady, and in all of the years of work with the UE. I began to feel that Chuck Conley was looking for help in moving in this direction. All of the old UE experiences in taking the offensive, in exposing the real conspiracy, came forward in the course of our discussion. As it happened, the viability of the approaches we discussed that evening were never tested out in that case, as several months later the state dropped the charges against Dr. King and adopted other methods to harass the movement and its leadership. But the discussions had their effect. They opened up an ongoing relationship with Chuck Conley which was to lead, several years later, to a testing out of the approaches in a wholly different setting than any we had anticipated, when the life of a young Black man, Willie Seals, was at stake in Mobile, Alabama.

In the meantime, the possibility of federal enforcement of the constitutional promises of equality and freedom became ever less likely. In 1957 Congress passed a relatively meaningless civil rights statute without any effective remedies. They made it quite clear that they had no intention of enforcing the constitutional commitments in any way. And the attention-getting confrontation at Little Rock, Arkansas, in the fall of 1957 was in effect merely a repetition of the complexity of the *Brown v. Board of Education* decision itself. Little Rock presented to the world the spectacle of the United States President calling out the national troops to enforce a federal court order desegregating a high school, but it also carried the hidden message of Eisenhower's real position—that the executive would take no steps of any kind to enforce desegregation *unless* there was willful disobedience to a final court order.

The white southern power structure learned the Little Rock lesson well. There are many ways to delay a court order indefinitely. Moreover, in the vast majority of all Southern situations there were never any court orders or other legal proceedings to enforce desegregation. No one, short of the national government, had the money or legal personnel to apply the Supreme Court decision outlawing school segregation to every other aspect of segregated life by bringing individual actions against every school district, every bus line, every movie theater, every hotel, every streetcar, every library, every restaurant, throughout the South.

When the national executive and the national legislature refused to face their responsibilities to enforce the national law, once again it was up to the people themselves. And so the movement toward popular enforcement of the Constitution surged forward again, on both national and southern fronts. On October 11, 1958, Dr. King and the SCLC leadership, together with A. Philip Randolph, returned to Washington to hold a Youth March for Integrated Schools, on which more than 30,000 people, including over 10,000 young southerners, demanded an immediate end to segregated schools. In May 1959, a second impressive Youth March was held in Washington. In the South itself, the movement catapulted into student sit-ins in lunchrooms, demanding an end to segregated eating places. Within several weeks in late 1960, over 300 Black students were arrested in eleven cities from Virginia to Mississippi. Campaigns of support sprang up all over the country, involving trade unionists and other civil rights supporters both Black and white, who picketed and leafleted the national chain stores that allowed segregation in their southern branches.

Within five years from the day that Rosa Parks had put herself on the line in that bus in Montgomery, a new people's movement was changing the entire political climate of the country. The mood of profound pessimism that had infected sections of the left, leading them to such devastating conclusions as we had experienced within the UE during the dirty decade, was now being challenged from one end of the South to the other. The lesson that people facing the harshest oppression had the courage and ability to organize and struggle together was hard to miss. The task of people's lawyers was still, just as it had been in the early years of the Cold War, to put their legal skills and abilities to work in the service of these struggling people.

Yet even in these first years of the growth of the southern movement and its emergence on the national scene, there were still some leaders of progressive organizations who clung to the mainstream approach, born out of the Cold War fear of the isolation of the left. To some of these people, the mainstream of the Black people's movement remained the NAACP. The same people who had urged the UE organizers and leaders to leave their "sinking ship" and merge with the mainstream AFL-CIO unions, now said to those of us who were excitedly throwing our support behind the new fighting southern mass movements, "Stay away. These new developments will undermine the NAACP's strategy of seeking alliance with powerful government and Democratic Party forces like the Kennedys, who will 'enforce civil rights' as soon as they have 'taken over' in the election of 1960."

To those of us who had helped to pull together In Friendship and then had thrown ourselves into the work around the Prayer Pilgrimage and the Youth Marches, this advice seemed to be sheer insanity. If nothing else, the experiences of the UE during the harsh years of the Cold War had taught us that in a period of growing oppression the only solid guarantee of survival was the strengthening and building of militant-led organizations of working people. From this came the perception that the heart of all social progress, whether in a period of repression or in one of forward movement, was the independent power and strength of the people themselves. The mass movements of Black people in the South were demonstrating that power and strength in a way which no one would have believed possible at the height of McCarthyism only six years earlier. Rosa Parks, Ella Baker, Martin Luther King, and the thousands of Black women and men in the towns and cities of the South had set us all on a path to rebuilding a new people's movement for equality and freedom. Where it would take us was hard to imagine during those formative days at the end of the dirty decade.

The subtle but fundamental shift in the role of lawyers within the civil rights movement was something I would really come to understand only after a sharp turn of events several years later, which threw me headlong into the daily struggles of the exploding southern Black Movement. But even now, before I had felt the full impact of this new development, I began to sense its implications for the future, as a result of experiences that occurred during an extremely difficult period of my personal life. In the fall of 1959, I had become seriously ill with an attack of meningitis. Following what seemed an endless period of hospitalization, rest, and only partial recuperation, the doctors surmised that the illness was probably incurable and that I was permanently cut off from a life of activity. I accepted the inevitability of cutting back drastically on the amount of time I could spend in legal activity. I was obliged to withdraw from active participation in the law firm and from most ongoing litigation. It was a very stressful time, not only for me but also for my wife, Susan, and for our children, Peter and Joanne. Without their patience, understanding, and ability to readjust their own lives, it is questionable whether I would have made it through those months.

It was particularly painful to drop out of active political life at this critical moment, when everything I had sensed as a possibility in the last few years was happening. The McCarthy tide of fear and defeatism was receding, and the rising movement of Black people was spreading rapidly from one end of the South to the other. The student sit-ins had sparked a whole new level of militant mass actions of many thousands of people calling for immediate enforcement of the constitutional promise of freedom and equality. And yet I myself was more and more removed from daily involvement in this momentous people's movement.

Then something happened which, in reestablishing ties that had been made during the stirring days of the Prayer Pilgrimage and the Youth Marches, built a bridge for me from the past to a future that might end my forced inactivity. Early one morning in July 1961, I received another call from Chuck Conley in Montgomery. He sounded tense and tired. Ever since the attempted perjury frameup of Dr. King, we had been in touch from time to time over legal questions that arose in the SCLC work. But this call was different. "Arthur," he said, "can you get down here to

Montgomery tonight? I'm going to need some real help." Never before had he made so urgent a plea. I asked him what was going on. "It's the Willie Seals case," he said. "They're going to execute him in two days unless we do something fast."

I knew little about the case other than what Conley had already told me. At the urgent request of the Mobile Non-Partisan Voters League, a Black community organization, Conley had come into the case at the very last moment. Willie Seals was a 24-year-old Black man, married and the father of a five-year-old child, who had been sentenced to death by an Alabama court for the supposed rape of a white woman. Among the incredible aspects of the case that had led Conley to agree to step in, despite being over his head with legal work arising from the growth of SCLC and the Montgomery struggles, was the fact that at the trial six witnesses had testified without contradiction that Seals was miles away from the scene of the supposed offense. There was only one problem with this testimony. All the witnesses were Black, and the all-white southern jury refused to accept the credibility of any Black testimony in a trial of a Black for rape of a white woman.

Conley needed an immediate answer to his urgent request. Something inside of me said, "Do this. You'll find the energy somewhere." Before the end of the day, I was on a plane to Montgomery.

On the flight down, my head was filled with thoughts about the special nature of this situation. There was nothing more ominous in southern society than the charge of rape of a white woman by a Black man. Nothing touched the heart of a racially segregated society built on the foundations of a slave economy more than this accusation. Since the earliest days of slavery, even the hint of such a charge had unleashed a reign of terror against the entire Black community, often resulting in the death of the alleged offender, either by lynching by the informal armed troops of the white power structure—the Ku Klux Klan or a local mob of whites organized for that purpose—or by a more formal "lynching" through the legal structure of the state.

Over the years, a formula had emerged out of these experiences for reminding the Black community of its inferior status whenever there was the slightest indication that resistance was beginning, or as the power structure put it, whenever the Blacks were starting to be "uppity." Pull out the charge of the "rape" of a white woman, round up dozens of Black men, beat them, torture them, terrorize their community, and then pick out one or two of them to hang. The lesson to the Black community was written in blood: if you cross the line, someone dies for it.

As I thought about this pattern, one aspect of the situation I was flying into struck me as different. The pattern was still there, and the lynching was about to occur, but now the Black community was fighting back. At the urgent request of an organization of the Black community, a Black lawyer had refused to be intimidated and had stepped into the battle. This the white power structure had not figured on. What would happen? Was there a chance for Willie Seals at this last minute, or would the lynching take place?

Chuck Conley and I talked over the frighteningly simple procedural situation as we drove through Montgomery from the airport to his office. He had not come into the case until after the Alabama Supreme Court had turned down the final appeal from the death sentence imposed by the trial judge after the guilty verdict. Conley had then quickly gone through all the necessary motions to exhaust every avenue of recourse in the state courts so that he could prepare for the last resort, an attack in the federal courts on the conviction as violating the United States Constitution. The way to get a case into the federal courts was to ask a federal judge to issue the ancient writ of habeas corpus, commanding the state authorities to "produce the body" of the prisoner before the federal court and to justify the lawfulness of the state proceeding under the federal constitution. The problem in this case was one of time. No southern federal judge would be willing to interfere with this state proceeding as long as any channel remained open for the state itself to hold up the execution, now scheduled for two days away, July 7. Conley explained to me that the Governor had scheduled a clemency hearing for the next afternoon, July 6, and since there was little likelihood of any reprieve, Conley must be ready later that afternoon to rush the habeas corpus papers before a federal judge to try to persuade that judge to hold up the execution scheduled for the next morning.

The task we faced that evening seemed, at the outset, over-whelming: how to fashion a habeas argument that would per-suade a southern federal judge to push aside centuries of in-grained prejudice and hold up the execution of a young Black who had been found guilty of the most horrible charge possi-ble within the context of a segregated society. As we went over the first drafts Conley had already prepared, one point seemed clear. We had to reach out to a deep-rooted feeling among federal judges which at some moments of crisis in the South in those days was leading a few of them to break away momentarily from the total support of the white power structure that normally charac-terized their functioning as judges. This was only two years after Little Rock. The supremacy of the federal Constitution and the special responsibility of federal judges to stand up and defend that supremacy were at the core of the few courageous decisions which southern federal appeals courts had since handed down. If we were to achieve the miracle of a stay of execution in the Seals case, we would have to frame the issues within the context of the fundamental constitutional confrontation that was rocking the South to its foundations.

For this reason, the issue could not be presented primarily as one of individual guilt or innocence, despite the many doubts about Seals' guilt that were now coming forward and which had already raised the most serious questions about the evidence that convicted him. As Conley laid out the underlying questions which in his view were decisive, one thing became clear to both of us. The case was exactly what the Black community leadership in Mobile said it was. It was a flagrant use of power by a totally seg-regated and discriminatory legal structure, without the slightest regard for the mandates of the federal Constitution. Willie Seals had been rounded up with forty other young Black men, without warrants or any other authority, two days after the episode. All of them were held incommunicado and beaten. After three days of intimidation and physical abuse, one of the men, Arthur Lott, was forced to sign a paper implicating himself and Seals. The city prosecutor immediately released this supposed confession to the newspapers, together with Seals' photograph. After the picture appeared in the papers, the white woman in the case for the first time "identified" Seals in a lineup. Shortly afterward, Lott repudiated the so-called confession as untrue and forced on him, and it was never even used at the trial. Seals was held in isolation without being arraigned or charged for over four months until an all-white grand jury indicted him. He was then tried before twelve white jurors in a totally segregated courtroom, and he was found guilty despite the testimony of six witnesses, all Black, that he was nowhere near the scene of the alleged crime at the time it was supposed to have occurred. Only the white woman, who had identified him after his picture was published in the papers, testified against him.

As Conley laid out these gross violations of the federal Constitution, it was hard to believe we were little more than twenty-four hours away from an execution. At one point I was so overwhelmed by the total disregard for the most elementary requirements of the Constitution that I blurted out to him, "How in hell did the Alabama Supreme Court get around every United States Supreme Court decision for the past ten years?"

Conley's response shook me awake to the reality of Alabama and to the grim prospects of the next twenty-four hours. "Oh," he said with a wry smile, "Seals had a lawyer at the trial, and the lawyer didn't raise any of the constitutional points. They have all been 'waived,' the state says."

My heart sank. There was no more elementary and fundamental rule of law than that of waiver. All of us as first-year law students had had it drummed into us. If a lawyer did not raise a constitutional point at a trial, it was "waived," dead for all purposes. It could never be used in an appeal. But there was something here that I simply could not understand. "It's one thing," I said, "to miss a complicated question—but *these* issues? How in God's name could any lawyer not raise the total unconstitutionality of an all-white grand jury and an all-white trial jury in a case like this?"

Conley brought it all home to me, and put the Seals case into the framework of southern reality, with the stark response, "The lawyer was white." That was what it was all about. No white lawyer could survive in the South who, in the defense of a Black client, raised any of these controversy-laden constitutional questions which went to the heart of the legitimacy of a segregated society. "How long do you think any white lawyer who went around challenging an all-white jury system or a segregated courtroom would keep practicing in Mobile?" Chuck asked me.

There it was in a nutshell. Only a tiny handful of Black lawyers were practicing in the South, because Black people had been almost totally excluded from the profession, not only by the general impact of the segregated society but also by the conscious policy of their exclusion from law schools in both the South and the North. Therefore, Black people were almost always represented by white lawyers. The United States Supreme Court had held for over ten years that the exclusion of Black people from juries was totally illegal. But unless white lawyers raised this constitutional question in the trial, it was "waived." And since white lawyers would never raise this explosive question, what was really waived was the United States Constitution itself—waived right out of the window.

That evening, I began to understand more clearly than ever before the built-in contradictions in this business of being a lawyer. In law school, no one would ever have challenged the concept, which was advanced as steadily as a platitude in first-year orientation lectures and graduation addresses, that the highest obligation of the legal profession was to be the conscious guardian of the constitutional rights of the American people. Yet here in Alabama I was discovering the truth about the role of the legal profession throughout one huge section of the country, that it was the conscious instrument whereby the basic rights of millions of Americans were totally erased.

This became the key for us that evening. This was the approach to the federal judge. Alabama had virtually conceded the most serious violations of the United States Constitution in the proceedings against Seals, but these violations had been "waived" by the white lawyer. We had to argue reality. If the Constitution meant anything at all, the refusal of a white lawyer to raise the constitutional mandate against a segregated system of justice in behalf of a Black defendant could not mean the abandonment of that right by the Black defendant. Otherwise the federal courts would be abetting a conspiracy to refuse to apply the principles of *Brown v. Board of Education* to the system of justice itself.

At stake here was more than the life of a young man, as crucial as that was. Seals' case presented a challenge to the entire system of segregated justice and to the role of the white-dominated legal profession in perpetuating it. At one point the seriousness of this threat became crystal clear when Conley proposed challenging the competency of even the Alabama Supreme Court to sit on the case, since it was elected by a voting constituency from which Black citizens were almost totally excluded.

For a moment I hesitated. Might this be too much for the federal judge to swallow? "My God," I said, "this means the conviction of every Black in Alabama is probably illegal."

Conley laughed, "They probably are." Then, in words I would often think of at crucial moments in the years ahead, he described the matter bluntly, "Better to put it sharply than to mince words." And deep down I felt he was right. The more we tied the fate of the individual, Willie Seals, to the overall confrontation between the assertion of federal power and the effort to perpetuate the system of segregation, the more chance we had of touching a raw nerve in the federal judiciary.

The next morning the die was cast. Our approach was set, our papers prepared. Conley would go through the motions of the clemency hearing and, after the inevitable denial, rush to Birmingham, 150 miles away, where Federal Judge Lynne was sitting, to present the habeas corpus application and ask him for an emergency stay of execution pending later hearings on the charges in the habeas papers. I would wait in Montgomery at Conley's office in case any last-minute work had to be done. Whether or not I would leave for New York in the evening after hearing from him about the results of the day would depend on the nature of those results. In the back of both our minds was the thought that an emergency search for a member of the United States Court of Appeals might become essential that evening, to ask that judge for a stay of the execution.

The minute the phone rang early in the evening and Chuck started to talk, I knew that the miracle had happened. "Relax," he said. "We did it. Judge Lynne signed the stay, and I just served it on the warden at Kilby Prison."

The next day I was flying back to New York, more than a little exhausted. I had not worked so hard since the meningitis hit in

167

the fall of 1959. My mind kept jumping from thoughts of the work that lay ahead, preparing for the hearings that would have to be held before Judge Lynne to prove the charges in the habeas papers, to thoughts of the difference between the experience in Montgomery and the tragic frustration of that afternoon years before in New Haven when Jerome Frank had turned us down. It would take a long time to come to understand all the reasons for the difference between the two periods, but one of them was clear. In a struggle against the impact of a repressive structure upon the life of an individual, success depended largely upon the ability to merge the fight for the individual with the overall fight against the structure itself. What emerged sharply out of those twenty-four hours in Montgomery was the fact that one of the crucial tasks of a people's lawyer had to be to make this bridge between the individual defense and the strategic assault upon the entire repressive structure. Whether the state of Alabama liked it or not, the fight to save the life of Willie Seals was merging with the fight of the Black people of Mobile and of all the South against the entire system of segregated justice and the historic use of that machinery to keep the Black people in their inferior status in every aspect of life. To assist in this merger, to use all the skills and art of lawyering to accomplish it, was the highest challenge for a people's lawyer thrown into the midst of such a struggle.

The federal hearings in the Willie Seals case, scheduled for September and October, were going to be massive undertakings, requiring tremendous preparation. We planned, in effect, to place on trial the whole legal structure of Alabama. Conley would continue to function as chief counsel, with the overall legal responsibility. This was the seed of a recognition, which was to grow and develop throughout the southern movement, of the central importance of the leadership of Black lawyers rooted in the communities from which the struggles sprang. But this handful of lawyers, as the experience in Montgomery also showed, would urgently need the assistance of other lawyers from outside the area if they were not to be drowned in the ocean of legal actions that continually flowed from the legal apparatus of the southern states. More and more lawyers from all over the country would have to be found who were willing and ready to accept this new role as supporters to the southern lawyers who were already doing battle in their own communities.

As I could in no way physically undertake my full share of the preparation for the Seals hearings, I personally understood the need to find more help. Despite the incapacitating effects of the illness, which persisted in lingering on, I knew I must continue to play a role in this struggle, no matter how limited it would have to be. Thus the best contribution I could make was to enlist others in the fight. I immediately turned for help to those lawyers with whom I had worked so closely in all the UE legal struggles. This was no accident. Once again the task was to find ways to put the skills and techniques of the lawyer to work to meet the needs of people standing up for their rights and searching for ways to fight back. The experience that the UE lawyers had gained in striving for the same goal could prove invaluable at this wholly different moment of history.

With this in mind, I called Conley early in September to tell him that Morton Stavis from Newark and Martin Bradley from Buffalo had agreed to step into the work on the Seals case and help him in preparations for the hearings. Their agreement to shoulder major responsibility in the Seals case was one of the first steps in a development that a few years later would make history in the American bar when hundreds of lawyers from all parts of the country went South to assist in the intense legal work arising from the Black movement's challenge to the entrenched white power structure.

While preparing for the Seals hearings, Bradley made a trip to Mobile, where a development occurred that was to prove crucial for the work of people's lawyers in the South. Returning from the trip, Bradley told us about the strong community involvement with the case in Mobile. The Black leadership of the Mobile Non-Partisan Voters League was deeply committed to the struggle to save Seals' life. A whole network of people, including employees of the postal system who therefore knew street locations, had been set up to check the thousands of names on the jury lists in order to provide proof of the almost total exclusion of Black people from the jury rolls. Bradley filled us in on discussions that he had taken part in which revealed an understanding of the inseparable relationship between the fight for Seals' life and the battle opening in Mobile against a totally segregated society—segregated in schools, in jobs, in every aspect of daily life. One of the leaders of the movement, John LeFlore, said to Bradley, "If they can kill Willie Seals, they can kill us all. That's the way the people think here. And if we can stop them from killing Willie, we've got real strength to move ahead."

In Mobile, Bradley also heard the first rumblings of a story that would haunt the fight for Seals in the days to come. Inside the Pritchard community, the Black section of Mobile where the attack was said to have occurred, a story was quietly circulating about the people who had lived across the street from where the raped woman's car broke down. The story was that they had seen two men pull her out of the car and drag her away, and that the two men were white policemen. Another story floated around to the effect that a day later someone had found, around the outhouse where the beating and attack were supposed to have taken place, a man's belt with a Mobile Police Department insignia on it.

These were only the vaguest rumors, and not until years later could anyone pin anything down. The people who might have been the witnesses had left Mobile, and no one knew where they had gone. But underneath the fear and terror which the mass roundups of young Black men had created in the neighborhood, there lurked the suspicion that the persistence of the police, the beatings, and the intensity of intimidation might very well be meant to divert attention from the real culprits. In the classic manner of the South, they might be covering up their own involvement by raising the old cry of "Black rapist." This suspicion fed the growing community determination, in the new spirit of struggle stemming from the bus boycott in Montgomery, to stand and fight back this time, even in the shadow of the lynch mob.

Stavis, Bradley, and Conley moved ahead with full-scale preparations for the fall hearings in the federal district court, while I helped in whatever limited ways I could. From their first experiences with Judge Lynne it was clear that, in a very real sense, all they were doing was building a record for the inevitable appeal to the highest federal court in the South, the United States Court of Appeals for the Fifth Circuit. Few district court federal judges in these days would have been willing to expose themselves to the controversy that a challenge to the entrenched power structure would entail. The original stay of execution was the most that could be expected from Judge Lynne. So it was no surprise when Conley called me late in November to say that Lynne had denied the granting of a writ of habeas corpus and had vacated his stay of execution. The judge had been so totally influenced by the explosive nature of the charge that he even refused to issue the necessary certificate of probable cause which was required to allow an appeal to the federal Court of Appeals.

Conley immediately appeared before a Court of Appeals judge, Richard Rives, who granted the necessary certificate. We all breathed a sigh of relief and pitched into the intensive work involved in preparing a brief for the argument before the federal court of appeals. Five days later, Conley called with the grim news that the Alabama Supreme Court, obviously not impressed with the possibility of action by the federal Court of Appeals, had reset Seals' execution for February 23, 1962. This was the fifth time in three years that the warden came into Seals' cell on death row in Kilby Prison to tell him the date on which he was to be electrocuted. Judge Rives responded by putting the whole appeal down for immediate argument on January 24 in New Orleans, where the Fifth Circuit met. The tension was building again, and once more we moved into an arena of work in which the entire atmosphere was shaped by the pressure of an impending date of execution.

As we worked feverishly on the last drafts of the brief, sending copies back and forth from Buffalo to New York to Newark to Montgomery, it was clear that this would be the critical confrontation. If we were unable to convince the federal Court of Appeals that saving the life of this young Black man involved the same fundamental issues of federal constitutional supremacy as did allowing the Black students to enter Little Rock High School four years before, we would not be able to pull it off. Deep down, we had the uneasy feeling that convincing the three white male southerners sitting on the federal appeals bench in New Orleans was not going to be easy in view of the traditional overtones of the rape charge.

And then, as we were putting the final touches on the brief, news hit us from Mobile that reminded us of the desperate lengths to which the white power structure was willing to go to stem the rising tide of Black insistence on enforcement of the national Constitution. Conley called to tell us that the chairperson of the Mobile Non-Partisan Voters League had been murdered by unidentified white gunmen, and at his funeral on January 7 the mayor of Mobile had openly warned John LeFlore, the top remaining officer of the association, that violence could also be expected to occur against him and other leaders of the association involved in the fight around Seals and the efforts to eliminate segregated facilities in Mobile. At an emergency meeting in Mobile, a decision had been made to send telegrams to President John Kennedy and Attorney General Robert Kennedy, requesting immediate and "effective protection for the leadership of the Mobile Committee and for the attorneys of Willie Seals."

In this tense atmosphere, we finished the brief and met Conley in New Orleans on January 24 for the argument. I had felt an irresistible compulsion to be present at this argument, no matter what the expenditure of energy, even if it was beyond the doctor's allowed quota. The developments in Mobile two weeks before had made it seem imperative in every way for me to be there physically at this critical confrontation.

This was the first time I had actually been in a southern courtroom. It turned out to be the beginning of a whole new road. As we sat at the counsel table, three distinguished looking judges walked in and sat down at the raised bench that faced us. Not knowing who these somber white southern male aristocrats of the judiciary were who held the life of Willie Seals in their hands, I dropped my eyes to the little piece of paper on which the Court Clerk had written their names: Judges Rives, Brown, and Wisdom. At that moment they were absolute strangers to me. I little dreamed that within three years, I would get to know them as closely as one ever gets to know an appellate judge. My first reaction to them was one of panic. What were we doing there? It was going to be a catastrophe! We could hardly expect three representatives of the southern white power structure to endorse a wholesale attack by a Black lawyer on their entire structure of segregated justice.

As they listened intently to Conley's eloquent account of the fundamental constitutional questions at stake and asked occasional friendly questions, I began to sense a fact that would remain deeply etched in my mind during the next years, as my life and work became intermeshed with the southern Freedom Movement. Something other than their own position in southern society was moving certain of these appellate federal judges. They themselves were caught in a deep conflict, the outcome of which was not always clear, between their roots in their own southern society and their special commitment, as representatives of the national judicial branch of government, to the concept of the supremacy of the mandates of the federal Constitution. To the degree that these judges felt that a given situation required a stand in support of the commands of the Constitution, it was not preordained that they would support the position toward which their own social background normally pulled them.

As my own experience with the southern federal appellate judges grew in the years ahead, I would come to understand much more fully the complexities of this situation, but that afternoon one fact stood out clearly, especially after the three judges had skillfully punctured the reply arguments of Alabama's attorney general, MacDonald Gallian, with incisive questions. This fact was that our task as people's lawyers in this case was to strengthen the pull within these judges, their sworn role as defenders of the national Constitution, which was moving them toward holding back Alabama's hand on the electric chair switch. And Conley's words back in July were proving to be true—"Better to put it sharply than mince words." That's the way he put it in his closing argument, avoiding the trap of responding to the technical distortions of the Alabama lawyers and sticking to the heart of the case, whether the simple commands of the United States Constitution applied to Black people in the South.

At the end of the attorney general's final argument, something happened which told us that this message was getting across. Judge Rives, acting as the presiding judge, leaned over the bench and, in emphatic tones, informed Alabama that the execution of Seals, now scheduled for February 23, was to be stayed "until the further order of this Court." You could have heard a pin drop in that courtroom. We had won the first and critical round, without even a formal application for a stay!

We left the courthouse jubilant. Stavis had to rush back to Newark for another trial, but Bradley, Conley, and I spent the evening celebrating at the home of Ben Smith, one of the few white southern lawyers willing to represent the Black civil rights movement, who had enthusiastically turned his office over to us during the Seals argument. As we sat there that evening and he filled us in on the countless stories of his own experiences with the southern federal judiciary, little did I dream that two years later I would be sitting in the same apartment, working through approaches designed to apply the same lessons, in a desperate effort to protect Ben Smith himself from the impact of Louisiana's attempt to use the full weight of its criminal procedure against him, in retaliation for the courageous role he was playing in the heart of a segregated society.

Our celebration that night in New Orleans was not premature. On May 30, the decision of the Fifth Circuit came down. It was a sweeping victory in every sense. The court went right to the heart of the system of segregated justice, holding that the exclusion of Black people from the jury rolls in Alabama was a fundamental violation of the United States Constitution and that the failure of a white lawyer to raise this question was in no way a "waiver of the rights of a Black defendant." On this critical point, the three judges went out of their way to assert a position which, in one blow, elevated the Seals decision to importance throughout the South. They said, "As judges of a Circuit comprising six states of the deep South, we think that it is our duty to take judicial notice that lawyers residing in many southern jurisdictions rarely, almost to the point of never, raise the issue of systematic exclusion of Negroes from juries." As for Seals himself, they threw out the original indictment and guilty verdict as unconstitutional, ordered the state of Alabama to establish a "constitutional" jury system without Black exclusion within eight months, and gave the state the right to reindict Seals and try him before "some court or tribunal so constituted as not to violate Seals' constitutional rights."

The decision threw the white power structure into a turmoil.

Gallian called it the worst decision since *Brown v. Board of Education* and termed the day of the decision the "South's new Black Monday." The leading newspaper in Montgomery warned that the decision might mean a total upheaval in southern judicial structure and might even challenge the validity of thousands of convictions of Black people during the past years.

For us, the decision had a different impact. It meant that the first stage of the fight had been won. We had held off the lynching. Nothing made us happier than the letter we received from John LeFlore on behalf of the Mobile Non-Partisan Voters League on the day after the decision, congratulating us on the "splendid victory" on behalf of Willie Seals and "for the cause of justice and fair play for all citizens."

But we also knew that this battle was only the first. Seals was still in prison on death row, and Alabama was not prepared to give up. Within two weeks the state made it known that it was going over the head of the Fifth Circuit and appealing to the United States Supreme Court. The reason given was that there could be no real exclusion of Blacks from jury service, because most Blacks in Alabama could not meet the standards of "good character" required for jury service. Shades of the slaveholder mentality! We prepared a cross-petition, suggesting that the Supreme Court go even further than the Fifth Circuit decision and end the whole case.

In February 1963, the Supreme Court turned down Alabama's petition, and the Fifth Circuit decision was upheld, sending the case back for a new trial. Second round won! But in March, Alabama reindicted Seals, and the whole process reopened. By April, Stavis, Bradley, Conley, and now another Black Alabama lawyer, Vernon Crawford from Mobile, had begun the long and tedious process of challenging Alabama's failure to change its jury system to meet the federal constitutional requirements despite the Fifth Circuit decision. What they now faced was the long-range problem that we would wrestle with for years and never really solve, the frustrating merry-go-round process, as we came to call it, of victory in the federal arena, then retrial in the still segregated state system, followed by victory again in the federal courts, and back to retrial in the states. Only the dedication of such lawyers as these could have seen Willie Seals through this process, which did not result in his final freedom until eleven years after his arrest, in 1971!

The first Seals victory of May 1962 had other immediate results besides saving Seals' life. All over the South, the opinion was used by the few lawyers, both Black and white, who had the courage to challenge the segregated system of justice. In Mobile, in Alabama, and throughout the South, the victory also gave an important boost to the morale of the struggling community movements. It meant that Blacks could win, that the lynch mob was not invariably victorious.

As for me, the Seals victory had a vital effect. During some of the worst days of my growing medical incapacitation, the case had said to me that I could still function and that it was important to hold fast to life in every respect. It also kept alive within me and in its own way heightened the vision of people's law. Thus, when a drastic change took place in my physical condition in January 1963, I was ready in every respect to start all over again.

The change occurred when, in order to undergo a new series of tests, I was temporarily taken completely off the intensive regime of medication I had been on since the first attack of meningitis. I suddenly found myself in another world. Within two days, all the symptoms which had virtually paralyzed me for over three years vanished. The verdict of the medical profession was swift. The medication prescribed to meet the original serious threat of meningitis had itself induced symtoms similar to those caused by the illness! The withdrawal of this medication was responsible for my sudden, spectacular recovery. I faced a whole new future, and because of my involvement in the Seals case, I faced it with confidence.

7

Thomas Wansley and the Danville Movement

The question now was where to head in order to continue functioning as a people's lawyer. The old law firm had long been dissolved. I was a little worried that I would have to spend a tremendous amount of time searching for new alternatives for functioning again as a people's lawyer. I was not sure where to begin. But then, in a wonderful way, the fight for Willie Seals' life, which had represented for me in the past a kind of life preserver, provided also the key to the future.

Late in March 1963, I received a phone call from an old classmate at Columbia Law School, William Kunstler, whom I had not heard from since graduation. He told me that in the past two years he had become heavily involved with southern civil rights cases as a lawyer for the American Civil Liberties Union and recently for the Gandhi Society, a legal support group for the SCLC. He had heard about my work in the Seals case and wanted my help in a similar situation he had just gotten into involving a young Black man, 17-year-old Thomas Wansley, sentenced to death a few weeks before in Lynchburg, Virginia, on the charge of raping a white woman. The lawyer defending Wansley had died suddenly of a heart attack after the trial, and Bill Kunstler and Len Holt, a Black lawyer from Norfolk, had stepped into the appeal on an emergency basis. I had met Holt a few times in the past at Lawyers Guild meetings and had always been impressed with his courage and his seemingly unending sources of energy. As Bill Kunstler talked, I felt an intensity about the situation which drew me in, in the same way that the tone of Chuck Conley's call from Montgomery had pulled me into the Seals case two years before. Once again, I was struck by the enormity of the distortions of the judicial system that sustained a segregated society.

Kunstler went over the situation with me in his office the next morning. Wansley, who was mentally retarded, had been sentenced to death on a charge of raping a white woman who could not even identify him at the trial. Three months before, in the same city, George Brooks, a 37-year-old, had been sentenced to only five years, the minimum sentence allowed by law, for admittedly raping an 11-year-old Black child in his automobile. There was one difference: Brooks was white, Wansley was Black. Bill pressed me to step in and virtually take over the preparation of the appeal. He and Holt were being pulled in a hundred different directions with arrests and prosecutions growing out of the sit-ins and other demonstrations that were escalating throughout the South. Virginia practice required that a full brief in the form of a petition for review be filed with the state's highest court if the execution, scheduled for June 6, was to be held up. This virtually full-time work would mean shelving my other tentative plans to explore different ways of functioning as a lawyer again. But I settled the question in my usual pragmatic fashion at such critical moments. "Do what has to be done now," I said to myself, "and the future will take care of itself."

I jumped into the work on the Wansley appeal. During the next two months, there were many long telephone calls to Holt in Virginia, as well as working discussions with Kunstler when I could grab hold of him between his frantic air trips to Mississippi, where he was working on a host of arrests and trials of Freedom Riders who were trying to desegregate public transportation. But most of my time was spent in long, lonely hours working feverishly against the deadline to formulate approaches that might conceivably move the Supreme Court of Virginia to hold up and then overrule the execution of Wansley.

As with Seals in Alabama, this case was filled with flagrant constitutional violations from the very moment of arrest. For the first five days of his imprisonment, this retarded youngster was held wholly without a lawyer while he was mercilessly grilled by the police, after which, to no one's surprise, they claimed to have extracted a confession from him. He was then indicted and tried by all-white, all-male juries. The trial took place in a totally segregated courtroom, where in his summation the prosecuting attorney passionately told the white male jury that, unless Wansley was electrocuted, "no white woman could walk safely on the public streets of Lynchburg." As outrageous as all of this was, the likelihood that the Supreme Court of Virginia would hold up the execution was slim.

As I struggled with the materials and papers on the case, one fact emerged as the best hope to move even the most conservative court. *No transcript existed for the trial.* I simply could not believe this when Kunstler first told me. A capital case without a written trial manuscript? How could we even ask for a review of the facts upon which the state proposed to put this young man to death if there was no written transcript of the trial? I listened in amazement as Holt explained on the phone that Virginia was one of the few states in the Union which did not require a written report of the proceedings in serious criminal trials. Wansley's original lawyer had implored the trial judge to postpone the trial a few days to give him time to get a court reporter at his own expense, and he had been turned down.

This was the special thrust we needed to shake even the highest appellate level of Virginia's segregated court system. A court structure which denied a defendant facing the electric chair a written report of the proceedings that led to the death sentence was, in the words of a weighty decision of the United States Supreme Court which had just been handed down, "shocking to the conscience." This situation brought me to grips once again with a fundamental question of approach that had emerged in the Seals case. It was essential to find ways to expose the manner in which a system of law that has as its central thrust the preservation of a racially segregated society also has the effect of destroying the most elementary concepts of justice for all people, white as well as Black. The failure to provide for a written transcript of all serious criminal proceedings did more than brush aside any meaningful right to appeal for any poor person in Virginia, Black or white, who could not afford the price of arranging to have a transcript made. It made a mockery out of any pretensions that the Virginia high court itself could have of sitting as an independent final appeals court. No appellate court could exercise its right to review the proceedings below it when there was nothing before it to review.

If there was to be any hope of success, the petition for Wansley's life had to raise the ultimate question of the integrity of the Virginia high court itself as an institution. This question, which I was struggling to express in the petition, was perhaps what led the Virginia Supreme Court to grant, in early May, our motion to stay the execution of Wansley. I then had a little less than a month to complete the appeals brief, have Kunstler read it before rushing off to another of his pressing Mississippi court dates, and get it in the mail to Holt for his signature as the Virginia lawyer responsible for the case, so that it could be filed in Richmond where the Virginia Supreme Court sat. At the argument in Richmond later in June, I was able to persuade the Virginia court that its own sense of integrity as an institution required the reversal of Wansley's conviction. But as in the case of Willie Seals, it would not be until many years later, as a result of the tireless and seemingly endless legal work of Bill Kunstler and Philip Hirschkopf, a civil rights lawyer from Washington, D.C., that the state criminal proceedings against Wansley would finally be dropped.

The work on the Wansley case proved to me that I was fully prepared to embark once again upon a life of full activity. The days of physical collapse and enforced inaction were over. When I had finished the almost one-hundred page petition in early June 1963, I had a deep feeling of satisfaction. I was back on the path again and I felt good. Where I would head and where it would take me I was not sure. But the door was wide open.

Then, only a few days later, in the same way that the call from Ella Baker about the Montgomery bus boycott had opened up wholly new horizons for me back in the last years of the Cold War, a call from Len Holt settled emphatically the direction of things for the years to come. I was confused as to where Holt was calling from. There was a great deal of noise in the background, and it did not sound like an office. When I asked him, "Where are you?" he shot back, "I'm in Danville, where are you?" And before I could respond to the tone of this remark—which seemed to imply that wherever I was, it ought to be there—he went on, "All hell has broken loose here. Get here tomorrow. We need help bad. Bring Bill if you can find him." The Black community in Danville, Virginia, Holt quickly explained, which like Montgomery and Mobile had been organizing and demonstrating against the segregated society, had been "too damn effective." During the last week the full weight of the legal power structure had descended upon them, with over two hundred arrests, power hoses, beatings, the works. He and the handful of Black lawyers in town needed help fast.

Late that night I located Kunstler in Jackson, Mississippi, where he was representing a number of Freedom Riders. He agreed to meet me in Danville. At that moment, I began to appreciate what was probably one of the most important abilities of a people's lawyer in the southern struggle—the ability to jump on a plane and get where you had to be fast.

We arrived in Danville the next day, on June 15. The events of the past week had so accelerated the situation in town that we were thrown, almost without any breathing space, into an intensive series of discussions with both the lawyers involved and the leaders of the community organization which was in the forefront of the erupting struggles, the Danville Christian Progressive Association. From these discussions, all focused on how to deal with the immediate problems over the next few days, we began to absorb what had been going on.

Danville was a city of some 50,000 people, at least a third of whom were Black. It lay deep in the southwest corner of Virginia, about ten miles from the North Carolina border. The city was built along the Dan River, and its major industry was the Dan River Mills, one of the largest textile mills in the South, employing over 12,000 people. Until 1960 the city had been, like all cities throughout the South, totally segregated. Then, inspired by the first student sit-ins in North Carolina, Danville students sat in at the public library, demanding an end to segregation in that building. As one of the student leaders who had participated in this first sit-in told me much later with a high degree of cynical pleasure, the building where it took place had been the last capital of the Confederacy after the fall of Richmond to the Union troops!

The immediate response of the Danville authorities to the library sit-in was simple. The public library was closed to the public. This was a standard first response of the white power structure throughout the South to demands for enforcement of the national Constitution. If the federal law required the desegregation of public facilities, shut them down. In anger and dismay, the Black leaders of the newly formed Danville Christian Progressive Association, Revs. Campbell and Dunlop, called for help from Len Holt, who was gaining a name throughout the South as a fearless civil rights fighter. Holt filed in federal court what had become known as an omnibus action to desegregate all public facilities. As a result, the court ordered the public library reopened.

Danville's official response to this federal mandate was unbelievable. All chairs and tables were removed from the library so that Blacks and whites would not be able to sit together in a public building. The arrogance of this action sparked several more sit-ins, which resulted in desegregating a few lunch counters in five-and-ten cent stores and one drugstore.

With these few exceptions, however, by the end of May 1963, segregation in Danville was still virtually unshaken by either federal court orders or protest activities. All the hotels, motels, restaurants, movie houses, hospitals, housing projects, public schools, and churches remained totally segregated. Black people were wholly relegated to menial cleaning jobs at the Dan River Mills. No Black representative sat on a single town board or commission. Nine years after the *Brown* decision outlawing segregation, the white power structure of Danville continued to enforce in virtually all respects the system of white supremacy inherited from the slave society of the Old Confederacy.

On May 31, the Black community of Danville made a historic move, inspired in part by the example of Birmingham, Alabama, where Black people were making front page news throughout the country by resisting the fire hoses of Chief of Police Bull Connor in their efforts to register to vote. On the initiative of the Black ministers in the leadership of the Danville Christian Progressive Association, a representative cross-section of the Black citizens of Danville marched through the streets to the city hall. Despite many differences with the association, the local leadership of the NAACP was much in presence, fully participating in the march and demonstration. It was a moment of overwhelming unity within the Black community, and the demands eloquently expressed on the steps of the city hall reflected the thinking of the whole community. The demands were for desegregation of all public facilities and all private facilities open to the public, equal job opportunities in both public and private employment for both white and Blacks alike, establishment of a biracial commission, and appointment of Black representatives to all boards and commissions of the city government. The May 31 march, which was the first in a plan for daily peaceful marches and demonstrations, represented the coming to maturity of what became known as the Danville movement.

The concept of a movement went beyond any single organization or individual. It was a coming together of all who were beginning to understand that only through united strength and direct action could they achieve the long-promised objectives of equality and freedom. In this process of coming together lay both the future strength and future weakness of the movement—the strength provided by the unprecedented unity it could have at critical moments, and the weakness inherent in the inability of the many different organizations and individuals always to subordinate their own special personal or political objectives to the movement's immediate needs.

But, as pointed out to us on June 15 by Ruth Harvey and Jerry Williams, two local Black lawyers involved in the struggle, the ones who best sensed the potential strength of the Danville movement were the members of the power structure itself. In words that reminded me of the discussions with the UE organizers over twelve years before in Evansville, Harvey and Williams sketched out what they bitterly termed the "Danville formula" for smashing the movement. It was a coordinated plan to use every instrument of power available to the ruling structure to intimidate and terrorize the Black community. After a week of peaceful marches and demonstrations, all hell broke loose. The plan was triggered by the most important symbol of law in town, Judge Aikens of the Corporation Court, Danville's municipal court. While Rev. Campbell was speaking on a street corner to a large group of marchers, suddenly Judge Aikens himself appeared, pushed his way through the crowd, and shouted into Campbell's face, "Disperse this meeting and break up the crowd." When Campbell refused, the Judge turned to the police chief, Eugene McCain, and ordered him to arrest Campbell and four other community leaders. They were immediately booked and charged with riotous and disorderly conduct and contributing to the delinquency of minors. This was merely a prelude to the pattern of intimidation about to unfold.

The next day another piece of the Danville formula was put in place. During a futile meeting supposedly to negotiate a settlement between the reluctant Mayor and the movement leaders, the city attorney suddenly walked in and announced that Judge Aikens had just issued a temporary injunction restraining the Black community and its leaders from engaging in any more of "these demonstrations." As Holt put it when he later handed us a copy of the injunction, "It has the effect of making it illegal to breathe in Danville."

But these were not the only prongs of the legal attack on the Danville movement. No one knew that at the very time of the meeting in the Mayor's office, in a room a few flights above, a special grand jury was in session to consider possible violations of Virginia's pre-Civil War "John Brown" statute, which punished "any person conspiring to incite the colored population to insurrection against the white population." Thus, when the movement leaders met again the next morning with the Mayor, they were greeted with the astounding news that three of them—Rev. Campbell, Rev. Dunlop, and Julius Adams—had just been indicted under the John Brown statute. These results from the two negotiating sessions with the power structure—first the injunction and then the indictments—led Dunlop to react angrily, "One more meeting with those white folks and we would have been electrocuted." Len Holt's moving account of the Danville summer, *An Act of Conscience*, written a year later, preserves this classic observation, together with Holt's response to Rev. Dunlop, "And that's not poetry!"

It seemed nothing could stop the Danville formula now. Armed with these sanctions of legality, on Monday, June 10, a day that was to go down in Danville history as the "Day of Infamy," the power structure let loose in full force. Despite the injunction, the movement had decided to resume demonstrations, and on Monday morning a group of about sixty high school students marched, singing and chanting, down the streets toward the city hall. They were led by a high school honor student, Thurman Echols. When they reached city hall, they were suddenly surrounded by the police. Waving copies of the injunction in their faces, the police grabbed Echols and two others in the lead and dragged them off under arrest.

The rest of the marchers, frightened, turned and ran down an alley between the city hall and the jail. Within minutes, the police had opened up on them with fire hoses. The students, hurled to the street by the force of the water, picked themselves up and ran frantically for protection toward the Black business area. The police caught up with them, threw them to the ground, and kicked and beat them. As Black people emerged from the stores to comfort or talk to the frightened youngsters, the police arrested them indiscriminately. Over fifty people were booked that morning for violation of the injunction.

The police then set a special trap for Echols' family. Since he was only sixteen, he was covered by the juvenile laws. He was urged by the police to call his mother and ask her to come and get him out of jail. When she arrived, she was promptly arrested on the charge of contributing to the delinquency of a minor by failing to keep her son from leading the demonstration. Allowed one call, she reached her husband and asked him to come and bail them both out. When he rushed over, he too was promptly arrested on the same charge.

The indiscriminate arrests throughout the Black community continued all day. That evening, a mass meeting was held at the Bibleway Holiness Church. One after another, people who had been beaten but escaped arrest came to the pulpit and told what had happened. At the end of the meeting Rev. McGhee called for volunteers to go with him to take part in a prayer vigil for those in jail. Fifty people, mostly women, left the church with the minister and marched downtown singing hymns. When they reached the alley beside the jail, they all knelt down in prayer.

Suddenly, one end of the narrow alley was sealed off by a large group of white men armed with clubs and truncheons. At the other end of the alley were dozens of firemen carrying heavy fire hoses. The Mayor stepped forward from the armed men, turned to the police chief, and said, "Give them all you've got." Two police dashed out, grabbed Rev. McGhee by the collar as he was kneeling in prayer, and dragged him aside, shouting, "You're under arrest for violating the injunction."

Then the trap closed in on the kneeling demonstrators. From one end of the alley the water roared out of the hoses, smashing the demonstrators to the ground. From the other end, the police rushed in with clubs and started to beat the demonstrators, women and men alike. Some tried to escape by hiding under parked cars but were yanked out and beaten harder for trying to escape. Of the fifty people who marched and prayed that evening, forty-seven were treated in the segregated public hospital that night. The records showed broken heads, fractured noses, fractured wrists, contusions, bruises, lacerations, and in some cases, lasting injury to sight and hearing.

The next morning, the Mayor announced that thirty state troopers, with tear gas and an armed tank, had moved into Danville to assist in "maintaining order." Random arrests continued in the Black community throughout the day. In the interests of efficiency, the police mimeographed arrest forms charging violation of the injunction. By nighttime two hundred arrests had been made, and the first trials were scheduled for the next Monday. The Danville movement responded by promptly holding the largest march yet, led by a Black minister, Rev. Chase. In response to urgent calls from the Danville movement, the Student Nonviolent Coordinating Committee and the SCLC immediately sent organizers and staff into the city for desperately needed assistance with the march. All the major television networks sent cameras into town. The eyes of the country were suddenly on Danville.

Overwhelmed by the prospect of the expense and drain of the impending two hundred criminal trials, the leadership of the Danville movement on the same day called an emergency meeting with the local Black lawyers and the leadership of the Virginia NAACP, to discover what help that organization, with its access to substantial national funds, could give in the litigation that lay ahead. This fateful meeting was to shape in many ways the part Kunstler and I would have in the months and years to come in fashioning the role of the people's lawyer in the freedom struggles of Black people in the South. The meeting was attended by Revs. Campbell and Dunlop representing the Danville movement; the five local lawyers, Ruth Harvey, Harry Wood, Jerry Williams, Andrew Muse, and George Woody; and a delegation from the Virginia NAACP leadership, including Lester Banks, the executive secretary, and Samuel Tucker, a lawyer from Norfolk who represented not only the NAACP Legal Redress Committee but also the powerful and wealthy NAACP Legal Defense and Education Fund, Inc., a separate entity from the NAACP which was known throughout the civil rights movement as the "Inc Fund." Len Holt was also at the meeting, along with Leo Branton, a prominent Black lawyer from Los Angeles who had just come to Danville.

Branton attempted tactfully to open what he sensed was going to be a tense discussion. He made it clear that, as he was not a "local" lawyer, he was "without an axe to grind." Then he put the problem directly. The situation in Danville was desperate, and the people there needed all the help that the NAACP could give. Tucker replied that although he had not yet discussed the matter fully with Jack Greenberg, head of the Inc Fund, he felt sure that they would underwrite all the legal expenses, whatever they might be. This wonderfully generous proposal seemed to be the much hoped-for offer of help.

But then the underlying tensions began to show. Campbell asked whether the Danville movement would have to consult with NAACP lawyers before engaging in demonstrations. Tucker's response was strained, "Since the NAACP will be footing the bill, we will want to be able to caution against anything unwise."

Then Campbell asked the most sensitive question of all, "What about Len Holt? Will he be one of the lawyers? Will the NAACP team of lawyers work with him?" Tucker's response was one that we were to hear to similar questions time and again during the years to follow, "NAACP money can go only to NAACP lawyers, and Holt is not an NAACP lawyer." There it was, out in the open. In a sense, this was a turning point for the Danville movement. The answer given by the two movement leaders present, Campbell and Dunlop, was simple and direct: "Ol' Snaky"—the Snake Doctor was a nickname affectionately bestowed upon Len Holt by movement people—"is the movement lawyer. If you want to put some people here to work with him, good. Otherwise, we're sorry."

This response of the Danville leadership, faced with the enormous expenses of the coming week's legal proceedings, was both courageous and principled. In part it stemmed from their past experience with the constant efforts of the NAACP leadership, both nationally and on a state level, to play down, if not discourage, mass demonstrative action—an experience that had led Campbell and Dunlop several years before to leave the local NAACP branch in Danville and form the Danville Christian Progressive Association, which became affiliated with the SCLC. In part the Danville leaders' response also stemmed from the confidence that they had in Len Holt, whose daily work had demonstrated his conviction that legal talents existed to facilitate, not deter, the direct action of people in struggle, and who over the past several years had himself come into conflict with the hesitancy of the Inc Fund and the NAACP leadership elsewhere in Virginia to become involved in legal struggles arising out of sit-ins or other direct action. But perhaps more fundamentally, the Danville leaders' response stemmed from their need to reaffirm the foundation stone of the Black Movement arising in Danville—that it was not the property of any one organization or the tool of any individual. It was not to be bought or sold for money. Its policies and methods of struggle were not to be conditioned on the approval of financial supporters. It was a movement of all who stood together to take effective action against the entrenched power structure, and it was owned by no one. This was the message relayed by Campbell and Dunlop that day in Danville, and it was to be repeated at different critical moments by leaders of the Black Movement throughout the South when any group offered help with strings attached.

This forthright decision by the Danville leadership forced Holt to move fast. On the one hand, he had to consolidate his relations with the five local Danville lawyers who had been NAACP lawyers for years and who remained so nominally. This required working out a response to the Danville formula that would make joint efforts seem sensible to them despite any reluctance from the national or state NAACP offices. On the other hand, he had to find help beyond Danville from lawyers not tied to the NAACP or the Inc Fund. And all of this had to be done in the few days left before the first of the now over two hundred trials opened in the Danville Corporation Court.

This situation prompted Holt to make two telephone calls. One was to George Crockett and Ernest Goodman in Detroit, urgently asking for help from the National Lawyers Guild Committee to Assist Southern Lawyers. The other call was to the two lawyers he was working closely with on the Wansley case, Bill Kunstler and myself.

So here we all were together in Danville on Saturday, June 15, at Ruth Harvey and Harry Wood's office: Holt, three of the five Danville lawyers—Harvey, Wood, and Williams—Dean Robb and Nate Conyers, the Guild Committee lawyers just sent down from Detroit, and Kunstler and myself. We were filled in on the latest development in the accelerating dynamics of the Danville formula. Just the day before the city council had unanimously passed a new ordinance, which made Judge Aikens' injunction look like a moderate measure. All picketing, all demonstrations, and all marching were declared illegal without a permit from the city itself. To make it clear that no one in the community was exempt from the thrust of these antimovement legal prohibitions, at the very moment that the ordinance had been announced at city hall, Holt himself, the movement lawyer, had been arrested at city hall for violation of the injunction.

The question now was what we as lawyers could do to help the movement survive, to keep it from being strangled by the net of legal proceedings the power structure had thrown on top of it.

How could we help to counter the atmosphere of fear and intimidation that the Danville formula was designed to create? These questions were central in our minds as we prepared for the Monday showdown.

One thing quickly emerged. No one was in the mood either to let the city continue its offensive or to assume the lawyer's conventional defensive posture. Before we knew it, we had agreed upon the necessity for a three-pronged head-on attack—on the injunction, the John Brown statute, and the new ordinance—as violating the fundamental protections of the national Constitution. Whether we succeeded or not, we all realized how important it was to the fighting morale of the movement for us to say loud and clear that the Danville formula in its totality was unconstitutional, illegal, and un-American.

As we divided up the responsibility for drafting the federal court complaints demanding injunctions against each of the ingredients of the Danville formula, I found myself back in the mood of the old UE struggles. No one asked, "Can we technically do this? Will it hold up in court?" We just had to do it. The objective of the movement was to fight back, and we as lawyers had to find the ways to assist that objective.

At one point a phone call came in telling us about the seriousness of the condition of Mrs. Mary Thomas, one of the women badly beaten on the night of June 10. Holt exploded with anger, "Let's bring a federal damage action for her and everyone hurt by the cops that night!" People in the room practically cheered. The idea of a federal damage action by a Black woman against Chief of Police McCain deeply touched the feeling of anger and the urge to fight back that gripped everyone involved in the Danville movement, lawyers and nonlawyers alike. So the damage actions were added to the assignment list, and responsibilities were assumed to talk with Mrs. Thomas and the others involved about their feelings concerning bringing such actions.

Then someone introduced a note of sober reality. How were we ever to handle the hundreds of trials facing us for violation of the injunction and the new ordinance? A great deal of money and time would be required for the long-drawn-out appeals after the inevitable convictions in Aiken's own court. It would be three or four years before we had any chance of winning finally in the United States Supreme Court, if then. This process could itself paralyze and destroy the movement, to say nothing of the atmosphere of fear that it would generate through the whole community, which might keep people from daring to participate in any more marches or demonstrations.

At this point, Kunstler reached into his briefcase and pulled out a sheet of paper, saying, "I just happen to have a draft petition to remove these cases from the state court into the federal court. It's an old Reconstruction statute we rediscovered down in Mississippi a couple of months ago. Why don't we try it here? It will stop Aikens dead."

This removal statute had been literally unearthed from the dead past by a brilliant young lawyer named William Higgs, the only white lawyer in Mississippi who had dared to become involved in the early Freedom Rider cases. It had been passed by the Reconstruction Congress back in 1866 to protect the newly emancipated Black people from criminal proceedings brought by elements of the old white slaveholding class who still controlled state governments in the southern states. The statute was simple. Whenever anyone was threatened with a state criminal proceeding in which their equal rights would not be protected, or whenever anyone was being prosecuted for asserting their equal rights under the federal Constitution, the defendants could instantly and automatically remove those cases from the state court into the federal court simply by filing a piece of paper in both courts announcing the act of removal.

This old Reconstruction remedy was exactly what was needed here in Danville. It had been created by the Radical Republicans in Congress right after the Civil War to remedy precisely the same problems that we faced in Danville almost a hundred years later—the white power structure's use of the state criminal apparatus to destroy attempts by the supposedly emancipated race to enforce the promises of freedom and equality made to them by the national government, both in the Constitution and in federal laws. There was only one problem. The removal statute had been buried for almost a hundred years. In the late 1870s and early 1880s the courts had manufactured unbelievable reasons why the federal civil rights removal statute could not be used. This was the same period in which the courts were burying the new constitutional promises of freedom and equality with judicial rationalizations which sanctioned the restoration throughout the South of a totally segregated society—the "separate but equal" concept.

Kunstler's suggestion went to the heart of the responsibilities we would have to assume as people's lawyers in the southern struggles. We would have to resurrect the old remedies fashioned by the Radical Reconstruction Congress. To achieve this, we would have to rip off the layers of rationalization that had later been carefully constructed to conceal the remedies themselves for so long. But at least the removal statute was still on the books. No one had ever bothered to repeal it. As someone cynically pointed out, the statute was like the Thirteenth Amendment itself, which had abolished slavery and all its trappings. No one had ever bothered to repeal that; they just buried it. Our task was to unbury the statute and use it, for it said openly what the Danville movement itself was saying: "remove" these obstacles to our marches, these state court criminal proceedings that detour us from our path.

As we drafted the removal petitions that afternoon, we were responding to an urgently felt need to find a legal approach that would, if even for a moment, remove the pressure from the movement people so that they could resume their marches and demonstrations. We were experiencing the same fundamental shift in the role of people's lawyers in the civil rights arena that I had first sensed back during the early days of the Montgomery bus boycott. Our primary responsibility at that moment was not to figure out how to fashion a legal solution to desegregate all of Danville from the public schools to the Dan River Mills. The Black people of Danville, as all over the South, were saying that they would enforce the constitutional promise of desegregation themselves through their own direct massive intervention in the life of their community, their state, and even, as we had seen in the Washington marches, their nation. The primary role of people's lawyers in the civil rights movement had shifted from the days before *Brown v. Board of Education.* Lawyers were no longer the central agents fighting to achieve the goals of freedom and equality through their own special arena, the courts of law. Their role now was vastly different. Their primary task was to find ways of helping the Black people themselves resist the efforts of the power structure to derail their own forward movement to enforce the constitutional promises of freedom and equality.

From time to time in the days to come there would continue to be opposition to this shift of direction in both the legal and the political communities nationwide. To some, this shift in the role of lawyers was a development to be resisted because it rejected the proposition that everyone, including the Black people, should rely primarily on the liberal sections of the business, professional, and academic communities, which were now predominant in the Kennedy administration, to come through on their old promises of freedom and equality. Efforts were therefore made to limit, and even discourage, the direct action of the Black Movement, on the grounds that such intervention might frighten off the liberal members of the power structure and "rock the boat."

As we worked on the removal petitions, we ran into a manifestation of this resistance. Jerry Williams, mindful of the delicate problem for himself and other local lawyers in continuing to function as NAACP lawyers while at the same time working with movement lawyers developing joint strategies and plans regardless of personal affiliation, put in a call to Jack Greenberg, director of the Inc Fund. He wanted Greenberg's advice on our use of the federal removal statute. The response was disturbing. Greenberg completely rejected all use of the Reconstruction statute, calling it a crazy idea amounting to "playing with the courts." When Williams reported this to us, there was an upset silence in the room. Then Holt broke the ice, saying, "Let's keep going." Long afterward, he confided to me that he himself had been full of reservations that day about using the removal statute, but deep inside him something said, "Try anything to stop them."

For a moment, the local Danville lawyers were in a bind. They were anxious not to break overtly with Greenberg, since Sam Tucker had promised them privately that the Virginia NAACP would try to help out financially with any legal work in which they were personally involved. Then one of the Detroit Guild lawyers came through with a lifesaver. He suggested that the removal of the cases be handled separately by each lawyer rather than in one overall move. Len Holt's clients, who were the first people to be tried on Monday, could thus appear on a separate removal petition. This would give the local lawyers a breathing spell to think over their approach to removal and talk it over a little more with the movement leaders before deciding. Everyone agreed to move ahead on this basis.

It could not have been a better solution. At the first day's proceedings on June 17, Judge Aikens acted as if the federal removal law simply did not exist. The first movement defendant was Ezell Barksdale, a 17-year-old high school senior who had been one of the leaders of the June 10 march. When Holt declared at the beginning of the trial that the judge had no power to continue the trial and that all the cases listed in Holt's petition were now removed to federal court, the judge simply stared at him and, to the astonishment of all the out-of-state lawyers present, fingered the gun he always kept on his desk. Then he said, "Let's proceed with the cases."

After a perfunctory trial, Aikens sentenced young Barksdale to forty-five days in jail, denied bail, and refused to stay the sentence pending an appeal. He then picked up from his desk a piece of typed paper, obviously prepared before the trial, and read a statement indicating why he intended to jail all the defendants without allowing the conventional bail pending appeal. "It is," he announced to an amazed courtroom, "the duty of this Court to bring this riot and insurrection to a peaceful termination as quickly as possible." The message was clear. Unless these proceedings were stopped in some way, the Danville movement faced the grim prospect of wholesale jailings in the immediate future.

At the close of the trial the five local Danville lawyers met with a number of movement leaders, including representatives of the local NAACP, and that evening they informed us that they had decided to work with us to remove all the remaining cases to the federal court. In many ways, this was an act of the greatest courage on their parts. As local lawyers, they were required to appear daily before Judge Aikens, yet the next morning they were prepared to tell him that Black people in Danville could not get a fair trial in his court. And when they signed the removal petition as NAACP lawyers, they were telling Jack Greenberg in New York City and everyone else in both the NAACP and the Inc Fund that no one except the people of Danville was going to tell them what was needed and whom they could work with in their own city.

That moment marked the beginning of a beautiful development in Danville, one that gave the movement its inner strength. This was the growth of a united team of movement lawyers who, during the tensions and agonies of the summer to come, would draw closer and closer together. Out of this experience I once again felt the impact of that basic lesson learned from the work with Dave Scribner and the UE lawyers in the Cold War years— the necessity for people's lawyers to overcome the divisive egotism of the legal profession and fashion a truly collective way of work.

When the next day's trial resulted in the same railroading and jailing of the defendant, it became strikingly clear that the only immediate hope lay in pressing hard on the removal petitions we had earlier filed in both the state and federal courts. But on that same day Sam Tucker took the question of bail for Barksdale on an emergency basis to a judge of the Virginia Supreme Court, and the response there was coldly negative. Everyone then agreed that unless we moved on our federal actions fast, the Danville formula, now enforced by the specter of immediate jail for any demonstrator, might well paralyze the movement.

Word came in that Federal Judge Thomas Jefferson Michie of the United States District Court for the Western District of Virginia had set down all our federal motions for injunctive relief, along with our removal petitions, for a hearing in Danville in the federal courthouse on the next Monday, June 24. After talking with Ruth Harvey and Len Holt, Bill Kunstler and I headed back to New York for a few days to take care of a lot of accumulated work, planning to return to Danville on Sunday to help prepare for the showdown in federal court. We also agreed that I would start digging into the background of the removal statute, to develop an argument as to why its burial had been premature and why it was still very much alive.

Late Friday night, Bill Kunstler called me in distress. He had just gotten a call from Ruth Harvey in Danville. "You won't believe this," he said. "They've just indicted Len under the John Brown statute, along with ten more leaders of the movement. The folks sent Len into New York when the rumors of the pending indictments started to circulate Friday morning, so that they can't jail him before Monday's hearing. They want us back in Danville fast." We left the next morning.

The new indictments hit the Danville movement hard. In addition to Len Holt, James Forman, Aaron Rollins, and Robert Zellner, leaders of SNCC, and Rev. Chase and Rev. Milton Reid, leaders of SCLC, had been indicted. This, along with the jailings under the injunction, was having its intended effect. People in the community were beginning to hold back from joining the marches and meetings. The Danville formula was getting a grip on the city.

When we all got together at Ruth Harvey's office in Danville on Saturday afternoon, the impact of the new indictments on the lawyers was obvious. One result of the indictment of Len Holt was to eliminate once and for all any feeling of division between the lawyers remaining from that original difficult meeting with the NAACP leadership two weeks earlier. The atmosphere of unity was overwhelming. When Kunstler and I suggested that a good response to Holt's indictment would be the formation of a formal lawyers' committee to handle jointly all legal matters of the Danville movement, there was enthusiastic agreement. The Danville Joint Legal Defense Committee was then and there set up, with Jerry Williams as director. Our first accomplishment was to send a telegram, signed by all of us, to Attorney General Robert Kennedy, demanding immediate federal intervention to stop the prosecutions of the Danville demonstrators and their lawyers. Then we got to work preparing for the hearing.

By evening, the legal team had been expanded by a powerful contingent from Washington, including Professor Chet Antieu of Georgetown Law School, Shelley Bowers of the Washington bar, and Philip Hirschkopf, then a third-year law student at Georgetown. Hirschkopf immediately went out to start interviewing the almost fifty participants in the June 10 prayer vigil to find the most effective witnesses while without any hesitation Antieu and

Bowers threw themselves into the legal preparations with the rest of us. I remember Antieu picking up a copy of the town ordinance and informing us with great dignity that even a first-year law student could tell that it was wholly unconstitutional. "My God," I said to Kunstler, "who would ever dream of finding a law professor in the middle of this kind of fight?" Working with Chet Antieu that summer did more than anything else to convince me that teaching and functioning as a people's lawyer were not totally irreconcilable.

On Monday morning when we arrived at the federal courtroom, the place was jammed with hundreds of Black people. Danville police lined the walls. We watched carefully as Judge Michie walked in and sat down on the dais. Michie, we had been warned, was a Virginia aristocrat and probably a millionaire. His decisions in the past had been technical in every respect and always favorable to the establishment. We had no real expectation that he would give us the sweeping relief we were demanding, and we prepared the leadership of the movement for this eventuality in the frankest way. The legal struggle would undoubtedly have to be continued on every appellate level, including, if necessary, the Supreme Court of the United States.

Our central objective was simply to use that courtroom to lay out fully, for all to see, the truth about the Danville formula. It was important for the hundreds of Danville Black people sitting there watching and listening to see that the movement was not dead or frightened, and that it was fighting back. We also wanted them to know that justice in the fullest sense was on their side— not the "justice" of the dominant white power structure, but the justice of the Constitution. The hearing had to be a learning experience for the people of the Danville movement.

In almost every way the hearing met these expectations. It was a powerful demonstration of a united people fighting back. The responsibilities were carefully divided among the entire team. Sam Tucker, who had been drawn much closer to the movement as a result of the events in Corporation Court during the past week, opened the case with a dramatic presentation of the events of the past month. Harry Wood took Rev. Campbell on the stand to describe the fruitless course of negotiations with the city leading up to the decision of May 31 to demonstrate, the peaceful, nonviolent nature of all of the following marches and parades, and the violence unleashed on the marchers by the city police. Andrew Muse handled the testimony of Rev. Thomas, the president of the local NAACP branch for the past four years, who described the atmosphere of the Corporation Court trials. When he said quietly, "The judge was wearing a gun," you could have heard a pin drop. Bill Kunstler took Rev. McGhee through the incredible story of the prayer vigil on the Day of Infamy, and Ruth Harvey questioned Mrs. Campbell, who told in moving words of the beating she had received that evening in the now infamous alley. Then, as the major witness on the nature of the state court trials, Len Holt himself took the stand and brilliantly laid out the picture.

The city's case was pitiful. To our astonishment, they produced Judge Aikens himself, and Chief of Police McCain. They succeeded only in strengthening the picture of arrogant brutality.

At the end of the factual presentation we were prepared to develop our legal arguments for immediate relief. I had been assigned the arguments around the necessity for the release of Barksdale and Smith, the two movement members jailed at the end of Aikens' first two injunction trials. At this point, there was a totally unexpected development. Now that the lawyers for the city were in a federal court, they could hardly take the position of wholly ignoring, as Aikens had, the federal removal statute. Here they had to concede that the cases had in fact been removed from the state court, and their only recourse was to demand that they be "remanded," that is, immediately returned to the state court. We had believed it inevitable that Judge Michie would grant the motion to remand and that we would then have to rush off to Baltimore to appear before the United States Court of Appeals for the Fourth Circuit to try to press for a speedy appeal from such an order. But at the end of the city's argument, Judge Michie quietly, and without any explanation, said that he was going to "reserve decision" on the city's motion to remand the cases.

My immediate reaction was that he must be hesitant to appear prejudiced against us, perhaps because of the strength of our case, and he thought it would look better if he took more time in considering the case before ruling against us. It seemed only faintly possible that we could actually have shaken him. In any event, for the time being the result of his "reserving decision" was that all the criminal cases remained in the federal court, out of the hands of the Danville power structure.

A wild thought suddenly hit me. After I quickly consulted with the others sitting at the counsel table, they nodded agreement. Holt's whispered comment was, "What do we have to lose?" I jumped to my feet and pointed out to Judge Michie that two of our clients, Barksdale and Smith, were being illegally held in a state jail, since their cases had been properly removed to federal court before their state court trials actually started. I reached down into my briefcase and pulled out one of the papers we had prepared for the argument. "We have here federal writs of habeas corpus for each of them. We would like your Honor to sign them right now, ordering our clients immediately released into your custody so that you can free them on reasonable bail."

Michie seemed taken aback by this request for immediate action. "But I have just told everyone I am going to reserve decisions on all the motions," he said with annoyance.

"You can't reserve this," I responded, trying hard to sound respectful. "The statute says you *shall* sign a federal writ of habeas corpus if a person remains in state custody after a petition for removal is filed." Quickly I looked down at the page of the federal statute lying open on the table, to reassure myself that the key word, "shall," was really there. I felt better. There it was, as I remembered it, having pointed out to Kunstler the night before the strangeness of the mandatory word "shall" in the original statute.

Judge Michie was quiet for a moment. Then he said abruptly, "I'll talk to counsel in my chambers."

As we walked into the Judge's back room, something inside of me said, "Push him hard. He's shaken." In his chambers, I went over the argument again, while the other movement lawyers chimed in. The response of the city lawyers was that for a federal judge to free these convicted criminals at this moment of racial tension in the city was absurd and the grossest interference with state's rights.

That did it. Having state's rights thrown at me in the last capital of the Confederacy made me even more determined. As I re-stated the argument as to the mandatory nature of the statute re-quiring that federal judges "shall" sign a writ of habeas corpus after a petition of removal has been filed, I hit again on the one note that would prove to have the potential for moving even cer-tain relatively conservative southern federal judges in a positive direction. This was a reminder of their special obligation under the Constitution to uphold and enforce national federal law as the supreme law of the land. When their commitment to enforce the federal law clashed with their equally strong commitment to support the southern power establishment, as it so often did when Black southerners demanded their constitutional promises of freedom and equality, there was no certainty as to which com-mitment would prevail at a given moment.

That afternoon in Judge Michie's chambers, I tried my best to use this conflict to our benefit by pounding away at the judge's overwhelming obligation to carry out the written word of the fed-eral law. This suddenly led me to do something impulsive. In the course of reiterating once more the meaning of the mandate in the statute to sign the writs then and there, I noticed that the judge had the statute book open on his desk. Without weighing any of the consequences of what might have been considered un-lawyerlike conduct, I jumped up, walked around the desk, and, as Kunstler has delightedly told people on occasion over the years, took Judge Michie's finger in my hand and placed it directly on the word "shall" in the statute, saying, "There it is, Judge. You *shall* sign the writ. That's the law." It was clear when I resumed my seat that something had rocked Judge Michie from his well-anchored base in the southern power structure. We all sat quietly for a moment, and then the judge lifted his pen and signed the writs of habeas lying before him which would free Barksdale and Smith.

Almost too stunned to believe what had happened, we picked up the signed writs and walked quickly out of the judge's cham-bers into the half-full courtroom. The word spread like electricity among the movement people who had waited for news: "Barks-dale and Smith are going to be freed!" People pressed around us joyfully and then rushed out to spread the unbelievable news through the city. By the time we had located one of the federal marshals assigned to the courthouse, who was required by law to serve federal papers, and had flashed Judge Michie's signature at him "commanding" the immediate release of our clients, someone had found a car, which was waiting for us outside the courthouse door. Ruth Harvey, Bill Kunstler, Jerry Williams, and I jammed into the car with the rather confused marshal and headed directly for the Danville City Farm, where Barksdale and Smith were being held as convicted prisoners.

By the time we got there, almost fifty people from the Black community had already gathered outside the gates waiting for us. Then came the supreme moment that no one, during the long hours of preparation and courtroom struggles, had ever really believed would occur. The gates opened, and two men, one very young and the other middle-aged, walked out with the federal marshal. The broad smiles of relief on their faces as they saw us all standing there waiting for them touched off a wave of jubilation that was unlike anything I had experienced for many years.

That evening at the High Street Baptist Church, this spirit took over as Barksdale and Smith walked into the crowded community gathering. The excitement of the audience grew as Rev. Campbell and Len Holt reported from the pulpit the events of the day. As in the earlier UE battles, once again I sensed the critical importance of even the most limited legal victories to the fighting morale of people in struggle. To have forced that federal judge to sign those writs did more than simply free two members of the movement. It said to every member of the Black community in Danville that the power structure was not invincible, that a hard fight could beat it back. In this spirit the exuberant meeting planned new marches and demonstrations for the days ahead.

It was no surprise, however, when the next day Judge Michie denied our motions for federal relief against the injunction, the John Brown statute, and the city ordinance. We immediately filed notices of appeal to the higher federal court, the Court of Appeals for the Fourth Circuit. Then two things happened which heightened the mood of optimism. Robert Kennedy's Department of Justice filed a long friend-of-the-court brief in our cases, saying, to the astonishment of us all, that they agreed with our federal removal petitions. On the same day, the SCLC staff announced that Rev. Martin Luther King was coming to town to support the Danville movement. Kunstler and I breathed a sign of relief and headed back to New York to prepare for the appeal and try to get a little rest and relaxation with our families.

But late on Tuesday night, July 2, Kunstler called me with news that undercut the mood of confidence in which we had left Danville. Judge Michie had just signed a sweeping federal injunction naming SCLC, the Student Nonviolent Coordinating Committee, and the Congress of Racial Equality as defendants, along with the entire leadership of the Danville movement. It was broader in scope than even Judge Aikens' state injunction, prohibiting any type of demonstrative activity and branding the movement and its supporters as a conspiracy in violation of federal law. As Ruth Harvey bitterly pointed out to Kunstler on the phone, the power structure was pulling out all the stops. A federal injunction would have a more fearsome effect on the community than a state injunction and might well produce that paralysis which the Danville formula had not yet achieved. Once again we were needed to help lift the burden of legal machinery, first state and now federal, from the back of the Danville movement. Would we head back to Danville and help to figure out what to do?

Within a week we were back in Danville, to argue once more before Judge Michie. On the morning of the argument we learned another key fact. Dan River Mills, worried about the developing situation, had moved its own public relations expert into the city administration to take over all public relations work. The stakes were rising. All over the country, people were watching Danville closely to see whether the old white power structure, this time spearheaded by a powerful corporate interest, could successfully repulse the challenge of a rising Black Freedom Movement.

Judge Michie clearly knew what the stakes were. As we argued before him, trying to convince him to dissolve the federal injunction that he had just issued against the movement, nothing we said could move him. Bill Kunstler brought up the precedent of Albany, Georgia, where he had recently persuaded a federal judge to dissolve a similar injunction. "Danville is not Albany,"

Michie snapped. His mind was set. What he was thinking could not have been plainer. No one, not the young leaders of SNCC, not even Martin Luther King, was going to agitate the until recently contented Blacks of Danville into upsetting the tranquillity of the last capital of the Confederacy.

By the afternoon Kunstler and I were in Baltimore in the chambers of Simon Sobeloff, the Chief Judge of the Federal Court of Appeals for the Fourth Circuit, which heard appeals from Virginia, Maryland, West Virginia, and North and South Carolina. We were there to present an emergency appeal from Judge Michie's refusal to dissolve his injunction against the Danville movement. Later we would come to know Judge Sobeloff well and to respect deeply his abilities as a legal thinker and his integrity and commitment to constitutional principles. But that afternoon we had nothing to go on in judging how to approach the argument. Once again, as in the old UE days and more recently in the fight for Willie Seals, my instinctive reaction was to "lay it all out," as the movement people did in the High Street meetings.

After Kunstler brought Judge Sobeloff up to date on the precedents of the Albany, Georgia, situation, I opened up with what Kunstler later jokingly called a "lecture" on the fundamental principles of the Federal Union. The judge listened quietly while I spelled out the idea that I would soon be developing in federal courts throughout the South, and then in Washington itself, before the highest court of all: the primary affirmative responsibility of the federal courts to protect and enforce the rights of Black people to freedom and equality as provided for in the Civil War amendments to the Constitution—the Thirteenth, Fourteenth, and Fifteenth Amendments—as well as to protect and enforce the rights of all people to exercise the democratic liberties provided for in the First Amendment. The federal injunction issued by Judge Michie, I emphasized, undermined and violated this fundamental duty of the federal courts.

After a few hours of argument, it was clear that Chief Judge Sobeloff himself was thinking within the framework of this conception. As we left his chambers, he told us that he was much in agreement with our approach and that he would inform Judge

Michie by phone that evening of his conclusion that the federal injunction against the Danville movement should be dissolved.

Word again spread like wildfire through the Black community. Not only was the federal injunction against the movement dissolved, but Martin Luther King was coming to town! A spirit of elation swept through the community. The next day hundreds of students marched through the streets, and over sixty were arrested. That evening I witnessed a gathering like none I had ever experienced. Thousands of cheering Black people jammed into the High Street Church. As Bill Kunstler and I sat there with Ruth Harvey, Jerry Williams, and the other Danville lawyers listening to Dr. King's impassioned speech, and as we all stood and held hands to sing the emotional words of "We Shall Overcome," I felt again that I was part of a mass movement of people striving together toward the highest goals. Our work as lawyers fell fully into place that evening. Our clients were the thousands jammed into that church. We were movement lawyers in every meaning which those words were coming to have.

And as movement lawyers, we had our work cut out for us through the rest of the summer. Judge Michie had remanded all the cases back to the state courts and refused our demand for federal injunctions against the power structure's legal and statutory tools for terrorizing the Danville movement. On July 16 all nine of us making up the Danville legal team appeared once again in Baltimore, to present to Judge Soboloff and two other members of the Fourth Circuit our appeals from Judge Michie's formal orders. We had worked long and hard on the arguments, and the presentations were strong and persuasive. The law students who had come down to Danville to work with us on the initiative of Professor Antieu had thrown themselves into historical research with intensity. They had succeeded in uncovering the enduring strength of the Reconstruction weapons, such as removal, fashioned so long ago and then buried for so many years after the betrayal of 1877. Our arguments, grounded in this historical reality, had a combined quality of passion and scholarship, which was to be the keystone of our legal battles throughout the civil rights movements.

Apparently because of the complexity of the constitutional

issues, the Baltimore judges decided a week later to hold off final decision until a further hearing on September 23. This gave us time to write the kind of exhaustive brief that we had not been able to during the hectic days of June and July. The team asked me to undertake this task, and so as Kunstler and I flew back to New York City, my head was filled with the appealing prospect of a relatively quiet August, preparing the brief and enjoying the delights of a postponed Block Island vacation with my family.

But once again we did not reckon with the Danville power structure. What we did not anticipate was that they would interpret the Circuit's delay in deciding the appeals as a green light to reopen every aspect of the Danville formula. The city manager called the two-month delay "good news." The Mayor said that it "ought to just about give us time to clean house." Within two days, the city pressed ahead with almost 250 trials under the original Aikens state court injunction. When on July 28, a Sunday, 80 people marched quietly in single file from the High Street Church to city hall, Police Chief McCain greeted them with the announcement, "Just keep marching and march on to jail. You're all under arrest." At four o'clock the next morning, Rev. Chase's home was broken into by the police, and he was arrested because of his children's participation in the Sunday march. During the next week almost 200 more arrests took place for violating the antipicketing ordinance, and trials were hurriedly called for the following week.

The last blow fell on August 5. As the first 47 of the now over 300 cases were being called up in court, the city lawyers made the astounding proposal that all of the Danville cases should be transferred to different cities all over the state, to be tried hundreds of miles away from Danville. The judge immediately agreed. Consternation and demoralization filled the community. The power structure once again seemed to be in absolute control.

I was in Detroit attending a meeting of the National Lawyers Guild Committee to Assist Southern Lawyers when news of the latest Danville developments caught up with me. Richard Goodman had stayed in Danville after we left, and he was full of information about the new setbacks. I discussed the situation with the other Guild members. Suddenly George Crockett cut through all the talk with the simple question, "Have you made a written motion before the court of appeals asking for an emergency injunction against *all* state court trials until the court of appeals' decision?"

This was clearly what we had to do. A call to the Danville lawyers found them in total agreement. A motion was filed, and two days later Kunstler, Harvey, Williams, and I were back in Baltimore before Judge Soboloff and his two colleagues to ask for an emergency injunction stopping all the trials wherever they were until after a final decision was reached by the federal court on our basic attacks on the Danville formula. This was our last means to lift the now overwhelming pressure off a faltering Danville movement.

We had less than an hour to present the motion, Judge Soboloff having slipped us into an already crowded court schedule. The others quickly presented the factual picture of the legal maneuvers used by the Danville power structure against the Black community. Then I had the task of justifying the extraordinary federal relief that we were seeking against those state court proceedings.

The justification that I put forward was, in embryonic form, a revolutionary approach to the role of the federal courts, which we were to develop the following year and finally bring to its fullest flower before the Supreme Court itself. This concept derived entirely from the practical reality of the Danville situation, but its theoretical implications were to upset years of legal precedents which had crippled the ability of the federal courts to protect citizens from harassment by state and local courts when those citizens were attempting to exercise their rights under the First Amendment. The proposition I advanced to Judge Soboloff and his colleagues was a simple one. The Black community of Danville had a right to exercise the fundamental liberties guaranteed by the First Amendment to protest, to march, to demonstrate against segregation. This could not be contested. But the pending state trials frightened off these citizens from exercising these fundamental rights. They created a "chilling effect" upon the use of the channels of democracy, the exercise of First Amendment freedoms. Anything that chilled the use of these rights, that deterred people from their exercise, was imminently dangerous to the democratic system itself, which the federal courts had the duty to protect under the Constitution. This was why the Court of Appeals had to enjoin at once the pending state court trials in Danville, until the basic questions of their underlying constitutionality could be settled.

After I finished, Judge Sobeloff told us to return in an hour for a ruling. When we did, he handed us and the lawyers for the city some papers. "This is our order," he said, and the three judges then stood up and left.

Out of a deep fear that the order would contain the one word "denied," I did not even want to look at it. But Ruth Harvey, who had been reading it to herself, suddenly said, "Listen to this," and read it aloud: "Upon consideration, after hearing counsel for the parties, it is this 8th day of August, 1963, ordered that Eugene Link, Commonwealth Attorney, and T. F. Tucker, Clerk, Corporation Court, Danville, Virginia, and all persons acting in concert with them or by their authority are hereby restrained and enjoined from bringing to trial any person for the alleged violation of said ordinance of the City of Danville and the injunctive orders of the Corporation Court of the City of Danville, until the determination of the above appeals which have been set for hearing at the term of this Court beginning on the 23rd day of September next." We had won! The unbelievable had happened. All the prosecutions were stopped. The movement was free to breathe and to fight.

Ruth Harvey and Jerry Williams rushed back to Danville, while Bill Kunstler and I stayed in Baltimore to file the order. As the news spread through the Black community of Danville that evening, over two thousand people, the largest gathering since King's appearance, poured into the High Street Baptist Church. For over five hours people shouted and sang in joy at the victory. Near the end of the meeting Ruth Harvey and Jerry Williams arrived from the airport, and in what she once told me was one of the most important moments of her life as a lawyer, Ruth Harvey read to the hushed assemblage the full text of the court's order. Then the jubilation really burst out with songs and shouts of victory. "Even the owners of the Dan River Mills could hear it," she said, "wherever they live."

For the remainder of August and September, at least until the next hearing in the Fourth Circuit on September 23, the power structure was stopped in its tracks. The Danville movement, like all of the civil rights movements throughout the South, would have many more tortuous turns, victories, and defeats along the road it had to travel during the next several years. As Ruth Harvey has pointed out, the struggle to eliminate the status of inferiority placed upon Black people in Danville by the institutions of slave society remains to this day, in the 1980s, an unfinished battle. But in the summer of 1963, the Danville movement had already taught invaluable lessons to the whole country about the nature of the people's struggle for the goals of a democratic society. Not the least of these lessons, which we as people's lawyers had helped to develop, was that the legal machinery of the power structure was not invincible. Danville had confirmed the truth of the refrain of one of the most powerful freedom songs now ringing through the South: "Don't let that injunction turn us around."

8

The Dombrowski Remedy and the Summer of '64

As I sat in the bus early one hot morning in late August 1963, heading for the nation's capital along with thousands of people from all over the country to take part in the March on Washington organized by the leadership of the exploding southern movement, I could not help thinking how deeply the summer in Danville had affected my own life as well as the course of events in the country itself. The years of illness and steady deterioration were over. I was once more fully involved in activity and struggle. But the intense demands of the Black Freedom Movement were forcing me into a way of work that was somewhat different from the style of work that I had grown used to during the 1950s. Formerly I had sometimes hesitated to assume a role out in front as a public figure in the legal arena. There were times when others battled for ideas or approaches that I myself had conceived and developed.

This tendency was in part the result of the younger lawyer's common hesitancy to take on the full responsibility of head-on legal combat. However, the sources of this reluctance to become an open participant, if not a leader, in the legal struggles also lay deep in the internal dynamics of the left, which encouraged a style of work that would protect itself from exposure and attack. It had become permissible or at times even desirable for those who were responsible for mapping fundamental political strategy to pass their ideas along quietly to others, who then took the public responsibility for putting them into practice. In a way, perhaps as a cover for personal insecurity, I had to a large degree permitted this process, nurtured by the political tensions of the Cold War, to shape my role and functioning in the legal arena.

The struggle in Danville had totally changed that old pattern of work. In presenting our arguments against the Danville formula, I had no choice but to stand up there myself, right out in front, and fight for ideas and concepts that I had played an important part in originating and shaping. This was a much more satisfying and fulfilling way of work. It also expressed a paramount truth for a people's lawyer: there is no more room in legal than in political battles for back room armchair theorizing. It is in the process of personally testing one's ideas and strategies in both legal arenas and movement discussions that they change and grow. In order to play an effective role in the formulation of ideas, a people's lawyer must be an integral part of that testing process.

This was one of the reasons that just before the March on Washington I had enthusiastically agreed to a proposal made to me by Bill Kunstler. He suggested that he, his brother Michael Kunstler, and I set up a law partnership in New York so that we could continue to do the kind of work we had started together in Virginia. The relationship with Bill Kunstler had thrown me headlong into daily participation on the front lines of the legal and political battles erupting in the South. We were constantly receiving calls for immediate help from all over the South. Directly after the March, we were due to head to Jackson, Mississippi, Americus, Georgia, and New Orleans. The ongoing relationship with Bill would provide a collective way of functioning that seemed essential if we were to survive and grow in the hectic struggles ahead.

Despite enormous differences between us, both Kunstler and I realized that we had the ability to work well together. The strengths of one, compensating for the weaknesses of the other, produced a powerful combination. On the one hand, Bill Kunstler had a drive and self-confidence that led him unhesitatingly into the center of the fray, sometimes without a thought-out plan or strategy. On the other hand, I often overplanned and hesitated too long, in a desire to think through all the consequences before moving ahead. In those first months of working together, we had already begun to learn from each other. As for Michael Kunstler, back in New York, he had an impressive ability to cope with the practical aspects of a daily law practice, which was essential to keep a firm afloat. So it was that we decided to set up the new firm of Kunstler, Kunstler, and Kinoy. The Danville summer had planted the seeds of what came to be known throughout the South as the "new KKK." It always evoked amusement in our movement clients when we would announce our appearance "for the record" in southern courtrooms as "K, K and K."

The March itself reinforced the decision we had made to start the firm. I stood at the end of the Lincoln Memorial looking around in amazement at the hundreds of thousands of people, Black and white, who had poured into the area and were listening with rapt attention to John Lewis, the head of SNCC. As we would learn later, the plan of struggle he was laying out for the civil rights movement had at the last moment been drastically curtailed by the frightened demands of the more conservative leaders of the March. But then for a moment all political questions, differences, hesitations, and confusions in the movement were washed away in the emotional waves surging from the platform as Martin Luther King spun out his never-to-be-forgotten message, "I have a dream."

Despite the vacillations and fears of important sections of the leadership, which had manifested themselves in the last-minute gagging of John Lewis, for a moment the magic of Dr. King united thousands of voices in one driving demand, which must have shaken the inner recesses of the national government as it thundered from the area in the words "Freedom now!" At that moment I could feel the relationship between the strength of those courageous people who had stood up against the clubs and fire hoses of the Danville establishment and the strength of these thousands of people gathered from all over the South and all over the country demanding immediate implementation of the forgotten promises of freedom and equality.

211

What I witnessed that afternoon in Washington was the strength that lay in the united national movement of Black people beginning to come together out of the local movements in towns and cities across the South. The heartaches and defeats in each community, as well as the victories and upsurges, were not to be measured solely in terms of the local gains in the battle against a segregated society, as important as these were. All were contributing, in a way sometimes hard to see in the intensity of the local struggles, to the creation of a national movement that had an enormous potential for the long run.

We were not the only ones in Washington who recognized the strength which was so evident that day. People on the highest level of the establishment, also sensing the growing power of the movement, were making their own plans to try to cut it off. But for me, to be a lawyer in the midst of this surging movement opened the path to fulfillment and personal satisfaction.

In the midst of the difficult work of setting up a new firm, a call from Jackson, Mississippi, introduced me to the tensions building in that stronghold of the white southern power structure. I discovered that what was called the "Jackson formula" there was being used to repress the kneel-in movement, a series of dramatic and emotional attempts to desegregate Jackson's all-white churches. This movement had started when three women students from Tougaloo College, two Black and one white, tried to enter an all-white Methodist Church to ask the congregation why Christians could not worship together. When they walked up to the church door, they found it barred by a white man. Bettye Poole, one of the Black students and a leader of the Jackson movement, asked the man the question that would reverberate throughout churches all over the country, "But what would Jesus do?" His blurted answer was, "Leave Christ out of this. What does He have to do with it?"

The state's response was heavy. The students were arrested, tried, and convicted for attempted trespass, for which they received twelve months at hard labor. That, of course, did nothing to halt the kneel-in movement. In answer to calls from Jackson and from outraged northern ministers working with the National Council of Churches, Kunstler and I went down to Jackson to help ease the legal pressure. We became immersed in federal re-moval and injunction proceedings, trying again, as in Danville, to reduce the impact of massive state arrests and trials.

By the end of the month, I was looking forward to a Lawyers Guild workshop in New Orleans early in October, to which we had been invited by George Crockett and Ernie Goodman. Not only would it give us a chance to pool our thinking as to legal strategies with other movement lawyers equally involved in these exploding legal situations, but it would be a chance to catch my breath after the Danville summer and the first hectic month of the new firm. It would also be an opportunity to renew my friendship with Ben Smith, who was chairing the workshop. Little did I real-ize that this workshop would be the occasion of a sudden turn of events that would shape the course of Ben Smith's life and work for years to come and would throw me, along with him, into one of the most intense legal battles of my life.

The workshop, the second southern conference sponsored by the Lawyers Guild Committee to Assist Southern Lawyers, was jointly sponsored by the Louisiana branch of the American Civil Liberties Union and the Louis A. Martinet Society, an association of Black lawyers in New Orleans. The first conference had been in Atlanta in 1962. This one was taking place at the Hilton Air-port Inn in New Orleans. It was not until Bill Kunstler and I drove over to the inn that we realized the significance of the con-ference being held there. This was to be the first integrated meet-ing of lawyers ever held in New Orleans. Ben Smith, Revis Or-tigue, president of the Martinet Society, and Leonard Dreyfus, president of the ACLU branch, had made New Orleans history by forcing the hotel to accept the conference on a completely open basis. All facilities were open to all fifty of us, Black and white, including the hitherto sacrosanct swimming pool.

This meeting marked a recognition of something that has al-ways been difficult for people's lawyers to understand and ac-cept—the necessity, in spite of the pressures of life, to take time off periodically to review and analyze their developing role and responsibilities at a particular moment in history. I was asked to give a talk, which gave me my first opportunity and incentive to generalize about the experiences of the Danville summer. In a way, to be forced to sit back and analyze what had really happened in terms of the lawyer's role was one of the most important moments of that summer.

The problem, I explained, that we faced in Danville was exactly the same problem other movement lawyers were facing in Gadsden, in Jackson, in Albany, all over the South. How could we meet a combined attack of all sectors of the power structure that utilized the entire arsenal of legal weapons at the disposal of the state? It was impossible to solve this problem by continuing to think in the old conceptual terms of mounting an individual defense in every situation, for we faced a totally new kind of reality. It was no longer a question of responding to ordinary, isolated legal procedures, but to a carefully worked out plan developed by the power structure to paralyze the movement. Our job was to find the legal techniques that would lift this repressive machinery off the backs of the people.

We could not do this, I pointed out, if we fell into the trap of pursuing each individual case tortuously through the state courts, ultimately seeking relief in the United States Supreme Court, while our movement clients remained for years in jail or under the cloud of a state conviction. Such an approach would stop the movement dead. The solution lay in the resurrection of the legal remedies created by the Radical Reconstruction Congress after the Civil War, which had permitted federal courts to grant immediate relief against state court proceedings that threatened to punish the recently emancipated Black people when they attempted to exercise their newly granted constitutional rights. These were the weapons of federal removal and federal injunctions against unconstitutional state proceedings, which we had used in Danville to mount a counterattack. This counterattack was not, and could not, be a matter of pulling out of the hat one or another technique at random. If the white establishment had a concerted plan for stopping the movement, the movement had to have a concerted plan for stopping the establishment.

Then I turned to the most painful reality of all those we had faced in Danville. We were faced head on with the many, complex legal theories that had been developed over the years to destroy the effectiveness of these Radical Reconstruction weapons.

Our task was to overcome these countless precedents which stood in the way. In words that were unknowingly prophetic of the immediate future in New Orleans, I said that the same challenge that we had faced in Danville in resurrecting the federal removal remedy would have to be faced in resurrecting the power of a federal court to issue injunctions to stop state statutes and proceedings which interfered with the exercise of fundamental constitutional rights. As lawyers, we could not accept the concept that if something was needed to protect people's constitutional rights, there was nothing we could do to help when the old cases said no. If the movement's ability to function needed protection, it was our job as lawyers to find a way; there was no other answer. We were no longer primarily lawyers in selected test cases. The legal work of people's lawyers must be totally integrated into the needs of the movement. If the movement could not exercise its First Amendment rights, then the lawyer had to figure out how to remedy this situation fast. "No one," I concluded, "can tell us, 'You can't do it.' We've got to do it."

The response was tremendous. Then, in the middle of the heated discussion that followed, something happened which was to put everything I had said to the test. Someone came into the room and whispered to Ben Smith. Out of the corner of my eye I saw him frown, jump up, and run over to where his law partner, Bruce Waltzer, was sitting. They both left the room quickly, without saying anything.

Later that evening, when the conference had reconvened without hearing from Smith or Waltzer, one of the New Orleans lawyers got up to answer a phone call in the next room. He came back with news that was devastating. Late that afternoon Smith and Waltzer had been arrested during a raid on their law office. Shortly afterward, Dr. James Dombrowski, director of the Southern Conference Educational Fund and one of the few white southern leaders of the civil rights movement, had been arrested on a similar warrant in a raid at the SCEF office. Someone asked quickly, "What's the charge? The answer came back in a puzzled tone. "Subversion, failure to register a subversive organization." "What are the subversive organizations?" someone else asked. The answer was blunt, "SCEF and the Guild." There was a sud-

215

den quiet among the lawyers, and then we all exploded. The Cold War McCarthy red-baiting attack was being resurrected in the middle of the southern movement. Unbelievable!

After a hectic twenty-four hours, we pieced together the events of that afternoon. At about three o'clock, a large moving van had driven up to the entrance of the SCEF office, along with a dozen policemen and twenty inmates from the House of Detention in fatigue uniforms. In charge of the raiding party was Colonel Alexander, staff director of the Joint Un-American Activities Committee of the Louisiana Legislature. The police jumped out with guns in their hands and broke down the door with a sledge hammer. They ransacked the office for over four hours, removing all the files, membership lists, and subscription lists to SCEF's newspaper, the *Southern Patriot,* all Jim Dombrowski's books—including, as a federal judge was to point out several months later, that "dangerous article," Thoreau's *Journal*—and even all the pictures and posters on the walls, including a poster for the March on Washington and a photograph inscribed to Dombrowski from Eleanor Roosevelt. They also grabbed Dombrowski's crutches, which he needed for a serious hip ailment, and ripped them apart, searching their insides. Then they arrested Jim Dombrowski and locked him up in the central jail.

The emergency call to Smith and Waltzer at the conference had informed them that the police had forced their way into their office as well and were ransacking their legal files. When the two lawyers rushed back to their office, they discovered that the police had already left. The office was in a shambles. Table lamps had been taken apart, pictures ripped off the walls, and every file pulled out and rummaged through. The police had left with a bundle of the files. Waltzer hurriedly called his wife, who told him that the police, along with a Mr. Rogers, the lawyer for the State Un-American Committee, were already at their house, ransacking everything. Waltzer rushed home, only to be placed under arrest and hustled to the central jail.

Smith was also arrested by a squad of police who were waiting for him at his apartment when he arrived. After being photographed and fingerprinted, he was pushed into the same cell with Dombrowski. An odd exchange took place there, which

Dombrowski would relate with bitter irony at movement meetings for years afterward. Seeing Smith come into the cell, Dombrowski jumped up, threw his arms around him, and said, "Am I glad to see my lawyer. How did you find me so fast?" Smith replied, "I may be your lawyer, but I'm your cellmate this time. We're in together on this one."

Twenty-four hours later, after Smith, Dombrowski, and Waltzer had been released pending a hearing on the charges, we sat down together to evaluate the situation. One thing was clear. As Smith had said to Dombrowski in the cell, we were all in this one together. The Louisiana attack was overwhelming. SCEF was the only organization of primarily white southerners committed to the Black freedom struggle. At that moment it was involved in the voter registration campaign in Louisiana. Smith and Waltzer were two of the handful of white lawyers who were totally engaged in the daily legal representation not only of SCEF but of every section of the civil rights movement throughout the state. In addition, Smith had assumed both regional and national responsibilities for enlisting legal resources into the southern freedom struggle. He was treasurer of SCEF, counsel for the Louisiana ACLU, and co-secretary of the National Lawyers Guild Committee to assist Southern Lawyers. Something very alarming was involved in these developments. As Earl Amedee, one of the New Orleans lawyers at the workshop said, "The people who arrested Ben Smith and Bruce Waltzer really arrested all of us."

Other than having heard him speak at mass meetings, this was the first time I had really met Jim Dombrowski. Now in his late sixties, he was one of the most respected, indeed beloved, organizers in the southern movement. In the 1930s he had helped to organize the Southern Conference for Human Welfare, one of the first interracial groups in the South to fight against segregation and the enforced inferior status of Black people. At our meeting, he put the situation very plainly. "They're desperate," he said. "They're going back to the weapons of the 1950s."

This was the heart of the matter. The Louisiana white power structure was growing fearful of the rising tide of the Black Movement, backed by an increasingly potent national movement, Black and white, as evidenced by the March on Washington, which now threatened the entire edifice of white supremacy. For almost ten years, the southern power structure had fought the freedom revolution with every concept in the book—nullification, interposition, and state's rights—always coupled with brute force, and yet they were losing ground fast. There was even talk of a new national civil rights statute. In desperation, the power structure was dredging up the old cry of "Communist conspiracy" to undermine and derail the Freedom Movement. As in the days of McCarthyism, the mechanisms of "subversive control" were being oiled up and mobilized.

As Dombrowski pointed out, "If they can get away with this, anything goes." If the power structure could illegalize SCEF and the Lawyers Guild, they could use this technique against any movement organization throughout the South. And if being a lawyer for the movement was a "subversive crime," no one who lifted a finger to help Black people was safe. This threat struck close to home for everyone sitting in that room. The most dangerous threat to the movement was the fear that would be spread by these outrageous charges, not only in Louisiana but throughout the South and the whole country, a fear that, as in the 1950s, could paralyze and then destroy the people's movements.

"What do we do?" everyone started to ask. To fight the state's "antisubversive" laws up through the courts of Louisiana in the normal course of state criminal proceedings was hopeless. It would take years before we ever reached the United States Supreme Court on appeal, and even the Supreme Court had never totally thrown out this kind of statute in the Cold War days. The prospect of this long, dreary process of a criminal trial in Louisiana courts and then the appeals up to the Louisiana Supreme Court, only to have each of these courts put another nail into the "subversive" coffin in which they were burying the movement, sent a chill through all of us. Then Ben Smith cut in with the words we needed to hear, "Remember what Arthur said yesterday? We counterattack. Let's take them head on."

Before the final meeting of the conference, Ben Smith made it clear to me that he wanted me and Bill Kunstler to work closely with him on whatever developed. When I said, "Of course," he put his arm around my shoulder with his characteristic affection and said quietly, "Well, no matter what happens, we'll give them hell." And at the closing session that evening, he proceeded to do just that. "My so-called crime," he said, "is the act of desegregation that we have borne witness to in this, the first really integrated bar association meeting in the history of this city." Then he attacked the state's antisubversion statute head on, saying, "The only reason these statutes have any meaning at all here in Louisiana is so a white man who helps desegregation can be branded a traitor to his people. That's why we have statutes about subversion." And finally he indicated what lay ahead for us. "I intend to go into the federal courts to get an injunction against these charges. I intend at all times to show the unconstitutional character of the state Anti-Subversive Control Act."

Smith had joined issue with the Louisiana power structure. The next day, Rev. Fred Shuttlesworth from Birmingham, co-chair of SCEF, publicly denounced the raids and arrests as the "first overt move of a carefully contrived conspiracy to smash the entire Freedom Movement." Our work as lawyers was to structure a counterattack that matched the seriousness of those words. Kunstler and I mapped out the first steps with Smith, Waltzer, and their close friend, Milton Brener, who had agreed to undertake responsibility as the local New Orleans lawyer in whatever cases should develop. Our very first moves would open up dimensions in the Louisiana attack that we had never dreamed existed.

As the first part of our counterattack, we agreed that I should draft a federal complaint charging a conspiracy under another old Reconstruction statute, which provided for federal relief against conspiracies that under the color of state law deprived citizens of equal rights guaranteed to them under the national Constitution. The complaint charged that the Louisiana Un-American Committee and the New Orleans Police Department and district attorney had conspired to use the antisubversive laws of the state to conduct raids and seize the files and property of SCEF, in order to harass and intimidate its members into abandoning their constitutional rights to fight for equality and against segregation in Louisiana. It demanded the immediate return of the seized files and property and, under the words of the statute, asked for damages of $500,000 against the conspirators.

Before this federal complaint with its supporting affidavits had been completed, Brener prepared a motion for the state court, asking to dismiss the arrest warrants as totally improper. We had little hope for success in this motion, but Brener felt that it ought to be tried. The hearing on this motion, which took place on October 25, taught me a lesson I would never forget: to take nothing for granted, even in a Louisiana courtroom. Brener skillfully led the state court judge to the point of actually agreeing that no evidence had been produced to justify the original warrants. The affidavits filed by the local prosecutor were insufficient, even under Louisiana law. This did not mean that the district attorney could not proceed with new affidavits, or that a local grand jury could not move ahead to indict, but it did mean that, for the moment, no actual proceedings against Dombrowski, Smith, or Waltzer even existed. The warrants of arrest were thus invalid.

As soon as the judge conceded this point, Brener seized the initiative. He jumped up and demanded that the Louisiana authorities immediately return all the confiscated materials to our clients. Then the roof blew off. The New Orleans district attorney wryly replied that this would be impossible, because although the files and records were still in the physical possession of the police, they were "legally" in the custody of the chairman of the Internal Security Subcommittee of the Judiciary Committee of the United States Senate, Senator James Eastland of Mississippi!

Brener and I stared at each other, dumbfounded. The district attorney then revealed that all the raids and arrests had been planned out together with Senator Eastland, the most powerful representative of the southern white power structure in Washington. J. G. Sourwine, his personal representative and counsel to the Senate Subcommittee, had actually been in New Orleans on the day after the raids, fully equipped with blank subpoenas signed by Eastland. All of the seized materials still remained in the physical possession of the state police in Baton Rouge, but as the result of a three-way deal worked out among the state police, the Louisiana Un-American Activities Committee, and the Senate Internal Security Subcommittee, control over the documents was technically in the hands of the Senate Subcommittee.

The state court judge shrugged his shoulders sadly at Brener and said, "I'm sorry. I don't have any power over the U.S. Senate." That was that. We had a hurried council of war with Dombrowski, Smith, and Waltzer. The stakes were even higher than we had thought. With Eastland calling the shots, it was now perfectly clear that the attack on SCEF was part of an all-out effort to apply the weapons of the Cold War to the Freedom Movement all over the South.

Faced with this situation, we decided to accelerate our counterattack. All that evening we worked to finalize the federal complaint, adding Eastland and Sourwine as defendants. We filed it in federal district court in New Orleans the next morning. We also asked the federal judge, Judge Ainsworth, for an emergency temporary restraining order prohibiting the state police from removing the documents and files from the state. When he asked us why the rush, we explained the new developments. He then told us to wait outside his chambers. A half-hour later, his clerk came out with the news that the judge had called Colonel Burbank of the state police in Baton Rouge, who had assured him that all the seized materials were still at the state police headquarters. On our emergency request for a restraining order, the judge set down a hearing in his chambers for the next Monday, and the clerk directed us to notify all the defendants by telegram. It looked as if our federal counterattack might actually be underway.

I had to head back to New York to catch up with a lot of work that had piled up. Things seemed relatively under control in New Orleans. But when Milt Brener called us Monday afternoon right after the hearing, we realized that we had completely underestimated the power and arrogance of the senator from Mississippi. Brener was almost incoherent with anger. The lawyer for the state police had showed up at the hearing with the news that late the previous night, at the direction of Eastland, Sourwine had arranged by telephone from Washington for a truck to appear at the Baton Rouge headquarters of the Louisiana state police, load up all the documents and files, and drive them across the state line into Mississippi, where they were now in the hands of a county clerk in Woodville. Thus they were outside the jurisdiction of Judge Ainsworth, whose orders could reach only into the federal district of Louisiana. Moreover, any order against the

Louisiana officials was now "moot," or meaningless, since they no longer had possession of the seized materials. As for Eastland and Sourwine, they were in Washington, and we had not even served them yet with the complaint. The question was what to do now. Brener's answer was direct. "Go after them in Washington."

Kunstler and I sat stunned in our New York office. The SCEF lists and files were now safely in Eastland territory in Mississippi, where they could be conveniently used for harassment by the power structure. Eastland could have them sent up to Washington whenever he wanted to. The only move left to us now was to start a federal action against him in Washington. At this thought we both hesitated. Was there any point to it? What federal judge would tangle with a Senate subcommittee and the senior senator from Mississippi? What about all those precedents that we remembered from law school about the absolute immunity of senators and Senate committees from legal interference? It seemed hopeless.

A telephone call from Jim Dombrowski the next morning settled our indecision. He was anxious to know what our next move would be. SCEF was getting out an issue of the *Southern Patriot,* and he wanted to include a full story about the conspiracy between Eastland and the Louisiana officials against SCEF and what we were doing to fight it. He and Shuttlesworth also wanted to put out a statement for distribution all over the South. When we mentioned our hesitancy about tackling Eastland in Washington, Dombrowski was not worried. He asked what the federal lawsuit would be called. When we said, "Dombrowski and SCEF against Burbank, Pfister, Eastland, and Sourwine," his reaction was, "Great! What a story that will make! We'll have to run off loads more copies of the *Patriot.*"

At that moment I thought back to Evansville and the enthusiastic reaction of the UE organizers to the federal action Dave Scribner and I had brought against the House subcommittee, and once again I realized that the test of whether we should move ahead against Eastland was not the strength of the legal precedents or the probability of success but, as Dombrowski reminded me, the importance of such a counterattack to the morale of the southern movement. When Dombrowski responded to my description of the legal hurdles that lay ahead by saying simply, "Why can't we sue a senator? Who's he?" that decided us. Within three days we had filed a federal complaint in the District of Columbia and served it on Eastland and Sourwine, demanding an injunction against the use of the files and records and the SCEF membership lists, their immediate return, and $500,000 in damages. For months afterward, the Eastland suit was used at meetings and rallies, person to person and door to door, to help organize marches and demonstrations throughout the South.

Over the next two years it came as no surprise that the federal district court in Washington and then the Court of Appeals agreed with the indignant senator and his subcommittee counsel that our suit violated the sanctity of the legislative process. What did come as a surprise three years later was my success in convincing all nine justices of the Supreme Court that at least with respect to the senator's counsel, Sourwine, it had been absolutely proper to start the lawsuit against him. Once again, when the news came in that we had won in the Supreme Court, I remembered that guiding concept which is sometimes so easy to forget, that when a legal move is needed to protect the people's struggles and the established law seems to be against it, if people's lawyers dig deep enough, they can often uncover the constitutional validity of the move despite the overlay of years of precedents that say they cannot do it.

Within a few days of filing our complaint back in Washington, however, the fight in Louisiana took a new turn. Up to this point, the power structure had been using the Louisiana antisubversive statute merely as a cover to legitimize its raids. Now, at an open hearing about the necessity to enforce the statutes, conducted in New Orleans by the Louisiana Un-American Activities Committee, the chairman of the committee, Representative Pfister, called for the immediate indictment of Jim Dombrowski, Ben Smith, and Bruce Waltzer under the antisubversion laws.

Ben was very troubled about this development when we talked that night. He told us that there was every indication the committee meant business. Pfister was a power in the state and could call the tune with the district attorney's office. Reports were floating around the New Orleans courthouse that a grand jury had al-

223

ready been impaneled for the specific purpose of handing down indictments as soon as possible. Formal indictments would mean months of full-time proceedings before state criminal courts and perhaps years of appeals winding their way through the state structure, ending up in the Louisiana Supreme Court, which, next to Mississippi, was probably the most reactionary court in the country. Then in the distant future there might be an appeal to the United States Supreme Court.

Smith drew a devastating conclusion. No matter what the ultimate decision would be, for the present we could expect the destruction of his and Waltzer's ability to function as movement lawyers, the derailing if not the total elimination of Dombrowski as one of the few experienced white organizers in the South, and the virtual illegalization of SCEF as an effective civil rights organization. Behind these terribly real possibilities loomed the most serious threat of all, the overwhelming probability that the resulting atmosphere of fear and intimidation would paralyze the Freedom Movement, first in Louisiana and then throughout the South.

As Ben Smith described this scenario, my own thinking crystallized. All of our experiences during that summer in Danville had been leading up to this moment. "Let's go all out," I urged. "Let's file a federal injunction against any criminal enforcement of the state statutes." Smith's response was immediate. "Can you have papers ready so we can file them in New Orleans by this Monday morning?" I said yes, thereby committing myself to one of the most overwhelming but most satisfying legal battles I had yet joined.

That weekend, as I worked around the clock to draw up the new federal complaint in time to catch the plane on Sunday for New Orleans, I had not the faintest idea that I was fashioning the foundation for an opinion that two years later would emerge from the nation's High Court to win the oldest historic accolade of the legal community—recognition as a "landmark decision." When, in that first handwritten draft, I wrote out the caption, *Dombrowski v. Pfister,* it never crossed my mind that these words would become part of the critical arsenal of weapons to be relied on by movement lawyers for years to come. What I was fully aware of was the enormity of the legal job we had undertaken by throwing down this gauntlet to the power structure. For years, no one had successfully persuaded a federal court to interfere with a state court criminal proceeding and stop it in its tracks as unconstitutional under the national Constitution. And, despite the turning of the McCarthy tide, no one had yet succeeded in persuading the federal courts, including the Supreme Court, to strike down the panoply of state antisubversive statutes as grossly violative of the First Amendment. The legacy of the Smith Act cases still lay heavy on the national legal scene. Yet no matter the odds against us, we had to proceed as though we expected to win. For if we did not act as if we believed we could win, no one else would believe it either.

And as I worked on the complaint, characterizing the events in Louisiana for what they were—a conspiracy to use the state antisubversive statutes as a means to intimidate and destroy the new movement of Black citizens and their white supporters—I began to feel the power in this legal position. It flowed from the relationship between the old but still ongoing struggle to defend the First Amendment liberties in the years of the Cold War and the new struggle to enforce the commitment to freedom and equality for Black people created by the Civil War Amendments. This combination of different yet interrelated constitutional commitments was to be a major source of strength in the legal battles to come.

The federal complaint was filed and served on Monday morning. This was none too soon, for on Wednesday the New Orleans papers announced that a grand jury had been convened by a state court judge to consider returning indictments against Dombrowski, Smith, and Waltzer under the antisubversive laws. The indictments were due a week later.

On Friday, when I was back in New York, Ben Smith called me in great excitement. It looked as if the Fifth Circuit was taking our complaint seriously. We had asked for the appointment of a three-judge federal court, comprising two district judges and one court of appeals judge, as the federal law required when there was a challenge to the constitutionality of a state statute. Chief Judge Elbert Tuttle had just appointed a three-judge court to sit on our case. The two district judges would be E. Garden West and Frank B. Ellis. Then, with a tone of deep respect in his voice, Ben Smith announced, "And John Minor Wisdom is the circuit judge sitting." He added, in a manner that reminded me of Len Holt's first phone call from Danville which had started everything off, "You better get down here fast. We've got work to do here Monday morning."

In light of the latest news that the grand jury was due to return indictments on Wednesday, and the three-judge court had been appointed, Ben Smith and I agreed to go through the motions at least of trying to get an emergency restraining order on Monday stopping those indictments until the federal court could hear our attack on the constitutionality of the state statutes. Under the rules, a single member of the three-judge court could grant such a restraining order. Ben Smith made arrangements for us to approach Judge Wisdom with this request.

At breakfast that Monday morning before we were due at the federal courthouse, Ben Smith filled me in a little on Judge Wisdom. The judge was, he felt, one of those rare human beings who had an unquestioned commitment to constitutional values. He had also displayed, in the tense and bitter civil rights cases of the last several years in which Smith had been involved, a courage that was exceptional, considering the passions of the period.

Although I remained deeply pessimistic as we walked into Judge Wisdom's chambers that morning, our experience with him confirmed the soundness of Ben Smith's appraisal. It was one of the highlights of my years as a people's lawyer. Under intense and incisive questioning by Judge Wisdom, we came to an understanding that was to shape a powerful weapon in the fight for people's liberties, known as the "Dombrowski remedy." What concerned Judge Wisdom most was the extent of his responsibilities as a federal court judge. Did he have the power, indeed the duty, to interfere with the impending state court criminal proceedings? His focus on this question forced me to sharpen my own thinking about the necessity for immediate federal action. I found myself almost thinking out loud in the discussion, reaching for ideas that would move him. And as in those critical moments months before with Judge Sobeloff in Baltimore, the concept that more than any other seemed to catch Judge Wisdom's attention was the primary responsibility of the federal system, including federal judges, to protect the fundamental national rights of citizens whenever they were threatened by acts of state authorities.

Here in Louisiana was a classic example of the necessity for federal intervention. The Louisiana authorities, along with Senator Eastland of Mississippi, were openly engaged in using Louisiana's antisubversive laws to intimidate, harass, and jail citizens who were invoking the national rights of assembly, guaranteed to them under the First Amendment to the federal Constitution, to form organizations to fight for the equality and freedom guaranteed to them under the Civil War Amendments. Under a federal system, a national court had the duty to protect these national rights. Thus, a federal judge would not be interfering with "state's rights" by intervening to stop impending state criminal trials that were designed to punish citizens for trying to use the very rights given to them under the national Constitution. Quite the contrary, by failing to act, a federal court would be abdicating its responsibility under the Constitution.

"Bold words," I thought to myself, as I finished my arguments—maybe too bold here in New Orleans, in the heart of the deep South. And then the unbelievable happened. "I agree with you," Judge Wisdom said. And he signed the temporary restraining order we had prepared the night before, prohibiting any state criminal indictments against Dombrowski, Smith, or Waltzer until after the three-judge federal court had heard and decided our challenge to the state antisubversive statutes.

The news of Judge Wisdom's temporary restraining order spread through the Louisiana movement and from one end of the South to the other. Time and again, SNCC and CORE organizers in Louisiana told us with delight how the news of that order had been received at local meetings. It greatly slowed the tempo of the power structure's attack. And once again, the lesson of the early UE battles was driven home—the tremendous value of winning something, even if limited in time and scope, in building the fighting morale of a people's movement.

Judge Wisdom's signing of the temporary restraining order also added an element of reality to the legal struggle itself. Here was a respected member of a high federal court saying in effect

227

that our approach was not insane or irresponsible but reflected the essence of the American constitutional system. As I prepared for the next major round, the full-scale arguments before all three federal judges set for December 9 in New Orleans, I had a growing sense that we, the representatives within the legal structure of the increasingly militant and activist Black Movement and their as yet small but growing group of white allies, were being cast by history into a strange role. When I got up before that three-judge court and took on the New Orleans district attorney and the attorney general of Louisiana, I would be challenging these powerful representatives of the establishment for abandoning the most elementary premises of the American constitutional system itself. We, the advocates for a movement that they were seeking to brand as "subversive to America," would be exposing the power structure and their lawyers as betraying the very principles upon which the constitutional structure was supposed to rest. *They* were the real subversives. This sense of the reversal of roles was to become a source of strength and confidence for me in the battles ahead.

In this atmosphere of growing confidence in both our own role and our assertions, Milt Brener and I worked out our strategy the night before the hearing. The panel was clearly loaded against us. In addition to Judge Wisdom, we would face two extremely conservative federal district court judges, Judges West and Ellis, who had been prosegregationist in a number of recent rulings. Judge Wisdom's views were hardly theirs. We wondered whether this called for a degree of caution in our approach. Then I recalled Chuck Conley's words of several years before in Montgomery that it was best to "lay it all out." Buttressed by the recent experiences in Danville, we decided to follow this approach and be completely blunt.

As in the first encounter with Judge Wisdom, our central thrust went to the nature of the federal union, which imposed upon the federal court the duty of intervening to protect the fundamental national rights of citizens, even if this meant applying remedies that had lain buried and forgotten for decades. Then we took a step which startled everyone, both the panel of judges and the state's lawyers sitting across from us. We offered, then and there, to put on witnesses to prove that these defendants were in fact engaged in a full-scale conspiracy to derail and destroy the civil rights movement of Louisiana and that their threatened use of the antisubversive laws of the state was solely for this purpose. One of the Louisiana lawyers jumped to his feet, shouting objections to our move, and Brener and I saw that we had touched a raw nerve. The last thing in the world that the state wanted was for us to turn this hearing into an open trial of the top officials of the establishment. This would risk exposure of their plans to smear and derail the Freedom Movement.

The lawyers for the state insisted that any testimony we might bring forward as to the motivations of state officials was utterly irrelevant. What was at stake here, they insisted, was the "inherent" right of the state of Louisiana to "self-preservation." The antisubversive statutes were critical weapons in the protection of that right. The use of these statutes by state officials must receive deference from everyone, including the federal courts. The right of the state itself to self-preservation took precedence over all other questions. When asked whether this included precedence over the rights of citizens under the national Constitution, these lawyers answered, "Trust us, trust the courts of Louisiana. The right of the existing state government to self-preservation is paramount. All other rights, all liberties, depend on that." Ten years later, I was to hear Robert Mardian make the same statements to the Supreme Court of the United States when urging legitimization of Nixon's claim of power to suspend provisions of the Constitution in the exercise of the same "inherent" right to self-preservation. This was the last ploy of a threatened establishment, heard first by me in the home state of that authority on native-grown reaction, Huey Long, who had so eloquently warned in the 1930s that "when fascism comes to this country, it will come wrapped in an American flag."

Louisiana's argument obviously unsettled Judges West and Ellis. After a brief whispered exchange between them and Judge Wisdom, we were told that the question of our being permitted to present evidence would be decided, along with other basic questions, at another session of the three-judge court in three weeks and that Judge Wisdom's emergency injunction against indictments would continue in effect until then. We all breathed a sigh of relief upon leaving the courtroom. As Ben Smith said with a wry smile, "At least they don't expect us to overthrow the state of Louisiana within the next three weeks."

When the three-judge court convened again in New Orleans on January 10, 1964, it was clear from the first words of Judge Wisdom, sitting as the senior judge of the three, that West and Ellis had taken over control of the proceedings. By a two-to-one vote, the court had rejected our offer of proof and had decided, Judge Wisdom dissenting, to hold that the Louisiana antisubversive statutes were constitutional on their face, resting on the fundamental right of the state to self-preservation. As a result, our request for an injunction against the threatened prosecutions was denied, and Judge Wisdom's temporary restraining order was vacated.

Although this result was not unexpected after the developments of the last hearing, it is never easy to listen to the message of defeat. After a quick discussion with Brener, Smith, and Waltzer, who looked as dejected as I felt at that moment, I jumped up and asked if the court would at least hold up the impending indictments until we could present our appeal to the Supreme Court. After a brief exchange on the bench, once again those ominous words rang out, "The court denies the request, Judge Wisdom dissenting."

That evening we took stock. The path ahead of us was clear. The state would now quickly indict Dombrowski, Smith, and Waltzer. Our course had to be to rush our appeal directly to Washington, to the Supreme Court, as the statute allowed. Everyone felt that we should also at least make the gesture of asking the Supreme Court for an emergency stay of the indictments pending its full consideration of our appeal, even though the chances of getting such an unusual order were slim. Having carried the fight this far, no one was in the mood to give up even the most remote chance of holding off the indictments.

We slapped together an application for the emergency order that same evening at Ben Smith's office, and I agreed to take it to Washington the next morning. At the last minute, however, I realized that, before going to the airport, I would have to stop in at Judge Wisdom's office, since he was the senior judge of the three, and get a copy of whatever order the judges had signed, to attach to our application. We had been so upset upon leaving the courtroom in the afternoon that we had forgotten to pick up the order from the clerk. As it happened, this was a fortunate oversight.

When I entered Judge Wisdom's chambers the next morning and told his law clerk why I was there and that I was planning to fly to Washington as soon as possible to present an emergency application to the Supreme Court, he said, "I'll see if the judge has a copy of the dismissal order on his desk." In a few minutes he came out with a strange smile on his face and said, "The judge would like to talk to you for a moment." As I walked into the inner office, I could not imagine what the judge would want to say to me. It turned out to be one thing, which was as warm an expression of support as I have ever received from anyone, much less a federal judge at the height of battle. He suggested that, since I was making an emergency application to the High Court that day, it might be helpful if he finished writing his dissenting opinion right then, so that I could take a copy with me. Would I be able to wait for him to finish it?

As I sat in his outer office waiting for his secretary to finish typing the opinion, I was overwhelmed by what this meant. Normally a dissenting opinion would have been filed perhaps a few weeks after the announcement of the decision by the three-judge court. For Judge Wisdom to have suggested that I wait for a copy of his opinion in this case before leaving for Washington could only mean that the implications of this struggle were not lost on him, and that he wanted to add his support in as powerful a way as he could. I glanced anxiously at my wristwatch as the hands moved closer and closer to flight time, and I continued to suffer acute agitation all through the hectic drive with Ben Smith out to the plane, followed by the mad run down the corridors of the New Orleans airport. But as I sat in the plane heading for Washington and read the eighteen-page opinion that Judge Wisdom had just finished, I knew that it was well worth the effort.

Judge Wisdom had brilliantly and passionately laid out the duties and responsibilities of the federal courts in a way that went right to the heart of the matter. Reacting to Louisiana's argument,

231

he wrote, "The crowning glory of the American federal system is not the protection of the States as sovereign states . . . The crowning glory of the Federal Union is the protection of the individual against governmental invasion of fundamental rights. The federal courts bear the brunt of protecting the individual's federally created constitutional rights against wrongful State action that is locally popular." Then he put forth the core of the theory we had been developing: "But this is not a new duty that started with the *School Segregation Cases*. It is close to the heart of the American federal Union. It is essential to workable federalism. The federal balance we all wish to preserve is in jeopardy when federal courts abstain from checking misuse of governmental power by the State in cases involving fundamental federally created rights."

The foregone conclusion of my trip to Washington was the denial by the Chief Justice of our request for an emergency stay. But the opinion of John Minor Wisdom must have had considerable influence upon the full Court when it later came to deciding the critical question of whether to consider the appeal and take the case on for decision. And for us, the Wisdom opinion had enormous impact. It softened the effect of the denial of the stay, which was the inevitability of state indictments of Dombrowski, Smith, and Waltzer. It said to us that this time we were not alone. John Minor Wisdom was with us all the way to the top.

So when the state indictments came down three days later, we felt prepared to make the necessary response, "We're taking this to the Supreme Court, and fast!" Dombrowski was indicted on two counts of violating the Communist Control Act and two charges of being executive director and a member of a "subversive organization," SCEF. He faced a ten-year sentence on both counts. Smith was indicted on three counts, for being treasurer of SCEF, a member of SCEF, and a member of the National Lawyers Guild, also a "subversive organization." Waltzer was indicted on one count, for being a member of the Lawyers Guild.

In every way, the counteroffensive launched back in October at the New Orleans workshop had prepared us and the movement throughout the South for this battle. We were going up to the High Court not defensively, not as a last resort after years of demoralization and defeat, but as part of an attack on the establishment's conspiracy against the movement. And after Judge Wisdom's opinion, we knew we were going up there not alone, not wholly isolated, but as champions of the best of America's constitutional promises. In this spirit, we later received the news of the decision of the Court to hear our appeals. "Next round Washington," Ben Smith jubilantly said to me when I told him that the Court had taken our case.

As the Black civil rights struggle grew in intensity and word got around about the helpful contributions people's lawyers could make, the requests mounted for our help elsewhere. Bill Kunstler reshaped a phrase from a popular western to sum up the tempo of our legal life: "Have writ, will travel." It became a daily necessity to find effective strategies to head off the massive efforts of the white power structure to destroy the movement. Mississippi especially became an area where we sharpened the weapons of legal battle first applied in Danville and New Orleans.

That the focus was now Mississippi was no accident. That state had been the breeding ground for the most repressive strategies of the slave system. And at this moment in history, when the southern power structure was being shaken to its roots, Mississippi was again generating the most effective techniques to quell the Black Movement. These combined a skillful use of the state legal machinery with the South's age-old weapons of the mask, the burning cross, the rope, and the gun.

The fundamental conviction underlying the developing movement in Mississippi was the same as that which had motivated the people in Montgomery and then in the student sit-ins throughout the South. This was the recognition that its substantive goals could be achieved only through direct massive activity of the southern Black people themselves. There was a growing realization that the 1954 decision in *Brown,* the national reaffirmation of the century-old constitutional promise of freedom and equality, was not self-enforcing in any respect. And in Mississippi, as everywhere in the South, it was clear from the start that the power structure was not prepared to accede in any way to the constitutional promises of freedom and equality for Black people. The Black people of Mississippi therefore took matters into their own hands, throwing down a challenge to the white power structure that was as serious in its long-range implications as had been the Black Reconstruction government so many years before.

The Black struggle in Mississippi had a special quality which heightened the tension for the power structure in that state. From the first days in 1961 when a handful of SNCC workers, led by Robert Moses, a brilliant Black student from New England and one of the most sensitive organizers I have ever worked with, went into the southwest section of the state, the work emphasized a demand for equality in participation in the political process. The SNCC organizers and the local people with whom they joined forces concentrated on helping to stimulate and develop programs of voter registration. Nothing frightened the entrenched white power structure more than these attempts. Ever since the national betrayal of 1877, when the white plantation owners had returned to power in the state, Black people had been totally excluded from the voting and political process. For a Black woman or man in 1961 to dare to appear at a courthouse and assert the right to vote was hardly the inconsequential act of civic virtue that it so often appeared to be in the rest of the country. In Mississippi it was an act of the highest courage.

Moses faced this experience himself during one of the first attempts at registration. In a town with the ironic name Liberty, he walked down the street toward the courthouse with three local Black residents who had decided to make an attempt to register to vote. A block from the courthouse he was attacked and beaten by a white man, who later turned out to be the sheriff's first cousin. Moses required eight stitches in his head, and two days later the sheriff's cousin was acquitted of assault charges by an all-white jury before a justice of the peace. No one registered in Liberty that week.

The experiences of the next several years showed time and again that the act of registration could not be an individual act but could occur only as part of large-scale demonstrative activities in which those participating drew courage from each other to confront the representatives of the power structure at the local courthouse. But slowly and patiently, in community after community, first in the southwest and then in the Delta region, Bob Moses and the SNCC workers helped to build local bases of

Black leadership, each of which organized, as soon as there was a feeling of readiness, mass marches to the local courthouse to demand the right to register to vote.

On November 2–5, 1963, the Mississippi movement lifted the struggle for equal participation in the political process to a new height by organizing a Freedom Vote to elect candidates for Governor and Lieutenant Governor. When the news broke that over 80,000 Black people had voted at this people's election, it catapulted the issue of Black disenfranchisement in Mississippi and the rest of the South into national attention. The potential dangers to the state power structure of a national confrontation suddenly heightened when the now highly enthusiastic and unified Mississippi movement, functioning through the Council of Federated Organizations, called for hundreds of volunteers from all over the country to come into Mississippi during the summer of 1964 to help in the registration drives and other activities. With the Mississippi Summer Project looming on the horizon and the whole country discussing the necessity for a new national civil rights act, the Mississippi white power structure faced its most serious crisis in years. It responded to this crisis by using a strategy known as the "Jackson formula," the Mississippi version of the strategies being employed all over the South to crush the Freedom Movement. The Jackson formula consisted of a massive use of the normal machinery of the state criminal law to frustrate and then cut off any efforts by the Black community to enforce what seemed to be national policy mandating equality.

The Mississippi authorities had developed this approach with considerable success as a response to the first Freedom Rides. Federal courts had long held that integration in interstate travel was constitutionally required. But no one had heeded this mandate in Mississippi until 1961, when the Freedom Riders arrived in Jackson to enforce the national command by organizing demonstrations of integrated travel on public transportation. These touched off similar demonstrations throughout the state. The state authorities faced a major dilemma. If they used the old state segregation statutes to arrest the demonstrators, it might invoke immediate federal judicial intervention. Since *Brown v. Board of Education,* state statutes that openly sanctioned segregation could no longer be relied on to enforce the continuing state policy of segregation. So Mississippi developed a new technique, which would become the principal response of the entire southern power structure to any attempt by the Black Movement to enforce desegregation. The state simply began a total, massive enforcement of all of the normal processes of the criminal law against the Freedom Riders. For example, hundreds of prosecutions for violation of conventional "breach of the peace" statutes were undertaken. From 1961 through 1963 these cases wound their weary way up through the Mississippi state courts, still without reaching the United States Supreme Court. Almost half a million dollars in bail bond money remained frozen in the state treasury. Thousands of dollars in fines were paid out, and countless days were spent in jail sentences.

The same techniques were used wholesale against the voter registration marches. As mass actions were organized to spur the voter registration drive, ordinary criminal law statutes dealing with such infractions as street littering, blocking traffic, disorderly conduct, and marching without a permit were used to harass and intimidate the movement. This large-scale legal persecution had a serious impact on the morale of the movement.

During the winter of 1963–1964, Bill Kunstler and I found ourselves involved in the huge task of trying to resist and overcome the Jackson formula. The techniques used had already become familiar to us in Danville, and the legal responses that had emerged out of our experiences there were desperately needed here in Mississippi. Every phone call, every trip into a crisis situation in Mississippi, invariably resulted in the utilization of a federal writ of removal to yank the cases out of the state courts. Sometimes we even used a federal injunction to slow up the state criminal proceedings, although the continued availability of federal injunctions still depended on the outcome of the *Dombrowski* arguments, yet to be held before the Supreme Court.

One evening in April 1964, Ben Smith called from Hattiesburg, Mississippi. I had rarely heard him so furious. He had gotten a call the day before from Hunter Morey in Jackson. Morey, of the COFO staff, was the legal coordinator for the state, playing the invaluable role of pulling together at critical moments whatever legal resources were available. He had told Smith about a march and demonstration on the right to register to vote that had taken place the afternoon before in front of the city courthouse in Hattiesburg, at which over thirty people had been pulled in on disorderly conduct charges. Morey had described the situation as run of the mill, with trials set for the end of the week, and he had asked Smith to come to Hattiesburg from New Orleans to file the removal writs.

By that time in the spring, our response to these mass state arrests was down pat. File civil rights removal petitions in the federal court, yank the cases out of the state court, bail our people out on federal bail, and "keep the movement moving," as it said in a gospel song that resounded at the end of many meetings. So Ben Smith had gone to Hattiesburg to handle the matter. But this time it had proved to be no routine removal.

"They're out to smash removal," Smith exploded to me. "What do you mean?" I asked, startled. It turned out that the district clerk at the federal courthouse in Hattiesburg had refused to accept Smith's removal petitions and had informed him that new rules were now in effect. A $500 costs bond had to be filed for every individual person removed, no more joint petitions were allowed, and, most extraordinary, no petitions were allowed to be filed unless signed by a local member of the Mississippi bar. The filing of the $500 bond for each person arrested was difficult enough, but the local lawyer requirement was impossible. In the whole state there was only a handful of lawyers, Black and white, who would dare to become involved in movement cases. The simple truth was that in almost all crisis situations, if lawyers from outside the state were not allowed to come in to help, there would be no lawyers for the Freedom Movement. All in all, the power structure had found a perfect way to derail our legal counteroffensive, if they could make it stick.

"Did you raise hell with the federal judge about the clerk's actions?" I asked. Smith laughed, "Guess who's sitting in Hattiesburg today? Harold Cox." My heart sank. Even my few months of involvement in Mississippi cases were enough to know that Cox, chief judge of the federal court for the Southern District of Mississippi, was as open a representative of the southern white power structure as ever sat on the federal bench. During a voter registration suit early in March 1964 he had openly attacked a group of Black would-be registrants as "a bunch of niggers." Kunstler and I had responded by filing a motion with the Fifth Circuit, which was still pending, calling for his disqualification from any civil rights cases. What we did not know at the time was that Cox had been a college roommate of Senator Eastland and was "his man" in the federal court system in every sense of the word.

For a moment we seemed to be caught in an impossible bind in the Hattiesburg situation. There appeared to be nothing in these cases for us to bring up to the Fifth Circuit. No action that could be formally appealed had been taken on the removal petitions. Word would soon spread through the state that our removal technique had been squashed. It would be a green light for wholesale arrests. The nightmare of hundreds and hundreds of local court trials loomed ahead. This was hardly the right atmosphere in which to launch the Mississippi Summer Project.

Suddenly, I thought of the papers I had just filed on appeal in Washington in the *Dombrowski* case. The recent words of Judge Wisdom in his dissenting opinion burned into my mind: "The crowning glory of the Federal Union is the protection of the individual against governmental invasion of fundamental rights. The federal courts bear the brunt of protecting the individual's federally created constitutional rights against wrongful state action that is locally popular." That did it. I threw a bold idea at Smith. "Let's mandamus Cox, right away, tomorrow. Let's battle it out in the circuit fast."

I could hear Ben Smith gasp on the other end of the phone. The ancient English writ of mandamus was called "an extraordinary writ," with good reason. It was the only way without a formal appeal that a high court could order a lower court judge to do anything. And we had nothing to appeal here, because Cox had not entered any kind of final order that could technically be challenged, having merely refused to tell the clerk to accept our removal petitions. This left only a writ of mandamus, the old Latin word for "we command you," which could order district judges to do something they refused to do. But from the earliest days this had been reserved only for the most extraordinary circumstances.

It took Ben Smith and me no more than two minutes to agree that this was an extraordinary situation, even if it did not say so in the law books. The problem now was to convince a Court of Appeals judge in New Orleans to entertain our application for a writ and call together an emergency panel of two other judges to hear us. But we had no other choice. If the federal Reconstruction remedies like removal were not to be buried once again, we had to face up to the responsibility of battling for their survival in the higher federal courts. Taking the fight with Cox to New Orleans, in what might appear to be a hopeless effort to save the federal removal remedy, was directly parallel to taking the *Dombrowski* case to the highest court in the land, in an effort to resurrect the federal injunctive remedy.

We moved fast that night. Smith called Waltzer in New Orleans to have him draft the necessary papers for an application for the extraordinary writ, to be ready the next day. I called Kunstler at his home in New York, and he quickly agreed with our approach. Then I threw myself into the task which, I was rapidly learning, proved to be one of the most difficult for a people's lawyer in the midst of the southern struggles: getting a reservation at the last minute on a flight to New Orleans. But working all night, Waltzer drafted the papers, I made my plane connections, and late the next morning the three of us found ourselves in the chambers of Judge Richard Rives, one of the senior judges of the Fifth Circuit.

I had a basically good feeling about our having been assigned by the clerk to see Judge Rives. I remembered with warmth the tone of his voice three years before when he had issued that courageous order from the bench stopping the execution of Willie Seals. After hearing a brief presentation from Ben Smith as to why our request for a mandamus was so urgent, he agreed to call together an emergency panel of two other judges and himself to hear our application. "Would you be ready by noon?" he asked.

We stared at each other in amazement and delight. Then we assured the judge that we would indeed be ready, left him our papers, and went out for a quick cup of coffee. As we sat in one of the sidewalk cafés lining the square, Smith reminded me of Judge

Rives's comment in the first New Orleans school segregation cases to come before the circuit several years before, in which he had condemned Louisiana's efforts to use the criminal law "to enforce the social philosophy of the state." This was the heart of the argument we had to put to the three judges that day. This was precisely what Mississippi was doing across the state line, "using the criminal law to enforce the social philosophy of the state." To prevent this, it was essential to preserve the federal remedy of removal.

In the argument before the panel, we maintained that the federal remedy of removal enacted back in the 1860s was an essential weapon for the defense of citizens seeking to implement basic rights guaranteed to them by the national Constitution. The rules of the local district court sanctioned by Judge Cox would undermine and render virtually useless this remedy which the Reconstruction Congress had provided. Under a system of federalism, the duty of the federal appeals court was to intervene immediately and protect the federal remedy.

One point more than any other seemed to move the three judges. The new Mississippi rule, which would throw out any petition for removal that was not signed by a local member of the Mississippi bar, would in reality virtually eliminate the removal remedy for Black citizens fighting for the right to register to vote, since only a tiny handful of lawyers in that state would represent them in this struggle. This struck home to the three judges listening to us. One of them remarked that Smith, the lawyer turned down by Judge Cox and the Mississippi clerk, was a member of the bar not only of the Louisiana federal court but also of the Fifth Circuit, which was supposed to be a step above the Mississippi District Court. Moreover, the judge pointed out, Smith was a member of the bar of the Supreme Court of the United States. "That ought to be credentials enough," he snapped.

Once again, as in the critical argument in the Seals case in the same courthouse, a fundamental question was emerging. Without lawyers, able and willing to fight for constitutional rights, the rights themselves were meaningless words written on a piece of paper. Without such lawyers, these rights either disappeared entirely or, worse, remained on the books but unenforced, as camouflage for a system which in reality was bereft of elementary democratic rights. This added another dimension to our role as people's lawyers. When we were speaking out in a courtroom for the rights and liberties of the people we represented, we were in truth representing *all* the people, through our fight for the life of the constitutional right itself. In the case at issue, without lawyers to use it, the Reconstruction remedy of federal removal was utterly meaningless for the Black people of Mississippi. If the duty of the federal court was to protect the removal remedy, Judge Cox's maneuver had to be rejected out of hand. And this was exactly what the emergency panel did that afternoon.

While we waited for a decision in Smith and Waltzer's office, the three judges met together and wrote out a short unanimous opinion, which we picked up from the courthouse at the end of the day. It was a sweeping victory for us, going far beyond our expectations. In no uncertain terms the court held that the $500 removal money bonds were not required, that individual petitions were not required, and that, most important, when local counsel were not available, a federal district court could not "close its doors" to people seeking federal removal who were represented by qualified lawyers who happened not to be members of the local state bar. In a delicate gesture, the judges then said they would hold off issuing the mandamus for fifteen days, giving Judge Cox time to comply "voluntarily" with their opinion. We had set back the strategy of the Mississippi power structure, put into motion by Judge Cox, which would once again have killed the removal remedy and drowned the movement in a flood of state criminal proceedings. At least for the immediate future, the path seemed clear for the statewide intensification of the mass activities designed to move ahead on the voter registration drive.

For Kunstler and myself, our area of work was becoming more defined. Increasingly, in a way we had never really contemplated, the arena of struggle within the federal judiciary was becoming the decisive one. Because of the special nature of the southern Black Movement—its struggle against powerful state governments—our use of federal legal forms and concepts was of critical importance.

But we also faced the harsh reality that even within the federal structure were powerful forces who were committed not to the underlying principles of the federal union but to the social and political objectives of the southern white power structure. Without the most bitter battle against those forces, the federal structure would not be available to play this role. Our experiences with Judge Michie in Danville, Judges West and Ellis in New Orleans, and now Judge Cox in Mississippi drove home this point. Just because a southern white man sat in the robes of a federal district judge did not mean that he was prepared in any respect to place the commands of the federal union above his own deeply entrenched ties to the white southern aristocracy.

This reality gave us lawyers for the Freedom Movement a strange responsibility within that level of the federal structure which had power over district court judges, the federal court of appeals. We were emerging within this arena as defenders of the true role of federal judges, spotlighting those who were betraying their supposed allegiance to the concepts underlying the federal union. And to the degree that we fulfilled this responsibility, we were able to reach out to certain other appellate judges in the South, like Wisdom, Rives, Sobeloff, and several others we would come to know. These judges, unlike so many of their southern colleagues, were resolving their own inner contradictions in the direction of fulfilling their sworn commitment as federal judges to the enforcement of the federal Constitution and of the national laws designed to implement its mandates.

As a result, we spent an increasing amount of time working directly with court of appeals judges, both individually and on emergency panels. It was virtually inevitable that in whatever situation we found ourselves, we would have to get "up to" the circuit. This meant we were constantly having to convince those appellate judges that unless they exercised their supervisory powers on an almost daily basis, no federal legal arena functioning in the South would be available to Black people. After a certain point, Kunstler, Smith, and I began to refer to our work as "riding circuit," the phrase from the early 1800s when lawyers literally lived with the circuit judges as they rode on horseback throughout the country, town to town, hearing cases.

Out of this constant contact, we developed an intimacy with

and mutual confidence in these circuit judges. We went back to them time after time, seeking their immediate intervention to force one district court judge after another to comply with the most elementary commands of federal law. We did not always convince them to move, but we sensed their growing respect for our insistence upon the vitality of national law. This was a strange role for radical movement lawyers to be in, champions of the federal system and invokers of the federal power. It was quite a contrast to the 1950s, when we spent so much of our energy in often fruitless efforts to resist the invocation of federal power. In many ways, these daily battles sowed the seeds of a deeper understanding of the nature of the Freedom Movement itself, which emerged as a struggle to fulfill the promises of a never completed democratic revolution.

That short opinion which the three circuit judges had hammered out affirming the removal remedy and forbidding Judge Cox or anyone else to obstruct its use showed that for the time being, federal civil rights removal was alive and well in Mississippi. We immediately arranged to mimeograph the decision, along with an explanatory memo, and mail it to the dozens of lawyers from all over the country who had begun to work in Mississippi with COFO during the winter and spring of 1964. This type of liaison and educational work with other lawyers was becoming one of our most important responsibilities for the Mississippi movement. In no way could the few dozen of us fulfill the legal needs of the exploding movement. Bob Moses and the COFO leadership looked to Bill Kunstler and me in New York, as well as to Ben Smith in New Orleans, to help reach out to the hundreds of additional lawyers throughout the country who would ultimately be needed by the Freedom Movement not only in Mississippi but throughout the South. We appealed for help from lawyers and lawyers' organizations of the most varied politics and commitments, from the National Lawyers Guild to the ACLU to the NAACP Inc Fund, as well as to the dozens of individual lawyers we each had such close ties with from past battles.

A feeling of warmth, affection, and mutual respect and trust began to develop among those of us who were cast together day after day at the center of the legal work involved in the movement: Bill Kunstler, Ben Smith, Bruce Waltzer, myself, and then Morty Stavis, who was once again throwing himself into the work as he had during the height of the Seals case. As in other intense periods of battle—during the Cold War, the Seals struggle, the Danville summer—once again I experienced one of the most exciting rewards of being a people's lawyer, the deep, close, human friendships that grew among those of us who were thrown side by side in the conflict. Often as I have thought back to those bonds of affection that tied us together, I have realized how rare this experience is generally among lawyers, whose lives and professional activities are as ego-oriented and elitist as any other group of people in the country.

I left New Orleans to head back to New York suffused by these feelings of warmth and solidarity, along with elation about the unexpected victory before the three-judge panel preserving the removal remedy. The way looked clear for the intense organizing that was planned for the Mississippi Summer Project. Eight hundred people were expected to come down to participate in the most massive voter registration drive that any southern state had ever seen. We were all set now to hold back the anticipated onslaught against them by the power structure through its use of the criminal law machinery of the state. Thanks to Judge Rives and his two colleagues, that old Reconstruction weapon of removal was ready and waiting for today's heirs of the slave power.

Yet once again, I wholly underestimated the strength, complexity, and resiliency of the power structure's strategy. One week later, on the night of April 24, all over the state the white establishment let us know what it had in store for us. COFO staff workers called in reports from every section of Mississippi that at 10:00 o'clock that evening, crosses were burned, many in counties where no one could remember it having happened before. The next morning the Jackson *Clairion-Ledger* reported that crosses had been burned simultaneously in sixty-four counties across the state. The Ku Klux Klan was loudly broadcasting its message that the time had returned for whites to resort to the ultimate weapon for keeping "the colored in their rightful place" the torch, the whip, the club, and the gun. This was the other arm of the Jackson formula. Whatever the criminal law machinery might not be able to achieve in the way of intimidation and paralysis of the Freedom Movement, open terrorism might well accomplish.

The very first night that I had spent in Jackson back in October 1963 when Kunstler had brought me there to help in the first kneel-in arrests, introduced me personally to the atmosphere of impending violence in which the movement people constantly lived. We were staying at Jeanette and Ed King's apartment near Tougaloo College, where Ed was the chaplain. Jeanette and Ed were two of the very few Mississippi white people who had committed themselves to the Freedom Movement, and their home had become a center of movement activity. As I sat there with a group of Black and white COFO staff workers, taking part in my first on-the-scene Mississippi strategy discussion, the reality of life in that state hit me directly. All of a sudden Ed King jumped up, ran over to where I was standing, and pulled me away from the window, which I had moved close to without realizing it. "Stay away from that window," he said sharply, pointing to three holes in the lower window pane. "Those are rifle shots. They came last night from our Klan friends out there." Then he pointed out the window to two cars parked down in the street. "They've been there every night for the last week." When I immediately asked, "Why don't you call the police?" everyone laughed, and with a touch of irony someone said, "Arthur's sure got a lot to learn about Mississippi. Some of them out there are probably off-duty state troopers."

By early May 1964, the atmosphere of open, violent harassment was intensifying all over the state. Hardly a single one of the weekly COFO reports failed to set forth an account of the beating of movement workers or the burning and bombing of churches or houses where movement people met or lived. Two statewide groups openly committed to violent measures "to keep the negroes in their places" had emerged publicly: the White Knights of the Klan, reborn after many years, and a new terrorist organization called Americans for the Preservation of the White Race. As we came closer and closer to the opening of the Mississippi Summer Project and the arrival of the hundreds of volunteers from all over the country, the violence pointedly rose. A week after the statewide cross burnings, three students who were working on an article on the voter registration project were grabbed by a crowd of white men on the street in McComb, badly beaten, and then told emphatically, "This is a warning for those coming down this summer."

The warning sounded even more bluntly at about 8:00 o'clock on the morning of Monday, June 22, when Hunter Morey called from the COFO office in Jackson. The tone of his voice made it all too clear that something very serious had happened. Three of our people, he told me, were missing, and it looked bad. Michael Schwerner, the Summer Project director for Meridian, James Chaney, a COFO staff worker for Meridian, and Andrew Goodman, who had just come in as a summer volunteer, had gone to Neshoba County at 11:00 A.M. the day before to check out reports of the burning of the Mt. Zion Methodist Church, just outside the town of Philadelphia. There had been no word from the three since then. I knew immediately what this meant. As a precaution, COFO workers going into difficult territory always checked in by phone to headquarters every four hours at least.

By 4:00 the previous afternoon, Morey reported, the Meridian COFO office had started making calls: there was no word of the three workers anywhere. Then a rumor had started, soon confirmed, that they had been arrested by Deputy Sheriff Price of Neshoba County, supposedly for speeding, and had been taken to the Philadelphia jail. But Ed King had also just heard an ominous report from a friend that stories were already circulating through Philadelphia and Neshoba County that the Klan had plans "to take care of" the three, and it was common knowledge that Price and Sheriff Rainey were working closely with the Klan, if they were not actually members.

I immediately asked Hunter Morey whether the FBI or the Justice Department had been asked to step in to protect our people against the possibility of a Klan lynching, assuming they were still in the Philadelphia jail. His response was devastating. At 10:00 P.M. the night before, Sherwin Kaplan, a law student working in the COFO office, had called an FBI agent in Jackson to tell him about our three missing people and the fears about what might happen to them at the Philadelphia jail. The agent's response was simple. "Nothing I can do now. Keep me informed."

Thirty minutes later, Morey continued, news had reached the COFO office that a Justice Department lawyer was actually in Meridian, less than a half-hour from Philadelphia. At once the COFO communications staff person, Robert Weil, called the Justice Department lawyer, a Mr. Schwelb, in Meridian, to ask him to check out the situation directly. After hearing all the information, including the latest reports and rumors about the arrests and the possible Klan action, the Justice Department lawyer replied, "The FBI is not a police force." Moreover, since he was not sure that any federal offense had actually occurred, there was "absolutely nothing" he or the FBI could do. Weil blew up at this and read him over the phone the section of the federal code, which Kunstler and I had provided to all the COFO staff people, requiring all federal agencies, including the Justice Department, to enforce the provisions of the federal law prohibiting conspiracies against citizens exercising their equal civil rights. The response of the Justice Department lawyer was the same. "We don't have any authority to act."

Morey then told me that at 1:00 A.M. that morning the SNCC office in Atlanta, having been told about the emergency situation, had called John Doar, Assistant Attorney General in Washington, who said that he would "look into the matter." Doar suggested "alerting the Mississippi State Highway Patrol." At 6:00 in the morning, the SNCC office again called Doar, who said that he had "invested the FBI with power to look into the matter." But just a few minutes before calling me, Hunter said, the FBI office in Jackson had curtly told the COFO people that they had heard nothing whatever from Washington. And at 7:00 in the morning the wife of the jailer at the Philadelphia jail finally admitted on the phone that the three had actually been in the jail and had been "released" sometime in the night. Yet there was still no sign or word of them anywhere.

The situation looked grim. The tie-in between the Neshoba Sheriff's office and the Klan sounded ominous. I quickly worked out with Hunter what calls we could make from our end in New York to try to pry loose the federal authorities in Washington, on the faint chance that there was still time for them to intervene in Neshoba to save the three. Kunstler and I were extremely skeptical as to whether anything could budge the federal structure in Washington, but we said we would do anything we could in this direction. By the end of the day the families of Goodman and Schwerner, together with the top national officers at CORE, had reached the highest levels in Washington, including Attorney General Robert Kennedy, and had been assured, "Everything will be done." But by nine o'clock that night, the FBI office in Jackson again blandly stated that it had received "no instructions" from anyone.

On Tuesday morning, the lawyers for the Goodman family, Henry Wolf and Martin Popper, both of whom were active in the Lawyers Guild, arranged a meeting with Robert Kennedy himself. Mr. and Mrs. Goodman and Mickey Schwerner's father, Nathan Schwerner, along with their congressmen, William Ryan and Ogden Reid, sat in on the meeting. The Attorney General told them that the Department of Justice was doing everything possible and that the President himself had expressed concern. The parents responded by indicating their concern not only that the federal government do everything possible to find the missing three but, even more important, that immediate steps be taken to provide federal protection for all civil rights workers throughout Mississippi and for all the Black people of the state who were demanding their right to register to vote. Kennedy replied that the government was going to ask all Mississippians who had any information about the missing three to come forward, promising them protection if they talked, but he avoided any discussion of federal protection for ongoing civil rights activity.

The families and the lawyers then met for about twenty minutes with President Lyndon Johnson, who assured them that the federal government "was doing everything it could." As they left the presidential office, the news came in that the station wagon driven by the three had been found a few miles out of Philadelphia near a swamp, charred and burned, without any sign of the young men themselves. That evening, the White House announced that the President was taking "decisive" action in the emergency by sending Allen Dulles, former head of the CIA, to Mississippi the next day as his "personal investigator," to report to him on what should be done. Dulles stayed in Jackson for a day and returned to Washington with his three recommendations for action. One was for the FBI to open a regional office in Jackson, another was for the civil rights workers in Mississippi to "stay out of danger areas," and the last and most incredible, in light of the events of the last week in Philadelphia, was for the civil rights workers to keep "local authorities advised of their whereabouts, and the location of their activities."

For all of us involved in the Mississippi movement, this last comment by the former head of the CIA fully exposed the bankruptcy of the executive branch of the national government at this moment of crisis. One did not have to be an expert in "intelligence gathering" to know what everyone in Neshoba County knew, that the "local authorities," Sheriff Rainey and Deputy Sheriff Price, had been fully informed of the "whereabouts" of the three civil rights workers. By the end of the week, when Dulles' conclusions were announced, Ed King had been told by people living in the county that it was common gossip that the three bodies had been buried by members of the Klan, including Rainey and Price, in a newly dug dam not far from where the burned-out car was found. The fact that it then took the authorities over a month to find the bodies of the murdered civil rights workers was hardly the result of the movement not keeping local authorities advised of their whereabouts.

Dulles' trip and his extraordinary recommendations highlighted the problem the movement faced. Bob Moses laid it out at an emergency meeting of the COFO state leadership in which, at his request, Kunstler and I took part. COFO, Moses reminded us, had pressed hard during the past months for some sign of a federal presence in Mississippi to offset the growing atmosphere of terror and violence. The events of the past week exposed the calculated refusal of the national executive to take any measures to protect the Freedom Movement and the Black people of Mississippi. As a result, the movement could expect a rapid acceleration of acts of violence. For example, Victoria Gray, one of the leaders of the newly organized Freedom Democratic Party, told us that a cross had been burned the night before in the front yard of one of the Freedom Vote organizers in Neshoba County, and a stone had been thrown into the window with a note attached, "You're next, nigger."

What was happening was crystal clear to all the COFO leaders.

The century-old conspiracy between the official state government power structure and their unofficial armed forces, the KKK, was in full operation, with the object of preserving a segregated society. One hundred years ago the radical Republican Congress had enacted legislation to prevent precisely this situation. And today, just as in the period of the betrayal of Reconstruction after 1877, those in control of the national government were failing to invoke this federal power to enforce the national commitment to freedom and equality for Black people. Instead, despite their brave words to the contrary, they were quietly searching out ways to ally themselves with the southern white power structure itself.

But as Moses and Vicky Gray and the other COFO leaders stressed, the movement in Mississippi had no intention of retreating, even after the events in Philadelphia. Civil rights workers would stay in Neshoba County and in all Mississippi, demanding federal protection not primarily for themselves but for the Black people of the state who were forced to live out their lives in an atmosphere of violence and terror. What was needed was an intensification of organizational activity in every arena—the voter registration activities at courthouses, the freedom schools being set up by the Summer Project throughout the state, and the freedom centers in every town and city.

Then Bob Moses turned to Kunstler and me and asked, "Can we do anything ourselves, with a lawsuit, to take the offensive, to expose the conspiracy, to demand federal protection, so that everyone—our own people, the Klan, the state police, the power structure, and Washington itself—sees that we're not afraid, we're not running, we're here to stay?" There it was, in almost the exact words that Jim Matles had used when news of the Evansville developments first hit us fifteen years ago. "Can you do something?" Once again, the people's movement was putting it squarely to us as people's lawyers: develop an approach which helps us to do what we have to do at this moment of struggle.

Within two or three days, Kunstler and I had drafted an exciting new federal complaint based on another old Reconstruction statute. In going through Title 42 of the United States Code, the volume of Reconstruction statutes that since the first days of Danville we had always jammed into our briefcases wherever we went, I had run across the statute which was made to order for the present crisis in Mississippi. Section 1989 of the Reconstruction laws was written to provide for situations where local, state, or federal officials were unable or unwilling to take measures to prevent the violation of federally guaranteed civil rights of citizens. In such emergencies, the statute provided for the appointment by federal judges of special federal commissioners in every county of the state, with the power to order the arrest and prosecution of persons violating any of the federal laws protecting civil rights. These special commissioners in turn had the power to appoint people within each county, with the full authority to issue warrants and arrest violators of civil rights laws and to call on any land or naval forces of the United States for immediate aid and assistance.

What excited me almost as much as the statute was the annotation that appeared under it. In words that seemed to have been written especially for us, it said that this statute had first been passed in 1866 "to provide an effective Federal police force to enforce civil rights where such enforcement was either prevented, actively opposed, or ignored by state officials and where men combined against civil rights." Further, these emergency commissioners were to be "especially empowered to concern themselves with conspiracies by private persons against the constitutional or statutory rights of persons through the use of violence or intimidation." It was almost too good to be true. This was precisely the situation we were in. We were facing a major conspiracy of state officials and clandestine terrorist organizations to use violence and force to stop Black citizens from attempting to enforce the civil rights guaranteed by the national Constitution, and no efforts were being made by state or federal authorities to prevent it. Section 1989 was begging to be invoked.

When we outlined the possibilities of such an action, the excitement among the COFO leadership was tremendous. Demanding the immediate appointment of emergency federal commissioners in every one of the 82 counties in Mississippi, with power to arrest civil rights violators, was exactly the kind of action around which people could organize community support and build morale. The federal lawsuit, now known by the appropriate title of "COFO against Sheriff Rainey," was filed on July 10 and had exactly the organizational and morale-building impact we had hoped for. Ironically, on the same day we filed the action, J. Edgar Hoover, national director of the FBI, opened a regional office in Jackson, but he announced publicly that this in no way represented a commitment to protect civil rights workers within the state. That, he said, was the task of the local authorities, in whom he had full confidence. When this statement was reported at a mass meeting that evening in Jackson, the groans were audible all over the hall, matched only by the cheers which greeted the news of the filing of the COFO action.

The suit became one of the most effective organizing tools ever used in the state. A hearing on our motion for the appointment of emergency federal commissioners to be placed at once inside every sheriff's office in the state was scheduled for July 23 in the federal courthouse in Meridian. The entire Mississippi movement became involved in preparing for the hearing. Teams of COFO organizers, summer volunteers, and whenever possible, one of the movement lawyers went into every section of the state where an act of violence had occurred over the past three years and met directly with the people involved, to take their affidavits supporting the sweeping charges of conspiracy. These teams carried with them mimeographed copies of our federal complaint, which became a teaching tool in and of itself. In addition, we experienced boldly with the taking of formal depositions from key defendants throughout the state. Carefully organized, the act of serving a federal subpoena on a local sheriff for the purpose of taking testimony was a sensational event in a town or local community. Although we were able to set up only a few of these events in the three weeks before the hearing, they proved so successful in raising morale in local situations that they became a regular tool in other actions during the next year.

In the course of preparing for the hearing, we also relearned a fundamental lesson. In helping to raise the morale of a people's movement, nothing is more crucial than to fashion forms of action which, if even for a moment, transform those attacked into the accusers, turning the tables and placing the people themselves in the rare position of being the prosecutors. Even the simple act of taking formal affidavits from people who had suffered the violence had a tremendous morale-building effect. For a COFO team to arrive a day after an episode of violence, explain to the people involved what we were doing to fight back, and then formally record the events for presentation to a federal court had a profound effect upon the entire community. They were no longer just isolated victims of an overwhelming force. They were part of an important, organized movement of people fighting back and demanding the enforcement of national law.

Perhaps even more fundamental was the lesson we relearned about organization while preparing for the hearing—a lesson that was much easier for the Black people of Mississippi and for the movement organizers from all over the country to come to grips with than it was for the lawyers. The ultimate purpose of the intensive activity in support of the COFO-Rainey lawsuit could not be any expectation that this legal thrust, sound as it was in principle and valid as it was in terms of historical background, could in and of itself provide the answer to the conspiracy of the white power structure against the Freedom Movement. Only the solid and lasting organization of the Black people themselves, in the towns and cities and throughout the state, demanding a share in the political process, could provide any meaningful defense against the violence and oppression of the power structure. A strong, broad-based movement was the most meaningful response to the murders of Chaney, Schwerner, and Goodman. Only to the degree that the lawsuit provided an arena in which people could learn to work together and to experience the possibility of fighting back did it serve a valuable purpose. And only to the degree that it said to people, in terms they could understand, that they had to rely on their own action, no one else's, did it play an important role in sharpening people's understanding of how to move ahead.

Within this perception of the real purpose of the legal struggle, no one was taken by surprise or much upset by the results of the hearing when it took place at the end of July in the federal district court. Judge Sidney Mize, panicked by the overwhelming nature of the evidence we had amassed to present before him, abruptly adjourned the hearing until the following week in Hattiesburg.

253

When the hearing was resumed the next week, the judge was all ready for us. After bitterly attacking the presence of "out-of-state" lawyers, and without even allowing an argument from us, he abruptly dismissed our entire action out of hand.

The reason for this unusual dismissal, without hearing us at all, was clear to the hundreds of movement people who packed into that courtroom. The one thing the Mississippi power structure wanted to avoid at all costs was an open hearing in which the conspiracy of Sheriff Rainey and Deputy Sheriff Price with the Klan would be exposed for the nation to see. Judge Mize had his work cut out for him by his commitment to the establishment. Get rid of the suit, no matter how. And he did.

Four months later, when I was arguing the appeal from his decision before a relatively conservative panel of Fifth Circuit judges in New Orleans, they were horrified at the abruptness and callousness of Judge Mize's refusal to hear our case. Without hesitation, they unanimously reversed his dismissal and ordered our case reinstated. But the desperation of the power structure to avoid any open exposure of the conspiracy in the state during the height of the Mississippi Summer Project had already backfired. The movement was in no sense derailed by Judge Mize's refusal to allow our hearing to take place. Instead, it continued to expose the conspiracy through intensified public activities all over the state, including those in the growing Mississippi Freedom Democratic Party, the independent political form springing out of the Freedom Movement. And when the bodies of Goodman, Schwerner, and Chaney were discovered, a week after Judge Mize's dismissal of our action, in the newly dug dam just beyond Philadelphia where Rainey, Price, and the gang of Klansmen had buried them late that evening in June, the movement's answer was expressed not in the federal courtroom, but in the first statewide convention of its own independent Mississippi Freedom Democratic Party held two days later. As lawyers, we pursued our appeal in the circuit, but deep down we knew that regardless of its outcome, the work we had done in initiating the legal counterattack had played a critically important part in helping the Freedom Movement stand up to the harsh actions of the power structure in Neshoba county and move forward to new heights of struggle in the months to come.

Late that winter, after a sharp reversal by the circuit of the district court's dismissal of our complaint demanding immediate federal action, the Justice Department faced a difficult dilemma. A failure to act now and convene federal grand juries to seek indictments under the old anti-Klan criminal statutes against the Klan murderers of Goodman, Schwerner, and Chaney would leave the Freedom Movement and its lawyers as the only visible enforcers of national law in the erupting cauldron of Mississippi. Rather than face this embarrassment, the Department finally, many months after they should have acted, obtained federal indictments against Price, Rainey, and the other Klansmen.

After long delaying sorties by their defense lawyers up to the Supreme Court itself, where the Court reaffirmed the validity of the Radical Reconstruction anti-KKK laws, convictions were finally upheld against Klan conspirators. The final jail sentences were minor considering the enormity of the offense, but the lessons of the struggle were clear. If the movement itself and the people's lawyers had not taken the offensive in the courts in the early days of July, there never would have been any action—however reluctant—by the federal Justice Department. The legal counterattack had strengthened the most important response of all to the conspiracy of government and Klan terror, organized political action of the Freedom Movement.

9

The Mississippi Challenge

As the freedom movement unfolded in Mississippi, a new dynamic was operating that would profoundly affect our role as people's lawyers. This was the growing awareness of the need for an independent political party of the people as the cutting edge of the movement for equality and freedom. From the first days of Bob Moses' work in the state, this understanding had been at the center of his approach. By the middle of the summer of 1964 the Mississippi Freedom Democratic Party had grown almost overnight into the largest predominantly Black grass roots political organization that the state had seen since the days of Black Reconstruction.

The MFDP sprang from the statewide Freedom Vote, organized by the Mississippi movement in the fall of 1963. In this "people's election" Black Mississippians had cast a "freedom ballot" for Dr. Aaron Henry, the state chairman of the NAACP and a founder of COFO, as Governor, and Ed King, the Tougaloo chaplain and movement leader in whose apartment I had been introduced so directly to the Jackson formula, as Lieutenant Governor. At a statewide convention of the MFDP, held in Jackson on April 26, 1964, over 200 people from all parts of the state met together and agreed to challenge the white-dominated regular Democratic Party, which had ruled Mississippi since the overthrow of the

Black Reconstruction government. A decision was made, which was to bring the MFDP into the national spotlight, to send a delegation in August to the Democratic National Convention in Atlantic City, to challenge the right of the regular all-white delegates to be seated as the representatives of Mississippi. Sixty-eight delegates and alternates were elected for this purpose. As a part of this process of openly confronting the Mississippi power structure, the Jackson convention further decided to run Black candidates for Congress in the regular Democratic Party primary elections in June. This gesture was meant to expose dramatically the almost total exclusion of Black people from the voting process.

On August 6, two days after the discovery of the bodies of the three murdered COFO workers, the MFDP held its second statewide convention in Jackson. With a deep sense of outrage at the murders, Ella Baker, the keynote speaker, expressed what every person sitting in that hall felt when she placed the central focus of attention on the Democratic National Convention in Atlantic City. This was a moment, she said, for the Black people of Mississippi and their growing supporters throughout the country to demand public repudiation of the regular party apparatus controlled by the white power structure. The newly elected chairman of the MFDP, Lawrence Guyot, a young COFO organizer from Pass Christian, Mississippi, was instructed by the MFDP members to deliver a letter to John Bailey, the chairman of the Democratic National Committee, demanding that the sixty-eight Freedom delegates and alternates be seated in Atlantic City in place of the all-white regular delegation, which had been selected, the MFDP charged, by a process from which Black people were totally excluded "in violation of the Constitution of the United States." Full-scale preparations were begun for the assault on Atlantic City. SNCC and CORE sent out word around the country for people to show up in Atlantic City for demonstrations of support for the MFDP delegation's demand for their rightful seats.

And then something happened in Atlantic City which enormously sharpened the understanding of the Mississippi movement leadership as to the dimensions of their struggle and, in its own way, had an impact on Bill Kunstler's and my relationship with that leadership and on our functioning as people's lawyers. During the hectic months preceding Atlantic City, Kunstler and I had not been fully aware of a rather delicate situation in one aspect of the legal work in Mississippi. Life was simply too busy for us to be concerned about the fact that we were not drawn into all of the in-depth discussions preparing for the Atlantic City challenge. We did know that Joseph Rauh, one of the most outstanding leaders of the liberal legal establishment in Washington, D.C., had come into the picture in the spring of 1964 as a lawyer for the MFDP, and that he had taken charge of the legal preparations for the Atlantic City challenge. Rauh was close to Walter Reuther, the president of the Auto Workers Union, and was intimate with the top leaders of the Democratic Party. He did not feel it necessary or appropriate to involve Kunstler or me in any of the legal discussions of strategy for the convention challenge, and frankly, considering the overload of work around *COFO v. Rainey* and the everyday crises of the movement, we were relieved not to be involved.

A few days after the second MFDP convention in Jackson on August 6, we began to have some contact with the Atlantic City preparations. In the middle of our frantic preparations for the first emergency COFO-Rainey appeal, Bob Moses buttonholed Kunstler and me and strongly suggested that we find a way to meet with Joe Rauh to find out, as he put it, whether Rauh needed our help in any way in Atlantic City. Kunstler and I worked out a stop-off in Washington on our next trip back to New York.

The visit with Rauh was strange. From the first words it was clear that he was not in the slightest degree interested in opening up any Atlantic City questions with us. As we left his office after only a few minutes of polite conversation, I realized that our exclusion from the preparatory work around the convention challenge had not been merely a form of division of labor among busy movement lawyers. The coldness that had emanated from Rauh was as marked as any I could remember over the years. But life was still too busy to be overly concerned about what seemed to be a conventional, if unhappy, encounter with the lawyer's traditional reluctance to share the spotlight. None of us was immune to that professional disease, so with a shrug we headed back to our own responsibilities.

The seriousness of the situation, involving far more than mere professional rivalry, did not hit us until after the events at Atlantic City, which rocked not only the Mississippi Freedom Movement but the whole country. Kunstler and I got a full report on what had happened there from the angry MFDP delegates on their return to Mississippi. People were beside themselves with frustration. Upon their arrival at Atlantic City, things had looked wonderful. Key delegations like California, Michigan, and New York were enthusiastically supporting the MFDP challenge to the Mississippi regulars. Reporters were circulating a story that the white regulars would lose hands down on a floor vote. But late the first night, word came through that President Lyndon Johnson himself had called in Senator Hubert Humphrey, his choice for Vice President, and instructed him that there was to be no break with the southern regulars. He must work something out. And Humphrey did. The next morning, the MFDP delegation was confronted with an unbelievable "compromise." All the regulars would be seated, while only two of the MFDP delegates would be seated, not as Mississippi representatives, but as delegates at large. A committee would be set up to examine ways of producing a "fairer" delegation *four years later,* in 1968. Humphrey then lined up all the influential national civil rights and trade union leaders he could find to support his pleas to the MFDP delegates to accept this so-called compromise and not "rock the boat" of the Democratic Party.

For the Mississippi movement this was a moment of crisis, and the MFDP's own lawyer, Joe Rauh, only intensified it. He could not have been more persuasive in attempting to get the MFDP to go along with Johnson and Humphrey. He argued that since the Republican conservative, Barry Goldwater, was threatening to break into the traditional Democratic Party stronghold of the solid South, this was no time to irritate the regular Mississippi Democrats.

After much soul-searching, the Mississippi Freedom delegation responded unanimously in the eloquent words of Fannie Lou Hamer, which would be repeated many times in Mississippi homes, halls and churches in the days to come. "We have compromised with compromises too long. We will not compromise now." When it became clear that nothing better would be offered,

260

the MFDP delegation, to the shock of President Johnson, Hubert Humphrey, and Joe Rauh, left Atlantic City, heads high, resolved to pursue a course of struggle independent of the control of the leadership of the national Democratic Party and those forces within the civil rights and labor movements and the liberal sector that had buckled to the pressures from above.

The power elite in Washington was stunned by this show of independence, strength, and courage. So-called sophisticated observers of the national political scene found it hard to believe that "uneducated Mississippi blacks" would turn down the guidance of "mature" liberals such as Humphrey and Rauh. There could be only one answer, or so Evans and Novak, the nationally known political commentators, wrote several days later in the New York *Herald Tribune.* What happened to the MFDP in Atlantic City "demonstrated some of the insidious dangers facing the civil rights movement in the South," stemming from the fact that the leaders of the MFDP were "dangerously oblivious to the Communist menace to the civil rights movement." A COFO leader pointed out bitterly one evening in Jackson as we were reading the Evans-Novak column, "They just don't think Mississippi Blacks are intelligent enough to see through the establishment maneuvering. We have to have Communists around to lead us by the hand!"

What became clearer and clearer after Atlantic City was that what the national power structure, both South and North, really feared was the potential lesson of the Mississippi experience for all America, the possibility of building a truly independent political party, controlled not by the establishment but by the people at the grass roots. The United States had not seen a political party like this for years.

As a result of the Atlantic City confrontation, the MFDP leadership accepted the reality of the abrupt termination of the legal relationship with Joe Rauh. Shortly thereafter, Bob Moses made it clear to us that the executive committee would like our thinking and advice as to the course of action to follow in the immediate days ahead in terms of the struggles in the political arena. The Mississippi leadership was now looking to Bill Kunstler, Ben Smith, and myself not only as the principal lawyers for the general legal work of the movement but as the lawyers for the political work of the MFDP as well.

And so early in September, Bill Kunstler and I sat in Ben Smith's apartment, in the French Quarter of New Orleans, going over the last draft of the *Dombrowski* brief to the Supreme Court, which was due in Washington at the end of the month, and began kicking around ideas about what kinds of legal and political moves were needed after the turn of events in Atlantic City. At that moment, I sensed again, as in the rough days of the dirty decade, one of the deepest dimensions of the role of a people's lawyer. Our ultimate function was not only to be skillful technicians creatively molding legal concepts to serve the needs of the peoples' movements, but also to be political beings in our own right, independent and equal members of the movement, participating in the formulation of policy and then aiding in its implementation.

This way of working was to lead to a growing acceptance of the lawyer as a political person on an equal level with the other movement people. This process had already begun to take place in Mississippi, and it was unexpectedly accelerated by the lesson of Atlantic City that this dimension of the lawyer as a political being had another side, typified by those lawyers within the movement whose politics tied them at moments of crisis to forces outside the movement. This had been the case with Rauh, whose connections with Johnson and Humphrey and the national leaders of the Democratic Party had proved to be closer than his ties with Bob Moses and Fannie Lou Hamer and the leaders of the MFDP. After this revelation, it was clear that the fundamental attitudes of people's lawyers must be close to those of the movements they were representing, if a sense of confidence and security was to emerge.

Many forces on the national scene, particularly within the Democratic Party, had counted on the influence of "liberal" establishment lawyers, especially Joe Rauh, to guide the growing southern Freedom Movement away from the dangerous perspective of independent political action and, in particular, away from all possibility of building an independent political party. As Evans and Novak had remarked in what we more and more real-

ized had been an incredibly frank description of the events in Atlantic City, "The one bridge between the Freedom party and political reality has been Joseph Rauh, who served as its lawyer."
But at Atlantic City, the Mississippi Freedom Movement dramatically abandoned this "political reality" of allowing their future
to rest solely in the hands of the leadership of the national Democratic Party and its century-old alliance with the southern white
power structure. The lawyer "bridge" was no longer available to
the establishment, for the movement had turned to people's lawyers whom they felt shared their growing conviction that if the
goals of freedom and equality were ever to be met, it was essential
to build organizations for political struggle free of control by the
power structure.

What we did not realize was how upset the establishment
would be at this turn of events. Late in September, the COFO office in Jackson showed us minutes of a meeting which had been
held in New York on September 18, called by the National
Council of Churches and attended by representatives of national
organizations that had participated in the Mississippi Summer
Project. Some of the people at the meeting, led primarily by representatives of the NAACP, had bitterly criticized the MFDP and
COFO leadership, singling out Bob Moses as a "dictator" for
forcing the rejection of Humphrey's "compromise" at Atlantic
City. An open attack had then been launched on all of us COFO
and MFDP lawyers who were associated with the National Lawyers Guild, and the objective of eliminating us from any role or
influence in the Mississippi movement had been placed squarely
on the agenda. Joe Rauh himself had said at the meeting that he
"would like to drive out the Lawyers Guild" because it was "im-
moral to take help from Communists."

When I read this comment in the minutes of the meeting that
the COFO office had sent us, I felt sickened and furiously angry.
In a week I would be filing a brief in the *Dombrowski* case in the
United States Supreme Court, exposing the unconstitutionality of
the efforts of the white power structure in Louisiana to jail people's lawyers like Ben Smith and Bruce Waltzer as "subversive"
because of their association with the National Lawyers Guild,
and here was the same attack being launched by the supposed

"friends" of the Freedom Movement! Ben Smith himself took it with a little more humor than I did. "We must be doing something right," he chuckled, "if they're all so afraid of us."

As in Danville, where the national NAACP had attempted to eliminate Len Holt as a movement lawyer, the pressure mounted on COFO and the MFDP to shift away from work with Kunstler, Smith, myself, and the recently established Lawyers Guild legal office in Jackson, being run so effectively by Claudia Shropshire. At the September 18 New York meeting, Courtland Cox, the representative of SNCC, and Andrew Young, representing SCLC, had resisted the pressures being applied by insisting on a full meeting at which Bob Moses and Jim Forman, one of the top national leaders of SNCC, could be present, as well as the MFDP leadership. At this meeting, held two weeks later, foundation funding and substantial material resources were openly tied to eliminating the influence of the "Guild lawyers." But the response of the movement was as direct as it had been in Danville a year and a half before. The Freedom Movement would make its own decisions as to whom it would work with, money or no money.

Fortunately, we lawyers were much too busy to pay any serious attention to these efforts to eliminate us from the work at hand. For myself, in addition to finalizing the *Dombrowski* brief for filing in Washington at the end of September, preparing for the *COFO v. Rainey* appeals, and throwing myself into the strategy discussions as to what was next after Atlantic City, I was about to start my first semester of teaching at Rutgers University School of Law in Newark, New Jersey.

I had not come easily to this major decision concerning my life's direction. Over the years, friends had occasionally asked me whether I had any regrets about the decision I had made years before when I had told Professors Cheatham and Gellhorn at Columbia Law School that I was in no way interested in teaching law. My response had always been that my feelings about not entering onto the academic road directly out of law school were still the same as they had been when I turned down Professors Matthiessen and Miller's proposals at Harvard several years earlier. It was not for me. Mine had to be a life not of study, contemplation, writing, and teaching, but of action.

Then in April 1964, in the middle of the feverish work around the first *Dombrowski* appeal, Walter Gellhorn called me from Columbia. I had maintained close ties with him over the years and had received his invaluable advice about a number of sensitive civil liberties cases in the Cold War period. But when he said on the phone that he wanted me to take the time to have lunch with Willard Heckel, the dean of Rutgers Law School, to talk about the possibility of teaching there, I almost lost my temper. "Walter," I said, "you know I'm back in full-time practice, and totally committed to the civil rights legal work. I'm not giving that up for teaching." Then he brought me up short by opening up a wholly new direction. "Arthur," he replied, "talk to Willard Heckel. His is the one school in the country that might now understand that the practice of constitutional law is an essential foundation for teaching it."

As it turned out, this was precisely Willard Heckel's approach. To my amazement, he put to me the proposition that my ongoing practice of constitutional law, as it was developing in my work throughout the South, was in his opinion a proper part of the functioning of a professor of constitutional law. He expressed his conviction, which corresponded to my own experiences, that it was in the crucible of reality that the most insightful formulations of legal theory could be shaped and fashioned. As he talked, I remembered a letter I had received years before while at the Anzio beachhead in World War II. It was from Merle Curti, professor of American history at Columbia, with whom I had worked closely in a seminar before being drafted into the Army. Professor Curti had written to me that he felt I was caught in "the conflict between theory and practice—the search in the mind, and the actualities and responsibilities of the social struggle."

Dean Heckel's approach made a great deal of sense. If law teaching could provide the sorely needed economic base for continuing to function as a people's lawyer, and if it could also offer the opportunity for developing the theoretical insights opening up so dramatically in the courtrooms throughout the South and now in the Supreme Court itself, it might be the logical road to travel. And so, after much discussion at home with Susan, Peter, and Joanne, and at the law office with Bill and Mike Kunstler, I decided to let Dean Heckel raise the question with the Rutgers law faculty.

Late in the spring, I received a call from him telling me that the faculty had voted to offer me a position as a full professor with tenure, while accepting my commitment to the ongoing practice of constitutional law in the areas of the civil rights and civil liberties. And while I was down in Mississippi in July, just before the COFO-Rainey hearing, word came through that the university had approved the appointment. Over the years, I have never regretted the call I made to Willard Heckel from Hattiesburg, telling him I would be in Newark at the law school in September. In many ways that I could not conceive of at that moment, Willard Heckel's prophecy that an integration could be achieved between the real world and the law classroom has been fully borne out. He sowed the seeds of a resolution of that conflict which Merle Curti had warned me of between the "search in the mind" and the "actualities and responsibilities of the social struggle."

But in the fall of 1964 I had little time to contemplate the new avenues that might open up from this attempt to bring together the different worlds of active legal practice as a people's lawyer and the remoteness of the university classroom. After agreeing on the final formulations for the *Dombrowski* Supreme Court brief, Ben Smith, Bill Kunstler, and I drove over to Oxford, Mississippi, to take part with the COFO leadership in a two-day meeting to think through the next moves to make following the confrontation in Atlantic City. Out of that weekend was born an idea which would lift the Freedom Movement to new heights and shake the foundations of establishment rule both in Mississippi and in the nation's capital.

Everyone agreed that a way must be found to make clear the national significance of the emergence of the MFDP. This was no one-shot operation designed merely to capture the spotlight at the Democratic National Convention but an expanding organization representing thousands of Black people and a growing number of white supporters. It was essential, Bob Moses stressed, to find a way to continue to force the country's attention on the problem of meeting, as a nation, the unfulfilled commitments of equality and freedom to Black people. The last four years of sweat, blood, and sacrifice in Mississippi, culminating in the summer of 1964, had proved to the movement one fundamental historical truth—that the grass roots struggles of the Black people in the deep South for the enforcement of the most elementary promise of equality required, in addition to their own collective strength, massive national intervention—legislative, judicial, and political—to destroy the centuries-old oppressive machinery that the power structure used to maintain the segregated society. As Atlantic City had made clear, any reliance on the national leadership of the Democratic Party to produce this intervention did not reckon with the strength of the alliance between the northern industrial establishment and the southern power structure. Moses drove home the point that the southern movement itself must swiftly find ways to thrust the issue onto the national scene. We must also reach out across the country to other movements, organizations, and social forces that would support the demand for massive national intervention against the white power structure's continued exclusion of Black people from the most elementary political processes.

Out of Bob Moses' overview, a new approach began to develop at the convention, which stemmed from the experiences of the movement in the Freedom Vote of 1963. Nothing could be clearer than the mockery of the regular elections held in Mississippi. Despite the voter registration drive, Black people were still virtually excluded from the voting process. But when a democratic method of registration and voting had been structured for the first time since Reconstruction in the freedom elections, over 80,000 Black people participated and cast their ballots for freedom candidates. Suddenly an idea took hold of everyone at the meeting. Why not challenge head-on the legitimacy of the regular elections? If the members of Congress from Mississippi were supposed to represent the people of Mississippi, and Black people were totally excluded from that vote, the members of Congress elected at those elections had no right to say they represented the people. Why not challenge directly their right to sit in Congress? If anything, as one of the COFO workers pointed out, Fannie Lou Hamer, Annie Devine, and Victoria Gray, the MFDP candidates for Congress, who had been pushed aside in the last regular Democratic primary vote in June by the total exclusion of Black people from the process, would have more right to sit in Congress if they were elected at a separate Freedom Vote next November than any of the white men who would be elected at the regular election.

That was it. Why not mount a full-scale challenge to the regular Mississippi Congress members? But how to do it in the most effective way? Here the movement people turned to us, the lawyers. Was there some move that could accomplish all of the necessary objectives—strengthen the grass-roots structure of the MFDP, raise the morale of the active organizers, force the issue into the national arena, and provide opportunities of reaching out for allies throughout the country? This question went to the heart of our responsibilities as people's lawyers. Our task was to find a legitimate, realistic form for such a campaign, which would yet be fluid and flexible enough to meet the pressing organizational and political needs of the moment.

Once again, we discovered the answer buried within the framework of the legal system itself. I could hardly believe my eyes when I stumbled across a federal statute from the old days that was exactly what we were looking for. It provided that when someone wished to challenge an election to the House of Representatives as improper or illegal, the "contestant," as that person was called, was required to serve a "notice of challenge" in writing on the person challenged, with a copy sent to the Clerk of the House. The "contestor," as the person challenged was called, was required to serve an answer. The contestants could then take evidence in support of their charges of illegality or impropriety in the elections. Subpoenas had to be issued to anyone from whom the contestant wished to take testimony on the challenge. The statute provided for enforcing these subpoenas and for taking testimony anywhere in the United States. After the taking of testimony, the evidence would be submitted to the Clerk of the House, who was required to print it up both for the public and for every member of the House. The decision on the challenge to the election would then be made first by the Committee on Elections and finally by the House of Representatives itself.

This formal procedure seemed too good to be true. After the two November elections, regular and freedom, we could publicly challenge the members of Congress formally elected from Mississippi, demand the seating of the MFDP candidates, and take the offensive organizationally from one end of the state to the other, armed with the federal subpoena power which the Justice Department itself had been hesitant to use against the power structure—as shown in their failure to invoke the federal criminal laws immediately after the murder of the three civil rights workers in Philadelphia, Mississippi. I could just see the expression on Sheriff Rainey's face as we slapped a federal subpoena on him "commanding" his presence at a hearing of ours! To cap it all, we could force a national hearing within Congress itself on the illegality of the regular Mississippi elections. This would provide the occasion for reaching out all over the country for national support.

And then came the best part. In checking the annotations on the statute, I discovered that this was the very procedure which southern Black people had used during Radical Reconstruction to challenge the white plantation owners seated in Congress. It had been effectively buried since then, along with all the other weapons of possible federal intervention against the white power structure.

As quickly as possible, we pulled together a memo for the MFDP leadership proposing this approach based on the federal statute. Larry Guyot's response was wildly enthusiastic, and planning went into high gear. Freedom elections for Congress took place from October 31 through November 2 in three of the five congressional districts in the state, with Fannie Lou Hamer, Victoria Gray, and Annie Devine, the MFDP candidates, winning against the white regulars on the ballots. A national campaign in favor of the Challenge was planned, with support committees set up in New York, Philadelphia, Boston, Detroit, Chicago, San Francisco, Newark, and Pittsburgh. The Washington office of the MFDP was expanded with the addition of two full-time staff workers. Everything was now heading toward the organization of a mass delegation to Washington for the opening of Congress on January 4, 1965, to support whatever action developed within the House.

The timetable of the Challenge campaign, spelled out by the

statute, called for formal challenges to be filed within thirty days after the contested election. The other side would then have thirty days to answer, or up to January 1, 1965, just before the opening of Congress. Thereafter we would have up to forty days, or through January and part of February, for the taking of testimony.

The scope of the campaign and the tightness of the timetable meant that we had to organize our own work as lawyers as never before. And because of the close relationship between the legal process and the political campaign, a merger of legal and political roles was inevitable. The work around the Challenge brought these two different aspects in the life of a people's lawyer closer together than almost any other struggle in which I was ever involved.

I felt this most keenly when Larry Guyot asked me to the first conference called by the MFDP in Washington late in November, where the mobilization of national support for the Challenge would be set in motion. Because of the press of the legal work, I was a little hesitant to go, and I questioned him whether a lawyer was really needed for anything at such a conference. Guyot replied, "We need a Challenge lawyer to help explain why it's really important." And he was absolutely right.

As I stood before that group of community organizers from all over the country, side by side with Vicky Gray, Annie Devine, Fannie Lou Hamer, and Larry Guyot, explaining the urgency of organizing support for the Challenge, I felt myself speaking primarily not as a lawyer but as a political person. Of course, I elaborated upon many of the legal concepts behind the Challenge, based on the unfulfilled promises of the Constitution itself. But what touched me most and what I tried passionately to make clear was my deep sense of the historical importance of being a part of this reaching out of the southern Freedom Movement to people's movements, white and Black alike, from different parts of the country. When I had finished speaking, I knew that my role at the meeting was much more than that of merely a legal technician, as helpful as that can often be. This became clearer when Fannie Lou Hamer came up to me afterward and said that she felt people had really been listening as I talked. Then, with a smile, she said something that I have often remembered in meetings or in courtrooms when I find myself slightly carried away by the occasion, "You must have been a Baptist preacher in your other life."

The conference set in motion the organization of rallies and public meetings all over the country. Kunstler, Smith, and I were called upon constantly to speak along with the MFDP leaders. We grew closer and closer to each other as we spent hours together working out the tactical details of how to convince as many congresspeople as possible to support us in the Challenge on that first day of the new session. On December 5, formal notices of challenge were served on the five white men elected at the regular November elections. The five contestants were Fannie Lou Hamer, Victoria Gray, and Annie Devine, the MFDP candidates, and a representative of the Black community from each of the two congressional districts in which we had not been able to hold freedom elections, Augusta Wheaton and Rev. Allen Johnson. And on December 24, Representative William Fitz Ryan, who had responded positively to the Challenge from the first moment in November when a delegation of Black and white community activists and trade unionists from his own district, the upper west side of Manhattan, had come to enlist his support, announced publicly that he and sixteen other members of the House of Representatives were prepared to challenge the right of the Mississippi regulars to be sworn in on the first day of the new Congress.

As the final step in our preparations, with the active help of the Lawyers Guild we lined up over one hundred lawyers to come into Mississippi from January 20 to February 12 for an intensive period of evidence-taking on both the exclusion of Black people from the voting process and the climate of terror and intimidation in the state. Briefing sessions to prepare these lawyers politically and technically for this unprecedented legal operation were held in four different sections of the country. COFO and MFDP workers throughout Mississippi organized teams of local people to prepare the communities to give the testimony and to work with the lawyers. In every sense, we were ready for that moment of history when Representative Ryan would rise to his feet and challenge the right of the representatives of the Mississippi white power structure to be sworn in as representatives of the people of Mississippi.

Everything was building for January 4. Early that morning over six hundred people from Mississippi arrived by bus in Washington to join several thousand people from other parts of the country. At a preliminary briefing at the Lincoln Memorial Temple, Larry Guyot deeply touched the feelings of everyone crowded into the hall when he said that the Challenge "will once again bring to America's attention the repression and intimidation under which Mississippi's Negroes live and die." Fannie Lou Hamer sounded the note that became the theme of the undertaking, saying, "We are here for our own people—and we are here for all the people."

In that spirit, everyone left the hall for different tasks. Most of the Mississippi people had been assigned to a massive, last-minute lobbying effort in the offices of Congress, while everyone else headed for picket lines at the Justice Department and White House. At noon everyone was to gather at the steps to the Capitol building. Those who could not get into the visitor's gallery would conduct a silent vigil in front of the Capitol during the session itself.

On the morning of January 4, Bill Kunstler and I were closeted with Representative Ryan in his office, together with Guyot and the three main MFDP challengers, for a final tactical discussion before Congress opened at noon. In the few weeks before the opening day, we had all developed a feeling of confidence in Ryan. He not only had agreed to open the challenges in the House but had taken the leadership in seeking support for a "fairness resolution," providing that no one should be permitted to sit in the Mississippi seats until the MFDP challenges were finally decided by the entire House.

Ryan quickly reviewed the situation with us as things then stood. The first formal act of the new Congress would be the swearing in of all the new members by the Speaker of the House, John McCormick. Ryan and a number of other members of the House—he was not at all sure how many—would then invoke an ancient tradition we had unearthed in plowing through the oldest records of Congress. If a member objected to the swearing in of any other member, that member could be required by the Speaker to stand aside while everyone else was sworn in. The House would then have to handle separately the question of how to proceed. Ryan warned us that there was no indication yet what action the Speaker would take at that critical moment, but he was prepared to throw down the gauntlet and launch the Challenge.

Then Ryan cut to the heart of what was happening in Washington that day. He looked at us all sitting in his office and said quietly, "I'm with you all the way on this. You should know that I've rarely seen such fear in the top level upstairs as they seem to have of what you folks are doing here." We knew what he meant. For the past two weeks stories had been circulating around the Capitol that top figures in the Democratic Party and in the White House itself were frantically urging Congress members not to vote to refuse to seat the Mississippi regulars. Those high in the establishment were frightened, as no grass-roots development had affected them for many years, by the implications of this effort of southern Black people to reach out for national ties and relationships with labor and community people all over the country. Such a development not only threatened the future of the southern white power structure but also had the potential of challenging the historic method of control over the entire country that the national establishment had relied on for almost a century, the deep underlying alliance between the northern and southern power structures, recemented after the burial of Radical Reconstruction in the Hayes-Tilden betrayal of 1877, and which manifested itself through its subtle and sometimes open control of the two-party system which had dominated political life in the country ever since.

This underlying sense of the history of the past and perspectives for the future lay heavy on us as we sat in the section of the gallery that had been reserved for the contestants and their lawyers, watching anxiously as the Speaker called the House to order for the first session of the Eighty-ninth Congress. As I looked around the galleries filled with hundreds of Black faces from Mississippi and all over, I thought to myself, "This must throw the fear of God into the Dixiecrats seated down there!" And then the long-awaited moment came. The Speaker called the name of Thomas Abernathy, First District of Mississippi, and Bill Ryan jumped to his feet. With the words, "I object, Mr. Speaker, to the swearing in of Mr. Abernathy," the Challenge was launched.

Almost before Ryan could lay out the basis for our statutory challenge, from every section of the House floor members jumped to their feet, calling out, "We join the gentleman from New York. We object to the swearing in of the Mississippi delegation." Over fifty members rose to join with Ryan. We looked at each other startled. We could hardly believe the sight. Nothing like this had happened on the floor of the House for many years. You could feel the waves of excitement speed through the packed galleries.

Then all eyes turned toward the Speaker. What would he do? Would he treat the Challenge seriously or try to brush it aside? The hall was deadly quiet. Then the words came out, "According to the rules of this House, the gentleman from Mississippi will step aside until all other members are sworn in." There it was. One after another, the five white representatives of the Mississippi power structure were objected to and then remained seated on the side, while every other member stood to be sworn in. It was an unbelievable moment. Everything welled up inside me and I could hardly restrain myself from jumping and cheering. Victoria Gray leaned over in her seat and whispered to me, "We did it. Even if just for this moment, we did it." That feeling was surging through every Black person from Mississippi in the packed galleries, and every Black and white supporter from the rest of the country. Although the fight had just begun, once again I was experiencing the inestimable value of even a moment of triumph, however brief, in strengthening and galvanizing the participants in a what may be long and often disheartening struggle.

The final outcome of the morning, though not total victory, was far better than any of us had expected. Carl Albert of Oklahoma, the majority leader and one of the most powerful leaders of the Democratic Party, put before the House a resolution permitting the Mississippi members to be sworn in but in effect recognizing the legitimacy of our Challenge by providing that the questions involved in the election of these members "should be dealt with under the laws governing contested elections." This would allow us to proceed with the rest of the Challenge—the taking of testimony that would lay the basis for a final decision by the House itself. Both Ryan and Representative James Roosevelt from California, President Franklin Roosevelt's son, urged that Carl Albert's resolution be defeated, so they could submit the "fairness" resolution providing that no one should be seated in the Mississippi seats until all the evidence had been taken and our challenges had been fully heard and debated by the House. As Roosevelt put it to the House, "They cannot win 'elections' based on murder and then claim the right to govern free men."

However, it was clear that the leadership of both the Democratic and the Republican parties did not want a formal showdown on the question of immediate seating. Albert jumped up and called for a voice vote on his resolution. To our surprise, Representative Edith Green of Oregon rose and demanded a roll call vote on Albert's motion. "Let everyone put themselves on the record on this one," she insisted. Since more than twenty percent of the members rose to support her, it went to a roll call. We were absolutely astounded by the number of House members who voted against Albert's motion, voting in effect not even to seat the Mississippi members pending our Challenge. We counted up 149 voting against Albert's motion and therefore standing with Bill Ryan and James Roosevelt. But the two party leaderships combined were able to muster 276 votes, and Albert's resolution passed, seating the Mississippi members pending our Challenge, but recognizing the legitimacy of the Challenge and directing the proceedings as required by the statutes to move ahead.

The meeting that evening at the Memorial Church was in the nature of a celebration. None of us had dreamed we would receive so much support on the floor of the House. Larry Guyot informed the assemblage that over one hundred lawyers were all set to come down to Mississippi to help with the next step, gathering the evidence needed to refute the unbelievable statements by the representatives of the regular Democrats that they had "no knowledge" of the exclusion of Black people from the voting process. The hall exploded with cheers. "We're ready, we'll show them," echoed throughout the church. The mood was fully captured in Guyot's cry ending the rally, "Back to work!" The movement was now totally geared up for massive grass-roots participation in the next stage of the Challenge, the taking of testimony to support the charges of illegal and unconstitutional elections.

The morning after the Challenge had been launched, I received a call from Michael Kunstler at the New York office which dramatically reminded me that a people's lawyer must often confront totally contradictory demands. Michael thought I should know that a notice from the Clerk of the Supreme Court had been sent to me at the office, informing me that oral argument in the *Dombrowski* appeal was set for January 24, 1965—barely three weeks away.

The next day I threw myself into preparation for the coming argument and tried to clear my head of all the tactical thinking of the last weeks' intense work on the Challenge, in order to re-enter the theoretical world of concepts that seemed to envelop the *Dombrowksi* Supreme Court argument. At first, I felt that these were two separate, distinct, and in many ways conflicting worlds. One was the world of political struggle around the Challenge, the other was the world of theoretical struggle around the impending Supreme Court argument. And then, as I immersed myself in the preparation, rereading our brief, John Wisdom's opinion, and Louisiana's opposition papers, it struck me once again that a people's lawyer is constantly faced with the necessity of synthesizing such seemingly opposing roles. Throughout the *Dombrowski* struggle we had been fashioning a legal weapon to counter the power structure's attack on the people's movement within the judicial arena, whereas throughout the Challenge we had been fashioning a weapon to be used by the people's movement against the power structure within the political arena. These two very different approaches called for different skills, different techniques, different vocabularies. But it gradually dawned on me how close and interconnected the two struggles really were. At the heart of both battles was the direct mass action of the Black people of the South to enforce the constitutional promise of equal participation in the political processes of the nation. In the Dombrowski, Smith, and Waltzer arrests, the state antisubversive statutes were being used by the state against the movement's major

276

voter registration campaigns; in the Challenge, statutory procedures were being used by the Freedom Movement to enforce the
constitutional guarantee of the right to vote. In both arenas, we
were calling on the highest branches of the national government,
the Congress and the Supreme Court, to meet their responsibilities to enforce the constitutional mandates to protect the fundamental rights of Black citizens.

This growing recognition of the strong connection between the
two struggles helped me to face the difficult problems of preparing for what was my first experience arguing before the nation's
highest court. What had to emerge out of my argument was the
centrality to the case of the national commitment to enforce the
constitutional promise of equality in the right to vote. From this
flowed all the complicated theoretical questions we had spelled
out in the brief. I faced a dilemma which was one I would run
into every time in the future I prepared a Supreme Court argument. It was whether to be "lawyer-like," to discuss the intricacies
of the conceptual problems "calmly" and "carefully," as so many
friends in the profession advised me, or to lay it out much more
bluntly, to "say it like it is," as my movement friends put it.

The night before the argument, as I sat in a Washington hotel
room stewing over my notes, the answer came to me. I had noticed in the Washington newspapers that on the day following our
argument, the Justice Department would be arguing in another
case before the Court that the voter registration statutes of Louisiana were unconstitutional. There was a general feeling that without much dissent the Court would agree that these laws, part
of the Jim Crow legislation of the 1880s and 1890s, must be
thrown out. This was my window into reality, and it shaped my
argument the next morning. "What is the good," I would ask the
Court, "of striking down unconstitutional voting laws in Louisiana if, on the other hand, we permit the harassment and intimidation of civil rights workers seeking to enforce the guarantee of the
right to vote?" This was the key to all of the complicated theoretical questions which at first seemed so overwhelming.

The next day as I stood before the Court, I faced what was in
many ways the most severe personal test since my re-emergence
from the years of illness. Openly, in the highest court in the land,

I was defending the approaches I had fashioned, rather than safely retreating, as I had done at times in the old days, behind the protective cover of having someone else put them forward. And as I spoke, I realized something that would guide me whenever I faced the same challenge again. The lawyer-like approach *was* in fact to "say it like it is." What was essential in an argument before the High Court was what was essential in any struggle: to cut through to reality. This was the heart of everything which happened that morning in Washington.

Leon Hubert, a member of the New Orleans bar and the Tulane Law School faculty and an old friend of Ben Smith and Bruce Waltzer, shared the argument with me. He dealt effectively with the question of the unconstitutionality of the antisubversive statutes. My focus was on the critical question of whether there was federal power to intervene and to enjoin these state court proceedings. As I approached this sensitive issue of federal-state relationships, I could sense the skepticism of several members of the Court. But when I addressed myself directly to the reality of the situation, I felt a response from across the bench. Chief Justice Warren and Justice White pulled back a little, almost startled, at my statement that Louisiana's intention was to use these antisubversive statutes against the entire civil rights movement involved in voter registration work. To make the point, I read a statement from the report of the Louisiana Un-American Activities Committee, the center of the conspiracy, "The Committee finds that the Southern Christian Leadership Conference and the Student Non-Violent Coordinating Committee are substantially under the control of the Communist Party through the influence of the Southern Conference Educational Fund and the Communists who manage it." I could practically hear the gasps across the bench. When Justice White asked if that report was in the record, I told him that Louisiana, apparently quite proud of it, had attached it as an exhibit to their brief in this Court.

As the meaning of this sank into the Court, I decided to make the point that went to the core of all the elaborate theoretical questions that the case presented. Pointing out to the Justices that they knew well that Martin Luther King, SCLC, and SNCC were leaders in the voter registration movements throughout the South, I emphasized that Louisiana was seeking sanction to use its antisubversive statutes to outlaw and undermine these voter registration and equality movements. This was contrary to the highest national policies and interests. I could not resist a final thrust at the antisubversive statutes, as being "in direct conflict with the essence of national security, a free people functioning in a democratic society." Everything else in our fine-spun theoretical arguments flowed from this. What was essential was a clear perception by the Justices of what was actually happening in Louisiana—the use of the state antisubversive statutes to interfere with the efforts of the Freedom Movement to enforce the national constitutional commitment to the equal participation of Black people in the political life of the nation.

On that note, I ended with as strong an appeal as I could make for the High Court to step in and require the federal district courts in the South to meet their constitutional responsibilities. Thinking specifically of Judges Cox and Mize in Mississippi and Judges West and Ellis in Louisiana, I said to the Justices that it was essential for them to reassert the primary duty and responsibility of the federal district courts to protect federal constitutional rights. Otherwise, I warned the Court, the only judicial tribunals in the deep South capable of protecting these rights would virtually close down. And such a closing down of the federal courts would create a constitutional crisis of major proportions.

This allowed me to deal with the trickiest technical obstacle of all to winning the case. Was there, in the words of the old English law, "an immediate and irreparable injury" sufficient for a court to issue an injunction? The answer to this question came from the harsh reality of the plans of the southern power structure. The effect of these statutes was to frighten people from using their elementary rights under the First Amendment to associate together in civil rights organizations, to speak freely, to assemble. Life in the South had shown that without the free exercise of these liberties, it was impossible to enforce the right to register and vote. And if people were afraid, if they were chilled in the use of their First Amendment rights, then the basic process of democracy, a free election system, would not exist in the South. And that, I put to the Court, was the greatest "immediate and irreparable injury" the nation could suffer.

With the light flashing on the rostrum, indicating that my time was up, I sat down. The members of the Court had been very quiet. I felt that they had listened carefully throughout my argument with very few interruptions. But when the lawyer for Louisiana got up to argue, they opened up on him with dozens of questions. Chief Justice Warren and Justice White prodded him about the vagueness of the definitions of "subversive" in the Louisiana statutes. At one point, Justice White stopped the Louisiana lawyer in mid-sentence and asked him whether he himself knew what a "subversive" organization was. The lawyer answered that if even one Communist belonged to it, it was probably subversive, if he was "wealthy enough to control it." Leon Hubert and I looked at each other and smiled, and Hubert quickly wrote me a note, "No rebuttal needed on this one."

As Leon Hubert, Bill Kunstler, and I left the Supreme Court building, along with Ben Smith and Bruce Waltzer who had come up from New Orleans for the argument, we shared a feeling that while we had been able to put our case in full, there was no telling how the Court would go. Smith was optimistic enough to predict that we had at least gotten two or three good dissents. Then we engaged for a while in the classic post-mortem, until Ben Smith cut short our useless speculation with a remark I have often remembered at similar moments, "I'm only sure of one thing. You all have done a really good job. What they'll do, they'll do." And soon we were talking of the wild developments taking place in Mississippi around the Challenge depositions, letting the afternoon's argument drop into the "waiting for a decision" receptacle that I was learning to keep at the back of my mind while life continued on other levels.

It was clear from what Kunstler and Smith said that the work on the Challenge was going extremely well. That work had forced us to enter an exciting new stage of our legal work. We had begun to function as a group to a much greater degree than ever before, consciously dividing responsibilities among ourselves. When I had been swept back into preparing for the *Dombrowski* Supreme Court argument, Smith and Kunstler had asked our old friend Morty Stavis to take over primary responsibility for organizing the activities of the now almost one hundred and fifty lawyers ready to go into the state to take depositions. Stavis was now down in Jackson, supervising this unbelievable influx of lawyers and setting up the testimony-taking teams.

Out of the intensity of the collective work relationship among Bill Kunstler, Ben Smith, Morty Stavis, and myself that winter, the idea developed that as movement lawyers we needed an organization of our own to encourage and strengthen this essential way of working together. This was the genesis of the Center for Constitutional Rights, which has grown and expanded in many directions over the years, and which to this day continues effectively to support the work of people's lawyers in every arena of legal struggle. Organizing the Center also marked a coming of age for us in terms of understanding our own role and responsibilities. Functioning in one of the most egocentric of professions, we had come to recognize the need for people's lawyers to find ways of working together in an ongoing planning group, tied to each other by mutual commitment.

The feedback coming in from the many lawyers who were involved in taking the Challenge testimony was astonishing. I could not remember another time over the years when there had been such a degree of excitement among lawyers. During the period allowed by the statute, depositions were taken from over six hundred witnesses in Mississippi. Teams of lawyers and COFO and MFDP organizers went into thirty-three counties to hold hearings at which testimony was taken. These hearings in turn generated discussions of the Challenge and of the MFDP, often resulting in an acceleration of organizational activity in the county. On carefully selected occasions, the lawyer-organizer teams used the federal subpoena power given to them by the statute to haul representatives of the power structure before gatherings of community people, where they were forced to testify to specific incidents of violence and intimidation and to the wholesale exclusion of Black people from the registration and voting process. Each of these occasions was an organizing experience of great importance. The net result of the concentrated drive, in addition to over 15,000 pages of testimony supporting the Challenge, was a strengthening of the MFDP organization all over the state.

At the same time that this activity was sweeping through Mississippi, the lawyer-organizer teams held hearings in nine northern cities, taking testimony not only from COFO Summer Project volunteers who had gone home but also from doctors, ministers, and lawyers who had been in Mississippi supporting the movement and had personally experienced the violence, fear, and repression. As a result of these hearings, Challenge support committees were set up throughout the country, which threw themselves into a massive lobbying effort to line up commitments from congresspeople for the final showdown in the House of Representatives sometime in the late summer or early fall.

As we sat in the Washington office of the MFDP late in March, going over the volumes of depositions and talking out the next steps with Michael Thelwell and Jan Goodman, who were working around the clock as the Washington coordinators of the Challenge, one thing was apparent to everyone. This deposition period had been a moment beyond belief for lawyers and movement organizers alike. It showed us all the practical reality of people's lawyering, which was the use of a legal skill or technique to help advance the organizing of a popular movement.

Other events in the winter of 1965 contributed to a heightened national concern with the issues of the Challenge. The introduction of the new Voting Rights Bill in Congress, providing for federal registrars in every county, offered exciting new avenues for the enforcement of the right to vote, if a powerful, organized movement existed strong enough to use these new opportunities. The Selma-to-Montgomery voting rights march, in which many of us took part, helped focus national attention on the questions that the Challenge was bringing to the fore.

On April 24, the MFDP took a major step to develop the national relationships necessary to prepare for the showdown in the House. The MFDP issued a call "to the American people of all communities, the Civil Rights Movement, the Churches, the Unions" to meet in Washington at a weekend conference to plan "the final national effort to unseat the Mississippi Congressmen, and what this Challenge will mean in terms of bringing truly free and open elections throughout the South." In words reflecting the need felt by so many activists in the rest of the country to find ways of organizing locally, the MFDP called for full discussion of "organizing in the north for FREE ELECTIONS in 1965. How do we

282

mobilize and focus the aroused conscience of the nation so that the shock of Selma, Montgomery, and Mississippi will be translated into action in their home communities?"

Over four hundred delegates from all over the country responded. In an atmosphere that was electric, they sat in the Metropolitan A.M.E. Church in Washington and listened to speeches from Larry Guyot, Fannie Lou Hamer, Victoria Gray, and Annie Devine. The appeal for a national mobilization for the final showdown of the Challenge met with strong support from James Farmer, the executive director of CORE, Jim Forman of SNCC, and Robert Spike of the National Council of Churches. At the closing session, Kunstler announced to cheers that over six hundred depositions had been filed that day, and I made a pitch for lining up the congressional votes needed when the Challenge came to the final floor vote. Once again, as at the initial MFDP conference in November, I found myself in a situation where the role of lawyer inevitably merged with that of political person. As I spoke, I was weighed down by the same feeling of overwhelming responsibility that I had felt three months earlier in this same city when before those nine Justices I took on the state of Louisiana and the entire southern power structure in the *Dombrowski* appeal. It was the same fight and the same basic issue, even though the form and context of the two moments were vastly different.

Nothing could have driven this home to me more potently than the message I received back at the law school on Monday morning. The Clerk of the Supreme Court had called. I anxiously returned the call, this being one of those Monday mornings when decisions were handed down. The news was beyond belief. We had won the *Dombrowski* case totally and completely. Justice Brennan had written the opinion. There were only two dissents, Justices Harlan and Clark. The Louisiana antisubversive statutes were declared to be unconstitutional, in violation of the First Amendment. The Federal District Court in Louisiana was ordered to issue an immediate injunction forbidding any prosecution of Dombrowski, Smith, or Waltzer.

None of us had dared to dream of such a victory. Jim Dombrowski had started sketching out a special issue of *The Southern*

Patriot before I even got off the phone. By the end of the day, word had spread from one end of the South to the other. SCEF had won! The Supreme Court of the United States had kicked Louisiana and Jim Eastland right in the teeth! The immediate impact of the victory on the morale of the entire Freedom Movement was overwhelming. Larry Guyot called me from Jackson that evening to get the details of the decision for a special MFDP bulletin. His comment was, "This is going to be great for the Challenge work."

But not until the next day, when I read the advance sheets of Justice Brennan's opinion, did I realize the historic sweep of the decision. Justice Brennan had gone the whole way in approving our fashioning of a federal weapon to restrain the use of state legal machinery which interfered with the exercise of fundamental democratic rights by the people of this country. In words that will live among the most important formulations of constitutional law, Justice Brennan wrote that governmental action which has "a chilling effect upon the exercise of First Amendment rights" must be condemned and prohibited by the federal courts. As I read the opinion, I thought about the many days we had spent developing the theoretical foundations for what was now clearly written out as the law of the land. Once again I was overwhelmed by the feeling, which I had experienced at key moments as a people's lawyer, that victory was not impossible. In different ways and in different forms, it was there to be reached for and utilized in the struggles ahead.

In less than a month, I would experience at first hand the close interaction between these two seemingly separate and distinct developments—the *Dombrowski* Supreme Court victory and the mounting preparations for the Mississippi Challenge. Everything was operating at full steam around the country. While we were jamming out a mammoth brief to be submitted to every member of Congress, summarizing the depositions and passionately demanding a vote of refusal to seat the representatives of the Mississippi power structure, the MFDP was taking the fight back into the streets of Jackson. Day after day, mass marches and demonstrations called for free and fair elections in Mississippi and an end to the atmosphere of terror and intimidation. Then the power structure hit back. Within two days in early June, over eight hundred people were arrested for violating a new local ordinance banning demonstrations near public buildings. The Jackson jail was filled to overflowing; a temporary stockade was set up in the fair grounds. Two hours after the first contingent of people had been pressed into the stockade, six demonstrators were taken to a nearby medical center for treatment of serious head and body injuries received in police beatings.

When the reports of these mass arrests reached us in New York, my heart sank. The Jackson formula was back in full play. But then a phone call from Claudia Shropshire, heading up the new Guild law office in Jackson, suddenly brought the recent Supreme Court decision in *Dombrowski* into the daily reality of the political activities of the thousands of people who were responding to the Mississippi Challenge. "Arthur," she said excitedly, "we're taking the decision in *Dombrowski* into the federal courts to get an order stopping up all the Challenge arrests."

And they did. Nothing could "chill the exercise of First Amendment rights" more than the power structure's use of the Mississippi antidemonstration ordinances. By early July, the Fifth Circuit had granted sweeping injunctions forbidding the massive arrests for demonstrating in support of the Challenge. The decision in *Dombrowski* had become, at least for that historical moment, a powerful weapon in protecting the day-to-day struggles of the Freedom Movement. Spirits among the MFDP leadership were high when the street demonstrations were resumed in Jackson.

The drive emanating from the streets of Jackson had an immediate effect in Washington. For weeks we had been stalled by the Clerk of the House who, under the direction of the House leadership, was holding up the printing of our mammoth collection of depositions, although under the statute printing was an essential step before the Challenge could be heard in the House. Responding to our frustration, Vicky Gray announced at an MFDP strategy meeting in Washington that she would settle the question. The next morning, she and twelve other MFDP members from Mississippi arrived at the Clerk's office on Capitol Hill. They announced to the Clerk and the waiting reporters that they were staying in the office until a decision was made to print the depositions. The news of their sit-in, demanding compliance with Congress' own rules, spread like wildfire through Capitol Hill. By the end of the day they had achieved what all our scholarly legal memos had failed to obtain for over a month. The Clerk rapidly retreated, and the depositions were ordered sent to the printer.

Over the summer, the strategic thinking of the Mississippi Black leadership as to the role of the Challenge became clearer. Increasingly the work was directed toward seeking out forces throughout the country who could identify with the southern Black struggle and begin to understand the relationship of the birth of an independent political party, free of the controls of the old two-party system, to their own interests and needs. Time and again the MFDP and COFO leadership stressed that the legislative showdown on the Challenge in September would probably not result in total victory, the repudiation of the elected representatives of the white power structure and the seating of the representatives of the Freedom Movement. But regardless of its outcome in Congress, the Challenge would be an enormous step forward to the degree that it strengthened the MFDP organizationally in Mississippi and established a national relationship between the southern Black Movement and its allies in the labor and other people's movements throughout the country. Most important of all, it would succeed to the degree that it spread beyond Mississippi the newly born idea of an independent political party outside the control of the power structure.

During the summer rumors were rampant on the Hill that the Democratic Party leaders in the House were quietly reassuring their angry southern colleagues that in one way or another they would get rid of the Challenge. But the plans of the Democratic leadership to cope with this challenge to the political status quo did not develop fully until two new events occurred to jar the establishment. In the course of searching out support for the Challenge, the Mississippi Black leadership entered into discussions with the leadership of a beginning popular movement destined within several years to rock the country to its very foundations, the anti-Vietnam War movement. At a strategy meeting toward the end of July, Guyot told us with some hesitation that the

MFDP had agreed to participate in an "Assembly of Unrepresented People." This was a demonstration planned for the following week in Washington against the rapidly expanding Vietnam War. At the same discussion, he filled us in on a new development in Mississippi about which he seemed a little uncertain as to how to respond. The local MFDP group in McComb was distributing leaflets urging Black mothers to tell their sons not to register for the draft.

This potential alliance with the newly developing antiwar movement generated a conflict within the Freedom Movement. On the one hand, it provided the opportunity for attracting new sources of national support, but on the other hand, it might provoke increased attacks from the entrenched right wing. The hesitations generated by this contradiction were apparent. The MFDP executive committee, Guyot told us, had decided to participate in the Assembly of Unrepresented People. Bob Moses was heading up a Mississippi delegation to march side by side with representatives of the antiwar movement. But at the same time, the MFDP leadership would not endorse the McComb antidraft leaflets. The McComb folk had a right to express their views on the Vietnam War, the MFDP leaders said, but the party was not yet ready to take the plunge and commit itself as an organization to an antiwar position.

The power structure had no equivalent hesitation. It was frankly terrified of the coming together of the Black Freedom Movement with other people's struggles. Upon hearing about this new possibility of a coalition between the Mississippi Freedom Movement and the exploding antiwar movement, Senators Eastland and John Stennis of Mississippi condemned the upcoming Challenge as evidence of a "most dangerous Communist conspiracy." The Mississippi American Legion denounced the McComb MFDP leaflets as "open treason." The director of the State Selective Service issued a hysterical call for a full-scale investigation of the MFDP by the Justice Department. Most serious of all were the secret steps taken by the Federal Bureau of Investigation, which we would not learn about until years later. That summer the FBI launched the infamous Cointelpro program, which had as its primary objective the disruption, if not destruction, of the

Freedom Movement, through the use of secret FBI agents and informers within the people's movements resorting to all manner of illegalities, including even assassination.

But as frightened as the power structure was by the threatening potential of the people's combined strength, it could not derail the MFDP. The first week in August, Bob Moses and his wife, Donna, marched side by side with David Dellinger and Staughton Lynd, two leading antiwar activists, down Pennsylvania Avenue in the Unrepresented People's demonstration. A can of red paint was thrown over all four of them by members of the right wing, vividly symbolizing its effort to "expose" the "red" conspiracy, but this act only heightened the impact of the coming together of the Freedom Movement and the new leadership of the antiwar movement.

Then in early September a totally unexpected development occurred. For the whole year following the crisis at the Democratic National Convention, those sections of the civil rights and labor movement most under the influence of Johnson, Humphrey, and Rauh had pulled far away from supporting the MFDP Challenge. Their anger at the independence shown at Atlantic City by the Black Mississippi leadership still cut deep. Their distance reflected their continued fear that the MFDP's posture threatened to "rock the boat" in terms of their own dependent relationship with the Democratic Party. But by September, as we prepared to join issue with Congress itself, the overwhelming strength of the MFDP position in the broadest sections of the Black and labor community overcame for a moment the fears and hesitations of the more conservative leaders of the civil rights and labor movement. Even the Leadership Conference on Civil Rights, though heavily influenced by Rauh and his friends high in the Democratic Party, at the last moment stood ready to resist the plans of the political establishment to forestall the Challenge. So when the telegrams arrived informing us, as lawyers for the Challenge, that we were to appear with the contestants for a closed hearing on September 13 before the Subcommittee on Elections of the House Administration Committee, we were ready for battle. It was with a feeling of great accomplishment and unified strength that we walked into that sanctum of establishment power, the subcommittee hearings room of the House of Representatives.

The subcommittee, totally controlled by southern Democrats, had turned down our telegraphed demand for open public hearings. Representative Robert Ashmore of South Carolina, the chairman of the subcommittee, abruptly slammed the doors in the faces of the more than two hundred Black people from Mississippi who jammed the corridor of the House building, having come up with us that morning. The nature of the confrontation that the establishment wanted to hide from the public eye was dramatically revealed by the physical setup of the room. On one side sat the five white male representatives of the Mississippi power structure, the regularly elected members of Congress, surrounded by their lawyers, impeccable in their buttoned-down suits, glaring at us. On our side, not three feet away from them, sat the five representatives of the Black people of Mississippi, Victoria Gray, Annie Devine, Fannie Lou Hamer, Rev. Johnson, and Augusta Wheaton. Kunstler, Stavis, Smith, William Higgs, the young lawyer from Mississippi who had worked so closely with us, and I stood squeezed in the back, since not enough seats had been provided for all of us.

From the first moment of the hearing, the approach of the Democratic and Republican leaders of the House was structured to avoid the issues of the Challenge. They had no way to meet the substance of our attack. The evidence was overwhelming that the Black people of Mississippi had been systematically excluded from the election process. The elections of the white representatives of the power structure sitting in that room were wholly unconstitutional. As no one could contest this fact, the leadership came up with an outrageous technicality. The challenges had to be dismissed, they said, without considering the substance of the charges, because the Black contestants had no "standing" to raise the challenges, and they had no standing because they had not appeared as "regular" candidates on the ballot for the general election. This was an absurd argument. How could a Black candidate be on the general election ballot if Black people were wholly excluded from voting in primaries? There was no way in Mississippi law to get on the general election ballot other than through the primary.

289

But that morning, logic and reason meant nothing. As the white Mississippi congressmen argued for dismissal, the essence of their position emerged. William Colmer, one of the five, called the Challenge a "dirty conspiracy" to undermine the fair state of Mississippi, indeed all the southern states, since anything that was said about the Mississippi elections could be said as well about all southern elections. No southerner was safe in his seat in the House unless these challenges were thrown out. What was involved here was "a conspiracy on a national level to disrupt and stop the functioning of the Congress." This was the deep fear gripping these representatives of the white power structure. Colmer went on unexpectedly to lash out at the role we lawyers had played in the preparation of the Challenge. It was, he said, plainly and simply a "well-organized, well-financed group conspiracy," at the heart of which was a bunch of lawyers who were threatening the "disruption" of Congress. At that moment, I remembered the words of Ben Smith after the first Louisiana attacks on him, "We must be doing something right." If ever I felt that we were reaching toward a sound and creative understanding of the role of a people's lawyer, it was when Colmer of Mississippi attacked us so directly.

The five MFDP candidates then presented our case. We all knew that we were witnessing a special moment in history. This was the first time since the burial of Black Reconstruction that representatives of the Black people of the South had stood formally before Congress demanding their rightful places there. Victoria Gray opened dramatically with the bitter words uttered by the last Black congressperson from Mississippi when in 1882 he had fought successfully on the floor of the House for his right to be seated: "You cannot consent to the elimination of colored people from the body politic, especially through questionable and fradulent methods, without consenting to your own downfall and your own destruction." This lesson of history was received in stony silence.

The other MFDP contestants spoke with equal fervor, insisting on the responsibility of Congress to enforce the Constitution and denouncing the subterfuge of the establishment's technical scheme to avoid the Challenge. In concluding, Fannie Lou Hamer interwove the political with the personal, which was one of her great strengths. Standing before the representatives of the white power structure of Mississippi and of the nation, she laid it out in a way which was unanswerable: "By sweeping this challenge under the rug now and dismissing this challenge, I think it would be wrong for the whole country. It is time for the American people to wake up. All we want is a chance to participate in the government of Mississippi. For all of the violence, all of the bombings, all of the people murdered in Mississippi because they wanted to vote, there hasn't been one person convicted. It is only when we speak what is right that we stand a chance at night of being blown to bits in our homes. Can we call this a free country where I am afraid to go to sleep in my own home in Mississippi? . . . It is time for the American people in this country to wake up. I might not live two hours after I get back home, but I want to be part of helping set the Negro free in Mississippi."

Her words left the room in somber silence. This was too much for Ashmore of Carolina. Before Morty Stavis could get in more than a few minutes of legal argument, Ashmore abruptly adjourned the hearings to the next morning. We spent that evening making calls all over the country to alert our supporters that a recommendation to dismiss the Challenge would undoubtedly come to the floor of the House by Friday. Several thousand people, including at least 1500 from Mississippi, were planning on coming to Washington at this last-minute notice in order to lend massive support to those congresspeople who were courageous enough to stand up against the establishment.

The next morning, when Stavis and I ripped into the rationale that the leadership had spun out for sidestepping the Challenge, it was in many ways the easiest legal argument either of us had ever had to make. The atmosphere had been so powerfully set by the movement leaders the day before that for once it was not only possible but essential for us as lawyers to play out a quiet, secondary, purely supportive role. I have rarely felt such satisfaction and pleasure as I did at being able to follow the presentations of the Mississippi spokespeople.

It was no surprise to anyone when the ten-person southern majority of the election subcommittee nevertheless forced through a recommendation that the Challenge be dismissed. The Committee on Administration, by a majority vote in which the conservative Democrats joined with the Republicans, then approved the recommendation. Bill Ryan's office called us Wednesday night to alert us to the fact that this recommendation would definitely come before the full House on Friday morning.

As once again we walked into the section of the House gallery reserved for the contestants and their lawyers, the same feelings swept through us as on that morning almost nine months earlier when the Challenge was launched. We were filled with a sense of strength and optimism, which flowed not from any empty illusion that the Challenge would prevail, but from a well-grounded consciousness that we were part of a people's movement which had effectively and creatively begun to fight. As we sat there waiting for the proceedings to begin, I looked around at the galleries and once again, as in January, saw the hundreds of faces of Black people from Mississippi and all over the country, now along with many white supporters.

Then something happened which set the tone for the proceeding. Accompanied by Bill Ryan and John Conyers, a new Black congressperson from Detroit, who as a Guild lawyer had helped out earlier in Mississippi, Fannie Lou Hamer, Victoria Gray, and Annie Devine were escorted by the sergeant-at-arms onto the floor of the House. A week before, we had discovered an old precedent of the House which held that contestants were entitled to floor privileges during the debate on their challenge. For the first time since the betrayal of Black Reconstruction, representatives of the Black people of the South were walking onto the floor of the House of Representatives. Guyot, sitting next to me, exclaimed the same words that Vicky Gray had spoken when Ryan started the Challenge off in January, "We did it! We did it!"

The spirit of the entire morning was set by the appearance of the three Black women from Mississippi in the well of the House. Bill Ryan opened the floor debate by calling the Challenge "one of the most crucial issues that will ever come before the House." He read a telegram from Martin Luther King, pledging full support to the Challenge. I realized the importance of this statement at this moment, considering the rumors that had circulated all summer concerning a supposed coolness on Dr. King's part toward MFDP and the Challenge. Then, to quash the expectations of the Democratic Party leadership that the more conservative elements of the labor and civil rights movements would not support this "ill-conceived" and "rash" Challenge, Ryan slowly read into the record the long list of names of labor, religious, and civil rights organizations who had joined together to oppose the tactic of dismissal without a full and fair hearing.

One after the other, members of the House took the floor to rip apart the flimsy reasons Ashmore of South Carolina had put forward for introducing the recommendation of dismissal. James Roosevelt pounded away at the inevitable conclusion from the evidence we had presented in the Challenge, saying "The record in the Mississippi contested election cases of 1965 bring before the House overruling evidence of the simple, stark factors upon which these cases rest—the almost total, systematic, and deliberate exclusion of the Negro citizens of Mississippi from the electoral processes of that State." Their exclusion put in question, he said, the basic sources of legitimacy for the institution of the House itself: "The unimpeachable facts of wholesale Negro disenfranchisement make a mockery out of the constitutional requirement that the Members of this House be chosen 'by the people of the several States.' "

The speech of John Conyers of Detroit was particularly impressive. I had met Conyers briefly two years before in Mississippi. From his first day in Washington, in January 1965, he had thrown himself into helping and guiding us through the treacherous pitfalls of the legislative channels of the House. Already we knew him as one of the most committed supporters of the people's movement in the House. As he laid out our case that morning, I knew we had found a friend high on Capitol Hill who would stand closely with us not only that morning, but in the long years to come.

As member after member took to the floor to support our right to a full and fair hearing and to oppose the recommendation of dismissal, it became apparent that we were receiving a solid and substantial show of support, which could not be held back unless the leadership of both parties joined together in a move to cut us off. But that is exactly what happened.

The final plea to dismiss the Challenge came from one of the

Mississippi members, Jamie Whitten, who had been challenged by Fannie Lou Hamer. Whitten's speech was received in an atmosphere of quiet embarrassment. I even thought I saw some members on the floor hold their heads in dismay as Whitten once again singled out the lawyers for the Challenge, in particular the National Lawyers Guild, as centrally responsible for this "well-organized, well-financed national effort" to create "dissension and turmoil."

As soon as he sat down, the top leadership of both parties went into speedy action to put into operation their quiet agreement to get rid of the Mississippi Challenge, no matter how. The Democratic majority leader, Albert, and the Republican leader, Gerald Ford of Michigan, read prepared statements which made it clear that both parties at the highest level wanted the Challenge dismissed. The final showdown was on their motion to dismiss the Challenge for the technical reason of "lack of standing" as found by the subcommittee. This motion was carefully shorn at the last minute of any implications that it "condoned" any practices of illegality in Mississippi. This was obviously a maneuver of the two parties designed to pull over some middle-of-the-road members who had been shaken by our presentation.

In the final roll call vote, the only surprise was the size of the opposition to the combined Democratic-Republican leadership. We received an unbelievable 143 votes opposing the dismissal of the Challenge, to 228 supporting the leadership. We had emerged beyond our wildest expectations with a solid body of support within the House. As I considered the result, I felt that we as people's lawyers, now not just a tiny band but hundreds of us all over the country, had fulfilled our responsibilities. We had found ways to use our knowledge, our skills, and our techniques for the purpose of assisting and advancing the struggle of millions of people for their fundamental rights to freedom, liberty, and equality. No people's lawyer could ask for a greater fulfillment of role than to have taken part in this historic Challenge. Sitting in the gallery observing the vote, I knew that we all—the Mississippi Freedom Movement, SNCC and COFO, the thousands and thousands of fighters, Black and white, throughout the South and throughout the nation—really had done it.

294

That evening Fannie Lou Hamer summed it all up for us when, at a meeting at the Lincoln Memorial Church, she said, "It's not over. We're coming back here, again, and again, and again." The Challenge was just the beginning of a long, hard struggle. This was what she, Annie Devine, Victoria Gray, and Larry Guyot all stressed as they spoke that evening. After the speeches were over and we were leaving, Fannie Lou Hamer grabbed hold of a few of us for a brief discussion. She wanted to make sure that none of the lawyers felt that the fight was over in any way. "We showed them we're for real," she said. "And now we have to build solidly in the state. Let's take the Challenge right to them in the Sunflower County elections this November." That discussion sowed the seeds for the political and legal battles soon to come in Eastland's own home plantation of Sunflower County—battles that would result a year later in an astounding victory in the Fifth Circuit, setting aside as unconstitutional, for the first time since Black Reconstruction, local elections which excluded Black voters.

The Challenge had achieved the objectives set forth by MFDP and COFO leadership a year before. It catapulted onto the national scene the obligation of the entire country to face the century-old betrayal of the commitment to freedom and equality for Black people. It set in motion a process for reaching out to other social forces throughout the country that would support the demand for massive intervention against the white power structure's continued exclusion of Black people from the political process. And perhaps most important, the Challenge aroused the people of the nation to the understanding that an independent political party of the people, free of the control of the establishment, was essential to any successful struggle for freedom and equality.

As we planned the next steps, we had no idea of the many problems that would develop, both within the Freedom Movement itself, South and North, and within the other people's movements throughout the country. These problems would complicate and in some ways undermine or postpone the perspectives that the Challenge had opened up, not only for the people of Mississippi but for all the people of the nation. But at that moment, one thing was clear. Those of us who as lawyers had found

295

ourselves a part of this movement had seen a full flowering of the concept of the people's lawyer in a way we had hardly dreamed possible in the bitter days of the 1950s. This maturing of vision as to role and responsibility would guide me through the difficult days to come, as the Vietnam War intensified and the harsh repression of the Nixon era began.

Arthur Kinoy dragged from HUAC hearing by three federal marshals after Representative Joe Pool, acting chairperson, ordered his removal, August 17, 1966.

Arthur Kinoy announcing appeal of his conviction for disorderly conduct at HUAC hearing, August 19, 1966.

Adam Clayton Powell (second from right), flanked by his attorneys Herbert Reid (right) and Arthur Kinoy, at news conference on Bimini after Supreme Court overruled his exclusion from Congress, June 1969.

Arthur Kinoy and daughter Joanne Kinoy in front of Foley Square courthouse in New York after grand jury hearing, January 5, 1971.

Arthur Kinoy arguing before Court of Appeals in Chicago Seven case, February 24, 1972. Foreground: Leonard Weinglass (left) and Bill Kunstler, trial lawyers.

10

HUAC,
Adam Clayton Powell,
and the Chicago Seven

I did not have long to wait to discover that the weapons of counterattack we had forged in *Dombrowski* and the southern Black Freedom Movement had a critical usefulness in arenas of battle seemingly far removed from the one in which they were born. Early in May 1965, while putting together the final draft of the Challenge brief in my new office at the law school in Newark, working with a number of students who had gotten excited about the possibility of immersing themselves in something a little more real than the latest casebook assignment in torts or contracts, I was interrupted by a call from Chicago. It was from Jeremiah Stamler, a close friend from my student activist days and now one of the world's leading cardiologists and research experts in the area of the causation and prevention of heart disease.

For years, Jerry Stamler had consistently identified himself with the movements of people's struggle, and he was now as outspoken an opponent of the rapidly escalating Vietnam War as he had been in the 1950s of the United States involvement in the Korean War. He sounded a little pressed over the phone as he asked if we could get together that evening in New York. My first reaction, in view of the impending deadline for the Challenge brief, was to say I could not make it that night. Then he dropped a bombshell. "Arthur," he said, "I've just been served with a subpoena from the House Un-American Activities Committee, returnable within the next two weeks here in Chicago. I've got to talk to you. What am I going to do?"

I was stunned. Although I had known that HUAC, that Cold War instrument of repression, was coming back to life as opposition to the Vietnam War grew all over the country, this was the first time in years it had touched me so closely. Jerry Stamler once again invoked in me the deepest responsibility of a people's lawyer, to be there at the moment of crisis and to think through, along with the people involved, the strategic direction to take. So we met, and out of our discussion emerged a whole new approach to the seemingly endless struggle against the committee.

Instead of falling into any of the defensive traps that had developed during the long, hard years of HUAC's attacks on the people's movements, we decided to apply the fundamental lesson we were learning so well in the southern struggles, to counterattack. If the vague words of the Louisiana antisubversive statutes created a "chilling effect" on the utilization of the First Amendment liberties, requiring the intervention of the federal courts to stop their enforcement, as had recently been commanded by the High Court in *Dombrowski,* why was not a similar attack possible on the congressional resolution that had set up HUAC? Nothing in the history of the country was more directly designed to "chill the exercise of the First Amendment liberties" by the people than the House Un-American Activities Committee. Why not challenge its power even to exist?

Jerry Stamler was tremendously excited by the possibilities of this approach. For years he had been involved in countless battles for democratic rights in Chicago. Now, because of his medical reputation, he was in a position of national and international prominence, and he wanted to use in a positive way the attention that the committee hearing would inevitably focus on him. Therefore, he was looking for a response to the subpoena that would reject out of hand the choice the committee had always presented: either become an informer and accomplice in smearing other people, or hide in a defensive posture by invoking the constitutional privilege not to talk. The application of the *Dom-*

browski concept to HUAC offered the possibility of a wholly different approach: a frontal attack upon the legitimacy of the committee itself. This was exactly what Stamler was searching for, an approach that would develop the widest possible opposition to the committee among the people with whom he worked, doctors and scientists throughout the country, by opening a dignified and persuasive attack on the legitimacy of the committee's very existence.

Then Jerry Stamler threw out a question at me that was to provide an opening into a new way of work for people's lawyers, permitting at critical moments the development of support from some of the most influential sections of the American bar. In his capacity as director of one of Chicago's most important heart research projects, he had worked for years with top business executives, including heads of the city's leading newspapers. When the subpoena was served, some of these people had suggested that their lawyers advise Stamler. These lawyers in turn had suggested that Albert Jenner, senior partner in an illustrious Chicago law firm and a highly respected figure in Illinois and national law, might be interested in participating in Stamler's defense before the committee. Jerry Stamler asked me if I would be willing to talk to Jenner in Chicago about the approach we were discussing. It would have a considerable impact in Chicago, he pointed out, if Albert Jenner were to join in this attack on the legitimacy of the committee.

At first, everything within me said "nonsense." But Jerry Stamler persuaded me it was worth a try. Two days later, we found ourselves in a marathon six-hour meeting in Bert Jenner's office in Chicago, talking through the fundamental questions involved with him and one of his young partners, Thomas Sullivan, who was to become a close friend and colleague during the years ahead. As I laid out the basic conceptual questions flowing from the *Dombrowski* approach, Jenner and Sullivan pulled out the reports of every case to which I had just referred and demanded an intense analysis of each and every problem. I felt that I was reliving the entire argument before the High Court. At the end of this exhausting session, Jenner and Sullivan exchanged glances, and Jenner said, "We're with you. It's sound. Let's draw up a federal complaint based on *Dombrowski,* and we'll ask for an injunction against the committee itself." To my amazement, he even added a suggestion on tactics, "We'll go with Dr. Stamler to the hearing. Then we'll tell the committee members we're taking them to court and advise Dr. Stamler to leave the hearing room since they have no authority to exist."

That evening in May 1965 as we left Bert Jenner's office, we had no way of knowing that this was the beginning of an almost eight-year legal and political battle with HUAC. The political struggle was brilliantly organized by Stamler, his wife Rose, a long-time experienced political activist, and Yolanda Hall and Milton Cohen, two other dedicated Chicago activists who had been subpoenaed along with Stamler and who had joined in the legal counterattack we launched. Once again, though in wholly different circumstances than in the past, I saw unfold one of the underlying precepts of the functioning of a people's lawyer, that the legal activity must stimulate and be totally interrelated with the development of mass action by the people themselves. In this case, it meant holding meetings, leafleting, filing petitions, lobbying, and fundraising in every sort of way, all directed toward obtaining from tens of thousands of people, mostly in the scientific, professional, and academic community, support for the legal attack on and public condemnation of HUAC.

The legal struggle opened with a dramatic confrontation in Chicago when Albert Jenner and Tom Sullivan publicly advised Jerry Stamler and Yolanda Hall to walk out of the hearing, since the committee was wholly without power to proceed. Milton Cohen, represented by two outstanding constitutional lawyers, Harry Kalven of the University of Chicago Law School and Richard Orlikoff of the Chicago bar, left the hearing on the same grounds. As a result, the Department of Justice initiated indictments against the three for contempt of Congress.

The battle came to a head four years later, in 1969, when the federal Court of Appeals for the Seventh Circuit ruled that our lawsuit, demanding a trial of the committee's constitutionality, was wholly proper. In powerful words reflective of Justice Brennan's statements in *Dombrowski,* the Appeals Court said, "The Congress has no more right, whether through legislation or investigation conducted under an overbroad enabling Act, to abridge the First Amendment freedoms of the people than do the other branches of the Government." The federal court ruled that we had the right to place in proof in a courtroom the long history of witchhunting by the committee, destructive of the elementary constitutional liberties of the people, and that, pending the result of such a trial, a federal injunction would be issued stopping the contempt of Congress indictments against Stamler, Hall, and Cohen. It was not much of a surprise when, rather than proceed with such an explosive trial, the government in 1973 chose to dismiss the contempt indictments, and a year later the House of Representatives itself pulled the rug out from under the committee by abolishing it.

The years of struggle around the Stamler-Hall-Cohen litigation, which went up and down twice to the Supreme Court, drove home once again the central lesson of people's law. The ability of the Stamlers, Hall, and Cohen to build over the years a broad defense committee, involving members of the academic and medical communities throughout the country, made possible the final sweeping victory over HUAC. And out of this long, intensive litigation emerged yet another critical perception about the functioning of a people's lawyer, which was later vividly reinforced when I stood alongside Bill Gossett in the Supreme Court in the warrantless wiretapping case. A people's lawyer, committed to the defense of elementary constitutional liberties, must learn to reach out to those more conservative sectors of the legal profession and the judiciary who are also unwilling to abandon these fundamental rights and freedoms and who are ready to accept the responsibility to fight for them. During the course of the Stamler-Hall-Cohen litigation, I had to develop the necessary respect for and ability to work with more conventional lawyers, including some rooted in the establishment. Increasingly over the years, as the threats to elementary constitutional liberties became more pronounced, the ability to be a patient but persuasive teacher and to argue with and win over others in the profession whose views on many questions were more conservative than mine, while at the same time learning from them many new ideas on tactics and approach, became a key factor in the practice of people's law. To operate in this way, I had to learn to suppress the arrogance that often flows from the deep conviction that one is right.

This kind of assault on the power of HUAC, rather than the inherently defensive posture of the 1950s, was the position assumed by those young leaders of the antiwar movement who in 1966, a year after the Stamler-Hall-Cohen hearings, were swept into the orbit of the committee attacks. When I proposed to a meeting of subpoenaed antiwar activists and their lawyers, hastily called together by Jack Pemberton, executive director of the American Civil Liberties Union, that we go into federal court in Washington a day before the scheduled hearings to ask for an injunction stopping the committee, the response was enthusiastic. A hesitation on the part of several of the lawyers, based on the still unknown outcome of the Stamler-Hall-Cohen action against the committee, was overridden by the excitement of the young activists who had been subpoenaed. Taking the offensive, challenging the legitimacy of the establishment's attacks on the rapidly expanding antiwar movement, was exactly the approach they were looking for.

Our strategy of counteroffensive against HUAC generated a great deal of bitterness and hostility on Capitol Hill, compounded by the aggressive political posture of the subpoenaed antiwar activists. Jerry Rubin, for example, created a stir when he appeared on Capitol Hill in a revolutionary war uniform, waving his committee subpoena. The last straw for the committee occurred the day before the hearings when, after filing the federal complaint challenging its constitutionality, I went through the motions of formally asking a federal judge for a temporary restraining order to stop the committee hearing. We were all prepared for a swift and routine denial, since no federal court had ever before interfered with a congressional committee hearing. But the unbelievable occurred. Judge Howard Corcoran, after listening to my arguments that *Dombrowski* required him to enjoin the committee from proceeding, looked up from the bench and quietly remarked, "I agree."

The sensation created on the Hill was simply not to be believed. The afternoon newspapers headlined this first court order in history forbidding a congressional committee from proceeding with a hearing. The committee members exploded with outrage on the floor of the House, supported by the southern Democrats and the Republicans. One would have thought Judge Corcoran had overthrown the entire structure of constitutional government by force and violence. The immediate consequences were not unexpected. By midnight, a hastily convened three-judge appellate panel had overruled Judge Corcoran's order and allowed the HUAC hearing to proceed the next morning, but it also reaffirmed our right to bring the suit and to be heard later in the week on the constitutionality of the committee. Even though Judge Corcoran's unexpected order had lasted less than a day, it had served a real purpose. No one on the Hill was now taking our attack on the committee casually.

This was underlined by a bizarre development at the hearing the next morning, which dramatized for me and others the built-in conflicts between the lawyer as a professional component of the judicial system and the lawyer as a part of the peoples' movements, indeed as a political being. I had not expected the fiercely hostile atmosphere which hit us as we walked into the congressional hearing room. To represent the many antiwar activists from around the country whom HUAC had subpoenaed in this carefully staged effort to smear the emerging anti-Vietnam War movement as "subversive" and "un-American," Jack Pemberton had pulled together a team of eight lawyers, who included Pemberton himself, Bill Kunstler, Frank Donner, Beverly Axelrod from San Francisco, Jerry Gutman from the New York ACLU, Joseph Forer from Washington, Ira Gollobin from New York, and myself. From the moment we appeared, it was clear that Joseph Pool of Texas, the acting chairperson, and the other members of the committee were furious not only at the activists but at the lawyers as well. It took me only a few minutes to realize that this was undoubtedly due to their outrage at the challenge we had hurled at them the day before in the federal injunction action, capturing so much public attention. As a newspaper reporter said to me later, "No one steals headlines away from Joe Pool without paying the consequences."

Among the subpoenaed witnesses whom Bill Kunstler and I had been assigned to represent was Walter Teague, a young antiwar activist from New York City. The committee counsel started to ask one of the "friendly" informer witnesses whether he knew Teague. Kunstler stood up and objected to any hostile testimony being given about our client in this open session instead of in executive session as provided by the committee's own rules. In addition, he objected to not being given what he characterized as "the American right" to cross-examine the "witness."

One of the members of the committee, John Ashbrook of Ohio, quickly moved that Kunstler's objections be overruled. As Pool was in the process of brushing Kunstler aside so the questioning could continue, I decided to take part in the exchange. It seemed to me that the denial of the right of cross-examination of hostile witnesses exposed the committee process as undemocratic and therefore illegitimate in its essence. This needed emphasis. I stood up, approached Pool, and said, "Mr. Chairman, I would like to be heard on that motion. I also am an attorney for Mr. Teague. Do I understand that it is the ruling of this committee that the fundamental right of cross-examination is not to be afforded to witnesses who are called before this committee whom the committee is attempting to defame?"

Pool snapped back at me, "You are arguing the question." This was a little too much, and I responded, with what I thought was remarkable control under the circumstances, "Of course. Lawyers always argue questions, Mr. Chairman." Ashbrook chimed in that I was "totally out of order" in even suggesting that the committee might consider "defaming" anyone. I quickly responded, "That question will be settled in federal court." And Pool snapped back, "Your objection is overruled." I thought fast and, in the most conventional of lawyers' language, said firmly, "May the record show that we take a strenuous objection to your ruling."

That did it. Pool exploded, screaming at me at the top of his voice, "Now sit down!" and banging his gavel violently on the table. That was the last thing I heard, because at that instant the heavy arm of a federal marshal grabbed me around the neck from behind and, lifting me off my feet, started to drag me out of the room. Looking around, I could see that three huge marshals had converged on me and were carrying me outside. One thought raced through my head as, choking and gasping from the arm crushing my throat, I managed to cry out to Pool, "Mr. Chairman, let the record show—Don't touch a lawyer—" Banging the gavel again, Pool shouted back, "Remove that lawyer!" While they pulled me, half-strangled, through the door, I was able to call out my last words, "Mr. Chairman—I will not be taken from this courtroom—I am an attorney-at-law—and I have a right to be heard—"

Those words, "Don't touch a lawyer" and "I will not be taken from this courtroom"—words people have reminded me of so many times over the years—triggered a sudden recognition on my part that what was happening at that moment resolved the underlying contradiction within a people's lawyer between our position in the established legal structure and our identification with the movements of fighting people. When the representatives of the establishment dragged me out, my first reaction was that they could not do this to a lawyer. Then the impact of what had just occurred sank in. By inflicting the same violence and repression upon me, a people's lawyer, as they regularly inflicted upon the people who dared to shake the structure of their power, they were saying that, as far as they were concerned, I had totally become a part of the movement I was representing. And so, in a profound sense, I felt wholly a part of the people's movement when they hustled me out of the hearing room, when they arrested me outside on a charge of disorderly conduct for using "loud and boisterous language" during the committee proceedings, and when they jammed me into a police van along with a dozen or more demonstrators who had been arrested for leafleting in protest against the committee hearings outside the House building.

The immediate reverberations from my being dragged out of the hearing were enormous. The picture of the three huge marshals wrestling me out of the hearing room hit the front pages of newspapers throughout the country. All major television channels had it on their news reports that night. While we were working together on the Stamler-Hall-Cohen case, Bert Jenner used to say with a half-smile that those pictures did more to bury HUAC than the tons of legal briefs we wrote and filed. Sullivan would agree, pointing out that the one thing Americans all over the country could not bear was the sight of three big men choking a little guy.

Immediately after I had been pulled out of the hearing room, the other lawyers representing the antiwar activists, a powerful cross-section of people's lawyers from all over the country, announced to the committee that under no circumstances would they proceed, and they all walked out. Witness after witness who were then called to testify that afternoon refused to do so without their lawyers. Meanwhile, as they booked, fingerprinted, and photographed me at the station house, I came to a quick decision that if they were going to arrest a lawyer for being a lawyer, they would have to live with it. I informed the presiding sergeant that I represented all the antiwar demonstrators lined up in the receiving cells and that I wanted an office immediately in which to talk to them. To my amazement, the sergeant quickly agreed, perhaps a little awed by all the reporters pushing into the station house, and for the next three hours I spent time in an empty cell, talking with each of the demonstrators who had been locked up with me. When Jerry Gutman arrived in the evening, having posted bail for me, he was stunned to find me, as he put it, "practicing law in the middle of a D.C. police station!"

The waves of support from all over the country almost drowned me as we prepared for the trial the next day. Lawyers from every part of the country who had worked with us in the South called to express their support, most of them offering to come to Washington to join the defense team. Dean Willard Heckel called from Newark early on the morning of the trial to read me a powerful statement of support that the Rutgers faculty had adopted at an emergency meeting on the night of the arrest. Larry Guyot called from Jackson to tell me that Martin Luther King, Stokely Carmichael, the chairperson of SNCC, and Floyd McKissick, the chairperson of CORE, planned to issue a joint call to set up a defense committee if the judge found me guilty that morning. It was thus with a feeling of overpowering strength and solidarity that I walked into Judge Harold Greene's courtroom that morning, surrounded by a dozen people's lawyers who had insisted on being part of the defense team. More than anything else, this feeling drove home to me a lesson that people's lawyers sometimes ignore—the emotional importance to movement people on trial of having concrete evidence of human solidarity and support as they face the establishment.

Despite what appeared to me to be a powerful case developed by Stavis, Kunstler, and Gutman, Judge Greene seemed determined not to step on congressional toes. At the end of the second day of trial, he solemnly announced that he was entering a verdict that I had been guilty of disorderly conduct in using "loud and boisterous language" in the committee hearing. When he turned to me and asked if I had anything to say before sentence was pronounced, my feelings were very mixed. On the one hand, I was not troubled in the slightest about the impact on me personally, for I was deeply confident that the outrageous conclusion that a lawyer could be criminally punished for proper if forceful conduct on behalf of a client during a legal proceeding would be thrown out by any appellate court. On the other hand, I was enraged at the judge's action. All of the anger of the past forty-eight hours surged up within me at the thought that a judge, a sworn defender of the Constitution, would be a party to so flagrant an effort to intimidate a lawyer who was willing to represent people being harassed by the repressive machinery of government.

In this frame of mind I stood up and, without notes or preparation, said, "Your Honor, needless to say, I am very disturbed and concerned about what has transpired today. I am not so concerned or disturbed, Your Honor, for myself. I intend to continue to the very best of my ability to pursue a vigorous defense of the constitutional liberties of American citizens in what I believe to be the highest and finest traditions of the American bar. I am deeply concerned and upset at the impact of what I consider to be one of the most extraordinary rulings in the history of our American law upon the rest of the American bar. I am concerned at the 'chilling and freezing effect,' to use the words of Mr. Justice Brennan in the *Dombrowski* opinion last year, upon other attorneys who are called upon to represent clients before the House Committee on Un-American Activities and the courts of the land, where the charges against the client are charges involving such inflammatory and publicly explosive questions as the exercise of opinions and beliefs contrary to the opinions of a given segment

307

of society at the moment. What I am concerned about is if an American lawyer, in arguing a point before an American court, must say to himself, 'Now, my voice is getting a little louder. The criminal sanction of the law is going to cut me off.' Or the lawyer who sits at a table and says to himself, 'I want to preserve a record for my client, but I better be careful. I know what happened to Professor Kinoy. He wanted to preserve a record in a very difficult tribunal.' I suggest Your Honor observe the functioning of that tribunal some day and that lawyer sitting here who will say to himself, 'If I press this objection, I stand the risk of a criminal sanction.' The danger of what has occurred here today is not to me. The danger is to the American bar. I have been led to believe—and it's the foundation stone upon which I build my life—that a free and independent American bar is the finest and ultimate guarantee and protection that the people of this country will have the opportunity to exercise the fundamental rights which they possess under the Constitution. And the degree to which the fear of criminal sanctions for practicing law is imposed, to that degree American lawyers, lawyers sitting here—"

At this point Judge Greene cut in with a curt reminder that I was supposed to be "addressing the Court for the purpose of discussing the question of sentence." I replied, "Your Honor may impose whatever Your Honor thinks is proper. I make no plea for mercy. I have no regrets or remorse for what I have done. I will do it again and again and again and again and again. I ask Your Honor, as a fellow member of the bar, that, whatever the procedural situations are, this case shall go to the Court of Appeals of the United States and, if need be, to the United States Supreme Court. Let's take it there, and let's take it fast, because I am deeply confident that when this case reaches the higher courts of this land, this decision today will be reversed."

As indeed it was reversed, by a unanimous court of appeals two years later, after a friend of the court brief had been filed by over one thousand lawyers and professors of law, and after a powerful argument had been presented by Professor Anthony Amsterdam, a leading constitutional lawyer and teacher, with whom I had worked closely during the days of the southern Freedom Movement. In the years that followed, I have often thought back to those moments before Judge Greene and remembered the words of commitment that I would "do it again and again and again and again." Perhaps at the heart of the concept of a people's lawyer— which in its own way was being tested in that committee room in Washington in 1966, just as it had been in Evansville, in Schenectady, in Judge Frank's living room in New Haven, in Danville, in Jackson, in New Orleans, and in the hundreds of other places over the long years since that walk around the Central Park reservoir in 1945—is the willingness to reexamine the role constantly as the struggle for freedom, equality, and a better life for all people erupts in endlessly new and different forms.

Perhaps the sharpest testing of the underlying concepts that have shaped my grasp of the role of a people's lawyer occurred as the result of an urgent phone call I received late in December 1966 from a member of Congress who had always been a strong supporter of the Freedom Movement: Adam Clayton Powell, the representative from the Eighteenth Congressional District of New York. I could tell immediately from the congressman's voice that something was terribly wrong. Could Bill Kunstler and I, he asked urgently, come to a meeting first thing in the morning at his office in Harlem? A number of experienced civil rights lawyers would be there to help him think through the news he had just received. When I asked him what had happened, he hit me with the information that the next day was to rock the country. Even though he had once again been overwhelmingly reelected as representative of the predominantly Black district of Harlem, the leadership of both the Democratic and the Republican parties had decided to refuse to allow him his seat in Congress when the House reconvened early in January.

This was shocking news. During the 1960s, Powell had become the most significant symbol of a Black elected official who actually exercised power. As chair of the House Education and Labor Committee, he had shaped the course of much of the important social legislation to emerge from Congress. In many ways he epitomized what had already surfaced in the voter registration struggles in Lowndes County, Alabama, as the demand for "Black Power," a demand that had quickly become the rallying cry of hundreds of thousands of young Black people all over the country.

For years, the power structure in the South and North had

been building a campaign against him, utilizing charges of tax evasion and payroll padding to undermine him. There may have been, within Powell's history and his way of life, as there always are within human beings, certain weaknesses that lent themselves to these exaggerated and distorted charges by the establishment. But no one ever dreamed that the power structure would move so drastically to rid the nation of the positive symbol that Adam Powell had become to so many Black people throughout the country. He was the living proof of the fact that registration to vote could actually result in Black people being elected to office.

When we met in Powell's office the next morning, the full impact of what had happened hit us. The southern Democrats were furious that, through the operation of a seniority system for the appointment of committee chairs which they themselves had originated generations ago, Powell, a Black representative of many years standing, had been functioning as the chair of one of the most powerful House committees. The southern Democrats had come to an agreement with the conservative northern Democrats, who bitterly opposed the prolabor bills pushed through the House by Powell, and with the House Republicans, led by the minority leader, Representative Gerald Ford, to pull the roof down once and for all on Powell. Having put together a majority, they were set to exclude him from being sworn in when the House reconvened, using as an excuse the pending charges of payroll padding and improprieties in office management, which in their judgment indicated that he was not fit to be a member of Congress. They had every intention of disregarding the fact that he had just been overwhelmingly reelected and met all three qualifications set out in the Constitution for membership in the House of Representatives, namely age, United States citizenship, and residence in his district.

That morning, Powell and the other representatives of the Black community of Harlem who were at the meeting made it clear that they were not going to take it. They were prepared to fight the House of Representatives all the way. In words that again reminded me of Jim Matles in the 1950s, Powell looked at us, the lawyers, and said simply, "Do something. How do we fight them?"

This threw at me one of the hardest legal and personal challenges I had faced in years. It came at a moment when the daily pressures of legal work and the new full-time responsibilities of law school teaching were becoming overwhelming. Yet I felt I had little choice. Aside from the official reasons given, in the deepest sense the move against Powell was the white power structure's response to the Mississippi Challenge of only a year and a half earlier. It was an assault on the entire concept of Black political power. The bold move to unseat Powell was not only an effort to destroy him as chair of the House Education and Labor Committee but, more important, an attempt to discredit and undermine the whole idea of Black political power by creating a caricature of the Black political leader as fraudulent and corrupt. In the oldest tradition of the past, it was designed to "slap down" the Black who had become "uppity" and to say to Black people throughout the country, "Stay in your place."

The fighting response of Powell and the Black citizens who had elected him as their representative was in the best traditions of the Freedom Movement. The responsibility of the people's lawyer was obvious once more. We had to find or fashion those legal weapons that could resist and defeat the move to exclude Powell from Congress.

Within the framework of the House of Representatives itself there was clearly no stopping the skillfully structured plan to exclude Powell. As lawyers, we would have to move along the path of trying to structure a lawsuit in the federal courts that would challenge the asserted right of the House to refuse to seat Powell. But this path too seemed totally blocked, because the Constitution itself stated in no uncertain terms that the House "shall be the judge of the qualifications of its members." No one had ever challenged the right of the House under this clause to take any action it pleased with respect to refusing to seat an elected member. Once again, as at so many other crucial moments in the past, we were faced with old legal doctrines and concepts which seemed to say that what we had to do was impossible.

And once again, despite the seemingly impossible barriers, we did it. An intense analysis of the entire constitutional framework of the situation provided a guide for the legal battle, which would

311

begin in the House of Representatives and move through the federal courts until the showdown before the United States Supreme Court two years later. The constitutional precept we grabbed for went "straight to the jugular," as Justice Hugo Black used to say in his lonely dissents of the 1950s. The refusal to seat Powell struck at one of the most elementary principles of democratic government, the right of the sovereign people to select their own representatives. This right was violated when a majority of the House refused to seat an elected member who, as they themselves conceded, met all of the written qualifications for membership in the House set down in the Constitution. What the House therefore argued, from the first moments of its action refusing to seat Powell, was that since the Constitution also stated that the House "was the sole judge of the qualifications" of its members, it had the "inherent" power to add to the stated written qualifications and thus deny a seat to anyone who, in the opinion of the majority of its members, lacked the character, integrity, or fitness required to be seated.

This assertion of an "inherent power" in a branch of the federal government to disregard the provisions of the Constitution, an argument that was to be advanced four years later by Nixon in the Detroit wiretap case, presented a constitutional question of a scope that we barely sensed during the first stages of the Powell litigation. From the very beginning of the legal battle we rested our arguments upon the premise that any such power in the House would undermine the elementary precept of democracy that the people had the sovereign right to elect their own representatives. What we did not fully realize until, with the help of students at Rutgers Law School, we had dug deeply into the history of the adoption of the Constitution was that this premise lay at the heart of the intentions of those who wrote the Constitution. James Madison himself had warned that to give the legislature any power to alter or add to these written qualifications would be "improper and dangerous" and that such power was the road by which "the Republic may be converted into an autocracy or an oligarchy." The battle to keep the House from refusing to seat Adam Powell was therefore related to one of the foundation stones in the structure of the American republic itself.

Emerging more clearly in my own consciousness as the Powell case developed was the recognition, which I had first sensed during the upsurges of the early 1960s, that in defending people's movements from attack, the people's lawyer was also time and again placed in the position of defending the most elementary concepts of the American constitutional system. This perception followed from the realization that at moments of tension and crisis, powerful sections of the establishment were not hesitant to move down the road that Madison had warned against pointedly two hundred years before—the road that might lead to abandonment of the basic institutions and concepts of constitutional democracy. So a sense of overwhelming responsibility engulfed me when, after we lost our appeal in the Powell case in the District of Columbia Court of Appeals, Professor Herbert Reid of Howard Law School, an outstanding constitutional lawyer with whom I had worked closely on the Powell case, called me in New York. He told me that Powell had decided that he wanted Herb Reid and me to take his case to the Supreme Court and share the argument there.

My feelings were very mixed. On the one hand, this was a strong show of confidence and support on the part of Powell. On the other, the responsibility it entailed was frightening. The atmosphere surrounding the case was increasingly grim, reflecting the climate of the country which had just resulted in the election of Richard Nixon as President. The alliance of southern Democrats and northern Conservatives which had launched the original attack on Powell was now in full control. The opinion of the District of Columbia Court of Appeals, sustaining the decision of the District Court in throwing out our action against the House as being beyond the power of the federal courts, was written by a judge of that court by the name of Warren Burger. His opinion spelled out in great detail why our request for judicial relief was groundless and without authority.

And then the final blow fell. Shortly before Nixon's election, Chief Justice Warren had resigned his position, but President Johnson had been unable to get Senate confirmation for a replacement. The resignation was waiting on Nixon's desk when he took office in January 1969, and one of his first acts as President was the appointment of Burger as the new Chief Justice, to replace Warren at the end of the term in June. Our appeal in the Powell case would be heard that term, while Warren still sat as Chief, but it would come to the Court as an opinion written against us by the very person who was about to become the new Chief Justice.

Herb Reid and I were deeply pessimistic as we prepared our arguments. We felt that the focus of the case must be our urgent plea that the Court reassert its historic role as the defender of the written Constitution. But we were sensitive to the growing feeling throughout the country, culminating in Nixon's election, that the moment had come to end the so-called activist role of the Supreme Court in the area of the rights of Black, poor, and working people. From one end of the nation to the other billboards now screamed the slogan that had so captivated the swelling conservative forces, "Impeach Earl Warren." In Washington itself, attacks were being launched on the liberal members of the Court. Pressure was mounting that would result in Justice Abe Fortas' resignation, and moves were being openly suggested in the House and Senate for impeachment proceedings against Justice Douglas.

As Reid and I, with the enthusiastic help of students at both Rutgers and Howard law schools, prepared our arguments and finalized our brief, one thing became clearer and clearer. The defense of the right of the people of the Eighteenth Congressional District to select their own representative as a manifestation of one of the fundamental principles of our constitutional democracy was merging with the necessary defense of the institution of the Supreme Court itself as the ultimate defender of the written Constitution. More and more, the interrelationship between these questions shaped our preparation for the argument, now set for April 21, 1969.

The argument before the Court that April morning reflected fully the mood we were in. I opened the argument by stating, "We rise this morning to argue this case with a sense of grave responsibility." I could not resist reminding the Court that, as Chief Justice Marshall had said in 1803 in the landmark decision first establishing the ultimate power of the Court to interpret the written Constitution, this case also was one of "peculiar delicacy." In our arguments, Herb Reid and I put to the Court the thesis that had become the center of our position, the duty of the Court to intervene when another branch of the government transgressed the limits of its power laid down in the written Constitution.

During those reminiscences that inevitably follow any Supreme Court case, Herb Reid and I have often said to each other that the arguments that morning must have affected the thinking of the Court in a powerful way. The decision, which came down within two months, went far beyond our wildest hopes. It was written by the Chief Justice, Earl Warren, as his last opinion, and in every sense it was a valedictory statement of the Warren Court. He affirmed for the Court our conclusion that the House of Representatives had no power to alter, ignore, or add to the written qualifications for membership in the House. Accordingly, he held for the Court that Adam Powell had been unconstitutionally excluded from his seat and that a declaratory judgment must be issued to that effect. And in words that reflected the oldest traditions of the nation, he restated the "responsibility of this Court to act as the ultimate interpreter of the Constitution."

This was Warren's final answer to the billboards calling for his impeachment. Neither he nor the members of the Court he spoke for were prepared to retreat from their historic responsibility to enforce the mandates of the written Constitution as the underlying guarantee that no branch of the government would transcend the limitations of power prescribed for it, and that the fundamental freedoms and liberties of all people would be preserved and protected. Earl Warren's life and work as Chief Justice had been dedicated to this proposition, and the powerful words in the Powell opinion reflected this commitment.

In every sense, the decision, now known in all the lawbooks as *Powell v. McCormick,* sharpened my understanding of the role of the people's lawyer. In accepting the responsibility of fashioning legal weapons of struggle, defense, and counterattack for the people's movements, we had to undertake the task of rejecting and then reshaping concepts and theories that seemed to stand in our way. We had to be fully prepared to defend those elementary principles of constitutional democracy that the power structure might attempt to brush aside in its moves to repress the people's movements. And as Herb Reid and I have often said to each other in our private moments of celebration, we also had to be prepared on occasion to win.

As the new Nixon administration launched its many-faceted program of legal moves designed to repress both the mounting opposition to the Vietnam War and the rising rage within the Black communities from one end of the country to the other, I drew much needed strength and support from the experiences in the Powell case. But there was little time quietly to assess the thrust of Earl Warren's valedictory or to think through the implications of the lessons we had learned in the course of that uphill battle, for a few weeks before the Powell argument in Washington, something overwhelming had happened in Chicago. On March 20, 1969, indictments were returned in that city against eight leaders of the anti-Vietnam War movement, arising out of demonstrations the past summer at the Democratic National Convention. Despite the fact that the Attorney-General under President Lyndon Johnson had publicly concluded that there was no basis for prosecuting the organizers of the Chicago demonstration, the new administration under Nixon had proceeded with these sweeping conspiracy indictments.

The trial, which began in September 1969, quickly became a focus of national attention. Once again, as in the 1950s, the court-room became an arena in which the power structure utilized every aspect of the legal machinery of the system to create an image of dissent designed to isolate, disrupt, and paralyze any movement of opposition to government policies. The trial of the Chicago antiwar demonstrators on the charge of conspiring to violate the so-called federal antiriot statute, which had been passed only a year before in frightened reaction to the angry uprisings within the Black ghettos throughout the country, rapidly developed all of these characteristics. In every sense, the trial became a testing ground for how people's lawyers and political activists thrown into the role of defendants could meet this challenge.

The dedicated, round-the-clock work of Leonard Weinglass and Bill Kunstler, who were the two full-time lawyers for the defendants during the six-month trial, continues to this day to be a model for the performance of people's lawyers. And the partici- pation in the trial proceedings of the eight antiwar leaders singled out by the government for attack—Dave Dellinger, Rennie Davis, Tom Hayden, Abbie Hoffman, Jerry Rubin, Bobby Seale, Lee Weiner, and John Froines—offered an invaluable example to learn from. The heights of success and the depths of frustration that characterized the daily experiences of these political defen- dants offer a unique opportunity for intensive study on the part of movement activists and organizers, who may face, once again, the difficult and frightening possibility of large-scale political trials. Such a study would be an important contribution to the strength- ening of people's lawyers and political activists in the days to come.

My teaching responsibilities at Rutgers, the final preparation for the Powell argument, and the effort of recovering from a wave of tachycardia heart episodes in early 1968 made any question of my own daily involvement in the trial a physical impossibility. But I was a consultant, and the occasional emergency phone call from Kunstler or Weinglass, suggesting that I come to Chicago that evening to talk through some immediate problem that had arisen, gave me an opportunity to meet with the five defendants with whom I had shared earlier experiences as a people's lawyer in the anti-Vietnam War movement—Dellinger, Hoffman, Rubin, Hayden, and Davis. At one point in the trial I was even called out to San Francisco to meet with Charles Garry, an old friend and one of the country's most experienced and dedicated people's lawyers, who was recovering from a serious illness. We talked over the advice he should give Bobby Seale, chairperson of the Black Panther Party, whom Garry was supposed to represent. Judge Julius Hoffman, the trial judge, in one of his many outra- geous moves, had refused Bobby Seale an adjournment to allow time for Garry to recover and represent him. When Seale had then insisted on his fundamental constitutional right to defend himself in the absence of his chosen lawyer, Judge Hoffman, in a series of moves that were to shock the country, had ordered Seale bound and gagged in the courtroom.

These sudden, emergency sessions gave me some feel for the

difficulties experienced by the lawyers and defendants in the Chicago trial. And when, after the trial resulted in convictions, I was asked to take a major role in preparing the appeal to the United States Court of Appeals, the enormity of the work seemed almost overwhelming. I faced a review of thousands of pages of trial transcripts, hundreds of appealable errors, both sweeping and technical, and a verdict of guilty that had resulted in five-year sentences for the convicted antiwar activists. But the most difficult problem was the need to erase the caricature of militant dissent created by the tactics of the prosecution, the judge, and the media. How could we turn this around and present the reality of the government's onslaught on the constitutional rights of Americans to protest and to demonstrate against government policies?

It quickly became clear that the task required the rapid construction of what over the years I had come to know was essential to the successful accomplishment of any major objective by a people's lawyer, the building of a collective team to share the work. Here I was fortunate to join forces with two skillful and determined lawyers, Doris Peterson and Helene Schwartz. We were very different people, in both our personalities and our ways of work. But something magical occurred. We gradually became bound together in a relationship of equality that enabled us to move swiftly ahead in a way none of us would have dreamed possible at the beginning of our work.

Building this working relationship was not simple, however, and it came at a critical moment in all our lives. I had just reached a difficult decision to end my marriage with Susan, a relationship of many years, and to build a new relationship with Barbara Webster. Doris Peterson had just made a major decision to return to the practice of law, after many years of inactivity as a lawyer, and Helene Schwartz, after several years of sometimes frustrating experiences in conventional law firms, was searching for areas of legal activity where she could more fully develop her own independence and capabilities. The enormity of the challenge we faced on the appeal forced all three of us to find ways to work together collectively and supportively and to share equally in the major decisions. One key to this process was learning to argue

318

with each other on terms of equality and without the overbearing oppressiveness of the "senior lawyer-junior lawyer" relationship. Even more important for us was the conscious effort to struggle against the ever-present tendency in so many of us in the legal world to accept the prevailing atmosphere of male domination over women co-workers.

It was not always easy to achieve all of this, and we had our rough moments. However, in recent years I have had occasion to reread the 547-page brief Helene Schwartz, Doris Peterson, and I wrote together. And I have no doubt that its quality and the impact it had on the court of appeals were largely due to the process of equal collective work we forged during those nine months together.

Our work in preparing the appeal centered around an assumption that had consistently run through our initial discussions with Kunstler, Weinglass, and the defendants. This assumption, which also reflected the fundamental premise of a people's lawyer, was to take the offensive. Our purpose was to expose the machinations of the government prosecutor, the trial judge, the FBI, and the entire Washington administration for what they were, a conscious conspiracy to utilize government power to undermine and destroy the elementary guarantees of freedom for the American people, the written guarantees of the First Amendment to the Constitution.

We had to abandon totally any defensive posture and to explain in detail how every step in the trial, starting with the utilization of a grossly unconstitutional federal statute, was part of a conscious effort to brush aside the constitutional commands of the First Amendment. The statute was designed to make criminal the interstate travel of persons supposedly crossing state lines with an intent to organize riots. It had come to be known as the "Rap Brown" statute because it was first used against Rap Brown, a leader of the Black Freedom Movement and the chairperson of SNCC. Generalized statements would have been wholly inadequate to expose the plan to use this statute to bury the First Amendment mandates. We had to analyze painstakingly every single move in the trial: every piece of evidence introduced by the government, every statement offered by the defendants. At the same time, we had to uncover each step in the trial proceedings which revealed that the government, in order to achieve its objective of burying the First Amendment freedoms, was willing to violate every guarantee of fairness and due process of law in a criminal trial also contained within the Constitution.

At the heart of the huge brief, one of the longest ever written in a federal appellate proceeding, was the proposition that the defendants had not been participating in any criminal activity. Rather, along with hundreds of thousands of people throughout the country, they had been exercising their basic constitutional right to assemble, to demonstrate, and to petition their government for a redress of grievances. These grievances, which were pressing and real, included the government's outrageous aggression in Vietnam as well as the most serious manifestations of racism, poverty, and injustice within the United States itself.

This perception of the defendants' activities explained the conspiracy trial in Chicago. In order to frighten, derail, and ultimately smash this constitutional movement of American people, the government had returned to the days of the Cold War, creating the spectacle of a political trial to illegalize the ideas, beliefs, and thoughts of the defendants. To achieve this objective, the government, again within the tradition of the past, had engaged in blatant abuses of due process of law. These included the partiality of the trial judge, the judicially condoned misconduct of the prosecutors, and the serious interference with the independence of the jury.

The institution of a political trial of these dimensions, designed to undermine First Amendment liberties, threatened not only those outspoken persons brought within its immediate sweep but all of American society. As history teaches, repressive moves against elementary liberties can so infect an entire society that no one dares raise a voice in protest because of the chilling fear of government prosecution and imprisonment. In the words of those who wrote the Bill of Rights, the legal proceedings in Chicago, unless halted, threatened the "very safety of the Republic itself," resting as it does on preservation of the fundamental liberties of the people.

This, then, was the picture of the Chicago conspiracy trial that we handed over to the Court of Appeals in Chicago late in 1971. And on February 8, 1972, Helene Schwartz and I shared the oral argument with Bill Kunstler, who participated not only to assist us in the argument but also to emphasize to the Court, through his skillful presentation, the outrageous nature of Judge Hoffman's characterizations of the trial lawyers and the defendants, which had culminated in his contempt of court citations of them all. Every one of these contempt citations was ultimately dismissed by the federal courts.

I was a little uneasy about what to present to the Court of Appeals that afternoon in Chicago. But in reality, the problem was precisely the same one that I had faced numerous times before and would encounter two weeks later in arguing the Detroit wiretap case before the Supreme Court. Either I could lay out the full picture, or I could stay with the literally hundreds of technical questions that might result in a reversal. And once again, as Chuck Conley had done years before in the Seals case, and as I was to do two weeks later in Washington, I put before the Court as fully and bluntly as I could the nature of the true conspiracy—the efforts of the government to bury the First Amendment through its criminal proceedings against the Chicago defendants.

Nine months later, the decision of the Seventh Circuit Court of Appeals came down. We won unanimously. Judge Thomas Fairchild, writing for the three members of the court, found serious grounds to reverse all the convictions, focusing mainly on the actions of the trial judge and the prosecutor to deprive the defendants of a fair trial. One of the three members of the panel, Judge Wilbur Pell, would have gone even further than the majority in reversing the convictions. He would have held that the antiriot statute was an unconstitutional violation of the First Amendment both on its face and as it had been utilized by the government in this case.

After the wonderful parties of celebration with Bill Kunstler, Len Weinglass, Dave Dellinger, and the other defendants, Doris Peterson, Helene Schwartz, and I got around to carefully reading the 121-page opinion of the Court of Appeals. One thing was completely obvious to us. Our basic strategy of conducting a full-scale offensive on the fundamental constitutional questions had been right on the nose. Even the two judges who focused on the fairness questions made it clear that the constitutional issues we had raised were very serious. It could not have been more evident that it was within this context that the Court as an entity had agreed on a full-scale reversal of the convictions. Naturally, we would have been even happier if the court had totally barred the antiriot statute as a repressive tool, but under the circumstances of the period, everyone in the people's movement responded to the decision of the Court of Appeals as a sweeping victory. The reversal of the Chicago conspiracy convictions in November, followed in June 1972 by the powerful decision of the Supreme Court in the Detroit warrantless wiretap case to reject the claim of the President to the inherent power to suspend the Constitution, represented major setbacks to the plans of the Nixon administration to repress the movement for ending the war in Vietnam.

In a personal way, I had already experienced the administration's determination to go to any lengths to sustain the Chicago conspiracy convictions. Four months before our brief was due to be filed, at a moment when the government knew full well how involved I was in round-the-clock work to complete the brief, it made a move which now, years afterward, seems to have been a crude attempt to prevent me from completing the job. One afternoon in October 1970, while I was hard at work on the brief in my law school office in Newark, two somber-looking individuals marched in holding FBI badges in their hands. After identifying themselves, they began firing questions at me. Where could they find my daughter, Joanne Kinoy? What was her address? They wanted to question her about her knowledge of someone else who knew a third person who might know someone the FBI was after in its search for antiwar activists to sweep up under new conspiracy charges. The men tried to assure me that she herself was under no suspicion of illegal activity.

I was furious. Here was the federal bureau once again engaging in the police harassment I had been fighting against for so many years. Only this time it was directed against me and my daughter, then a student at the University of Wisconsin in Madison.

I knew immediately how to respond. For years I had advised

movement activists that agents of the FBI had no power whatsoever to require answers to their questions and that a prudent, indeed a constitutionally protected response was to refuse to participate in any way whatsoever with their probing. It was hard to
believe that the agents had not anticipated this position from me.
In no uncertain terms I told them that I would not participate in
these probings into the antiwar movement and that, as Joanne's
father as well as her lawyer, my relationship with her should be
totally protected. The agents quickly left, and I assumed that this
ploy by the government was at an end.

I was wrong. To my amazement, about a month later, as I
walked out of a classroom at the law school, two FBI agents were
standing in the lobby waiting for me. Once again, after displaying
their badges, they threw the same questions at me about Joanne's
whereabouts. This was too much. It was simply not believable
that the Justice Department did not already know full well where
she was. Only two weeks before, she had come to Chicago to join
me in the federal courthouse while I argued preliminary matters
in the Chicago appeal. While she was sitting at the counsel table
with me, the United States Attorney for the Eastern District of
Chicago had walked over to talk about procedural questions on
the appeal. I introduced Joanne to him as my daughter, and we
casually chatted about her work as a student in Madison. Two
weeks later, a formal inquiry into her whereabouts by government agents was ridiculous. I firmly restated my previous position, and once again they turned and left the building. This time I
felt that the ploy was surely over.

However, a month later, in December, at a moment when Peterson, Schwartz, and I were swamped with final work on
the Chicago appeal, I was hit with the full brunt of the government's maneuvers to derail our work. This time the FBI agents
handed me a subpoena to appear before a federal grand jury in
Manhattan. Now if I continued to refuse to participate in their
probings, they could invoke the full power of a grand jury. This
was no longer a minor harassment technique. This was for real!

In view of my long-standing position against the witch-hunting
tactics of the Department of Justice in using grand juries as a
major weapon for harassing and intimidating political activists,

the FBI had to have known that I would never retreat from this position, especially when it involved me, personally, and my daughter. Late that evening, at an emergency meeting of lawyers and legal workers from the Center for Constitutional Rights, we put our heads together over this bizarre turn of events. Everyone was convinced that, although this move by the government was clearly designed to impede our preparations for the Chicago conspiracy appeal, we had no alternative but to stand firm and fight. Once again, the central strategy problem that always faces people's lawyers during attacks by the power structure was on the table: how to avoid the purely defensive stance that the government tactics were trying to force upon us, a position of refusing to comply with a federal subpoena, which would inevitably result in a long and protracted contempt-of-court proceeding and then, possibly, indefinite imprisonment for refusal to answer questions before a grand jury. Ways had to be found to turn the situation completely around, to place the government on the defensive for its harassing moves designed to hamstring my ability to continue functioning as a people's lawyer at this bitter moment of constitutional struggle.

In the days that followed, a fighting strategy emerged. A number of lawyers concerned about the implications of the government moves joined with the Center lawyers to structure a two-pronged counterattack, involving motions to quash the federal subpoena and an independent federal action, naming as defendants Attorney-General John Mitchell and J. Edgar Hoover, director of the FBI, along with the United States Attorney for the Southern District of New York and his assistant. This action sought both an injunction against the defendants' use of the federal grand jury for harassment purposes and damages for Joanne and myself for interference with our constitutional rights.

The sitting federal judge, Marvin Frankel, seemed as taken aback as I was at the number of distinguished lawyers who appeared in the Federal Court that morning in December to press this counteroffensive. Along with the Center lawyers, Professor John Lowenthal from the Rutgers faculty, Melvin Wulf, Norman Dorson, and Jeremiah Gutman from the American Civil Liberties Union, Victor Rabinowitz from the Emergency Civil Liberties Committee, Eric Seitz from the National Lawyers Guild, and Helene Schwartz and Doris Peterson from our Chicago appeals team all rose in the courtroom to represent me and Joanne at the opening of our attack on the government's harassment. The battle around this legal counterattack waged furiously for the next several weeks, up and down from the district court to the court of appeals. On every front and on every issue, our team of lawyers, joined after the first few days by Herb Reid and Ramsey Clark, the former Attorney-General under President Johnson, used every occasion to expose the underlying government design of harassment.

Then suddenly the government's house of cards fell apart. The government had been trying to create a distorted image of Joanne as some sort of fugitive, and after careful consideration we had all decided to dispel this image by having Joanne appear in the courtroom voluntarily and take the principled position of invoking her constitutional right not to participate in the grand jury questioning. The Department of Justice rushed to try to hold her in contempt of court, resorting to the provisions of a new immunity statute which had been designed to eliminate the constitutional protection of the privilege against self-incrimination. In a courageous decision, District Judge Constance Baker Motley held that the new federal immunity statute was unconstitutional on its face, violating the provisions of the Fifth Amendment, and that accordingly Joanne was fully protected in her invocation of her constitutional right not to participate in the grand jury questioning.

Judge Motley's opinion was in the great tradition of Judge Wisdom of Louisiana in the days of the *Dombrowski* battles, and although several years later the Supreme Court, in another situation, had a more conservative view of the immunity statute than Judge Motley's in Joanne's case, at that moment her decision had a sweeping effect. The structure of harassment totally collapsed. There was no longer any way the Department of Justice could pursue their subpoena against me or Joanne. Doris Peterson, Helene Schwartz, and I could return to full-scale work on the Chicago appeal, and Joanne could return to her life in Wisconsin and, ultimately, to the decisions that would lead her to attend law school and then to fashion in her own way her present activity as a progressive lawyer in Chicago.

Certain long-range aspects of what we all learned during those intense days remain with us even today. As frustrating as it may seem, the struggle of a people's lawyer to develop approaches that can open a counteroffensive, even during such rough moments as the government's use of the grand jury machinery to harass political activists, continues to be a central task. How, at a given moment, to shape the legal weapon required to counterattack is always a difficult question. But as I look back at those hectic moments when the government attempted to divert me from the responsibilities of the Chicago appeal, one thing is extremely clear. The key to our survival was found by Jim Reif and Nancy Stearns, two of the Center for Constitutional Rights lawyers, in the long hours spent fashioning a legal counterattack that completely changed the atmosphere in those courtrooms and allowed us to return to our work, which led ultimately to the victory in the appeals.

Over and over during the work around the Chicago appeals, I experienced the interrelation between the two paths of struggle that must be followed in any meaningful effort to defend the constitutional rights of the people. Just as during the southern work I had come to understand that legal battles to enforce freedom and equality had the potential of victory only when they were intertwined with the daily struggles of the Black people and their supporters to transform these constitutional promises into reality, so in the midst of our legal activity on the Chicago appeals the same understanding was driven home to me. Over the long haul, our legal battle to defend the First Amendment through the Chicago appeals had the potential of victory only because it was occurring in tandem with the constantly escalating daily efforts of vast numbers of people all over the country to transform the written words of the First Amendment into reality through the demonstrations, the mass marches, the picketing, the leafleting, and the political organizing directed against the war in Vietnam.

When we argued in Chicago that the use of the federal antiriot statute to sustain the arrests and convictions of the leaders of the antiwar movement was a dangerous assault on the continued existence of First Amendment liberties essential to the foundations of the republic, we were not talking about ephemeral, even mystical concepts spun out of ancient tomes by legal scholars or Fourth of July orators. We were talking about fundamental rights being exercised daily by the multitudes of Americans speaking out loud and clear in hundreds of different ways, from the national student shutdown of over four hundred colleges and universities in the spring of 1970 to protest the killing by the National Guard of student antiwar demonstrators at Kent State University in Ohio and at Jackson State University in Mississippi, to the hundreds of thousands of people who descended on the city of Washington, D.C., in the spring of 1971 to demand an end to the Vietnam War.

Through these massive demonstrations, through the countless acts of individual protest against the barbarism of the continuing war, through the increasing tempo of confrontational and symbolic actions, people were struggling to utilize and preserve the vitality and availability of the basic First Amendment liberties. We, as lawyers, were fighting to keep the First Amendment alive in the legal arena; the people were fighting to keep the First Amendment alive in the streets, in their homes, in their factories, in the legislative halls, in the political arena. Once again, the lesson was that the effort to safeguard essential constitutional liberties from the repressive moves of the establishment involved a two-pronged battle, whose parts were sometimes deeply meshed, sometimes seemingly independent, but always interrelated in impact and effect. One prong was the struggle of the people to use these basic liberties to meet their needs and solve their problems; the other prong was the struggle of people's lawyers within the courtroom to protect and preserve these liberties. All the experiences leading up to the victories in the union struggles of the 1950s, the southern struggles of the 1960s, the Powell case, the Chicago conspiracy appeals, and the Nixon-Mitchell wiretap case before the Supreme Court drove home the same point, that once this two-pronged offensive went into action, it was no longer preordained that the power structure was all powerful and that victory was impossible for the people's movements.

This vision that victory is a possibility for the people's movements and for people's lawyers has at times led a number of my co-workers in the struggle to term me an "irredeemable optimist." But it is this same vision that has always sustained me at difficult turning points, when I have had to remind myself that the skill, the art, and the creativity of a people's lawyer will have to be utilized over and over again on the long road of democratic peoples' struggles in this country, with no end in sight. And it is this vision that victory is a possibility, both now and in the future, which makes bearable the acceptance of the unending responsibilities of the people's lawyer.

As new movements of struggle have constantly erupted in the 1970s and early 1980s—among the Black people of the northern ghettos and once again throughout the South, among the Puerto Rican people fighting for freedom and independence in their island homeland, among the women of this country fighting so courageously for equality and freedom, among the working people responding to the devastating effects of unemployment and plant closings, and among all the people of the country facing the dangers of new military adventures abroad and the prospect of a nuclear holocaust—the concept of the people's lawyer has been tested successfully again and again. As we move ahead toward the goal for which each of these movements has struggled, for a life of freedom, equality, and happiness for all people, increasingly I have learned that for a people's lawyer to take her or his place as a political person in these struggles is the ultimate resolution of those contradictions which from the very beginning were inherent in the concept of the people's lawyer.

The many experiences during these long years will have much more to teach us. Those in power today are increasingly unable to cope with the problems of society. Linked with this inability is their deep, pathological fear of the people's movements that have risen in response to these problems. It is impossible to predict what form the next move toward the deadly experimentation with the abandonment of democratic forms may take. That history must repeat itself is not written in stone. Having had the cover of legality blown by the Supreme Court in the warrantless wiretapping decision in 1972, the establishment may in the future wholly circumvent that institutional obstacle. Or it may make new attempts to undermine the Supreme Court from within.

Recently, the theory of the inherent power of the President to suspend constitutional guarantees, with its frightening and dangerous implications, has been revived by the Reagan administration. The original architect of the inherent power theory still sits upon the Court. The exposure of FBI and CIA files during the years following Watergate revealed the continued existence of covert activities of the grossest nature. Once again, the most powerful forces in the country may be moving toward the goal of experimentation with undermining, and then eliminating, our most elementary democratic liberties.

The road ahead is very complex. The struggle to avert the ultimate disaster, the abandonment of constitutional government and the substitution of a rule by open terror and lawless force, can never, we have learned, be fought solely within the confines of the courtrooms, as important as that fight at a given instant may be. Next time, these judicial institutions may be bypassed entirely, the "executive order" not being unknown in our political history, or these institutions may fall from within, victims to a new conspiracy to obtain their complicity in the abandonment of legality.

A mood of regrouping and reassessment possesses us all. It touches me in many ways. The hesitations which in 1971 temporarily held me back from joining Bill Bender and Linda Huber in the Supreme Court wiretap case are still present within me. Only a new renaissance of popular initiative, a new upsurge of people's strength, can prevent the betrayal of democracy and open the door to a future consistent with the old dream of life, liberty, and the pursuit of happiness for every person in this land. This I know. But this means we must all examine our lives and our work, if the emergency of today is to be faced and the promise of tomorrow to be realized.

For me, as for others who consider themselves people's lawyers, there must be an ongoing reevaluation of our role in the struggles, the victories, and the defeats of the social movements of the people. How do we continue to fight the necessary, the inevitable battles within the judicial system, while simultaneously moving beyond the courtroom and stepping out onto the long, winding road of political struggle, wherever that road may lead? More and more, my own answers to the complicated challenge of the present may be found by continuing to reexamine moments of the past, when I found myself caught up in the interaction between struggling social movements and the legal institutions that surround and sometimes engulf these movements. To look back at these moments, to search for the seeds of a resolution of role, may help for what is to come. At least I think I will try.

Index

331

Index

Brener, Milton, 219, 220–222, 228, 229, 230
Brennan, William J., Jr., 18, 26, 35, 283, 284, 300, 307
Brooks, George, 178
Browder, Earl, 76
Brown, John R., 172
Brown, Rap, 319
Brown v. Board of Education (347 U.S. 483 [1954]), 143, 151, 153–154, 158, 166, 175, 233, 235
Buchanan, James, 37
Burbank, Colonel, 221
Burger, Warren, 18, 23, 27, 28, 35, 313–314
Button case. *See NAACP v. Button*

Campbell, Mrs., 198
Campbell, Reverend, 182, 184, 187–188, 197, 201
Canadian Broadcasting System, 141
Carey, James, 84, 136
Carmichael, Stokely, 306
Center for Constitutional Rights, 115, 281, 324
Central Intelligence Agency (CIA), 4, 13, 329
Chaney, James, 246, 253, 254, 255
Chase, Reverend, 186, 196, 205
Cheatham, Elliot, 46, 47, 48, 53, 264
Chicago. *See* Democratic Party; House Un-American Activities Committee
Chicago Seven case (*Dellinger v. U.S.,* 472 F.2d 340 [7th Cir. 1972]), 3, 316–327
Churchill, Winston, 62, 73
CIO. *See* Congress of Industrial Organizations
Civil rights movement, 115, 143; Montgomery bus boycott, 151–160; *Seals* case, 161–176; *Wansley* case, 177–180; Danville movement, 181–208; role of lawyers, 192–193; March on Washington, 209, 210–211, 217; subversive control aspects, 216, 218, 221, 225, 227, 229, 230, 278–279; MFDP efforts, 267–276, 280–283, 284–296
Clark, Charles, 124

Clark, Ramsey, 325
Clark, Tom, 283
COFO. *See* Council of Federated Organizations
COFO v. Rainey (339 F.2d 898 [5th Cir. 1964]), 250–255, 259, 264
Cohen, Milton, 300, 301
Cohn, Roy, 97–98, 99, 100, 103, 108, 110, 113, 131, 132, 133, 135, 141, 144
Cold War, 6, 22, 49, 89, 90, 93, 95, 104, 114; Churchill's speech, 62; role of big business, 129–138; McCarthy and, 130–142, 145. *See also* Rosenberg
Colmer, William, 290
Columbia Law School, 46–47, 98, 126
Committee for the Re-Election of the President, 36
Communism, 62, 63, 72–73, 81, 91–92, 99–100
Communist Party, 73–74, 75–84, 86, 89, 95, 138
Congress: Reconstruction era, 67–68, 191, 192, 214, 240, 250; 1957 civil rights act, 158; immunity of members, 222, 223; challenge to Mississippi delegation to, 267–276, 280–283, 284–296; and voting rights, 282; House efforts to exclude Powell, 309–316
Congress of Industrial Organizations (CIO), 65, 84, 98, 103, 107, 129, 137, 138
Congress of Racial Equality (CORE), 202, 227, 258
Conley, Charles, 157–158, 161, 162, 163, 167, 169, 170, 172, 174, 175, 178, 228, 321
Connor, Bull, 183
Conspiracy: charges against anti-Vietnam War activists, 4, 21; against labor, 67; against Communists, 76, 78, 81, 91; to violate civil rights, 219. *See also* Chicago Seven case
Constitution, 78, 146; assertion of Presidential power to suspend, 11, 24–26, 30–31; Civil War amendments, 203, 225, 227. *See also* Bill of Rights; specific amendments

Index

Contempt: of court, 82; of Congress, 105, 300. *See also* Emspak; House Un-American Activities Committee
Conyers, John, 292, 293
Conyers, Nate, 189
Corcoran, Howard, 302–303
Cordiner, Ralph, 134, 135
CORE. *See* Congress of Racial Equality
Cotton, Gene, 74
Council of Federated Organizations (COFO), 235, 243, 244, 246, 249, 251, 252, 253, 263, 264, 266, 271, 281, 286, 295
Cox, Courtland, 264
Cox, Harold, 237–238, 239, 240, 241, 242, 243, 279
Crawford, Vernon, 175
Crockett, George, 74, 189, 205, 213
Curti, Merle, 265, 266

Dan River Mills, 181, 182, 192, 202
Danville, Virginia, civil rights movement, 181–208, 210, 214
Danville Christian Progressive Association, 181, 182, 183, 188
Danville Joint Legal Defense Committee, 196
Darrow, Clarence, 40
Davis, Ben, 80–81
Davis, Rennie, 317
Dayton (Ohio) 1948 UE strike, 64–65
Dean, John, 25
Declaration of Independence, 78
Dellinger, David, 288, 317, 321. *See also* Chicago Seven case
Dellinger v. United States. See Chicago Seven case
Democratic National Committee headquarters. *See* Watergate
Democratic Party: 1968 Chicago Convention, 3, 4, 316; of Mississippi, 257, 260; 1964 Atlantic City Convention, 258–261, 267
Denaturalization proceedings, 104–105, 106, 133, 148
Dennis, Eugene, 81. *See also* Smith Act cases

Dennis v. United States. See Smith Act cases
Department of Justice, 21, 22, 112; and illegal wiretaps, 6, 8, 10; Internal Security Division, 12–13; and Smith Act cases, 73, 76, 83, 89; Palmer raids, 75; and denaturalization proceedings, 104–105, 148; under Kennedy, 201–202; and Mississippi struggles, 246, 247, 255; and HUAC, 300; harasses Joanne Kinoy, 322, 323, 324, 325–326
Detroit, 3–4. See also *United States v. U.S. District Court*
Devine, Annie, 267, 269, 270, 271, 283, 289, 292, 295
Dimitroff, Georgi, 79, 82
Dissent, repression of, 92, 320–321
District of Columbia v. Kinoy. See House Un-American Activities Committee
Doar, John, 247
Dombrowski, James: and Louisiana subversion case (*Dombrowski v. Eastland,* 387 U.S. 82 [1957]), 215–217, 218, 220–224, 225, 227, 232, 276, 284; the *Dombrowski* remedy case (*Dombrowski v. Pfister,* 380 U.S. 479 [1965], 224, 236, 238, 262, 263, 264, 266, 276–280, 283–284, 285, 298, 300–301, 302, 307, 325
Dombrowski v. Eastland. See Dombrowski case, Eastland's role
Dombrowski v. Pfister. See Dombrowski
Domestic security, 7
Donner, Frank, 74, 75, 83, 84, 86, 93–94, 105, 115, 116, 126, 142, 143, 303
Donner, Kinoy, and Perlin (law firm), 85, 90
Dorson, Norman, 324
Douglas, William O., 18, 27, 33, 35, 38, 95, 115–116, 120, 121, 314
Dowling, Richard, 46
Dred Scott v. Sanford (60 U.S. [19 How.] 393 [1857]), 37
Dreyfus, Leonard, 213
Dulles, Allen, 248–249
Dulles, John Foster, 139

Index

Index

Pell, Wilbur, 321
Pemberton, Jack, 302
Perl, Arnold, 94–95
Perlin, Marshall, 85, 94, 105, 115, 116, 120, 121, 122, 124, 126, 136
Peterson, Doris, 2, 318, 319, 321, 323, 325
Pfister, James H., 223. *See also* Dombrowski
Phillips, Wendell, 40
Plamondon, Lawrence, 3, 6, 8
Plumbers unit, 13
Polan, Myra Jordan, 90
Pollitt, Basil, 114
Pool, Joseph, 19, 303–305
Poole, Bettye, 212
Popper, Martin, 248
Powell, Adam Clayton, 27; case (*Powell v. McCormick*, 395 U.S. 486 [1969]), 309–316, 327
Powell, Lewis, 18, 27, 33–34, 35
Powell, Richard, 46, 47
Powell v. McCormick. See Powell
Prayer Pilgrimage, 155–156, 157, 160
President, 7, 9–10, 24–26, 30–31, 158–159, 229, 329
Pressman, Lee, 74
Price, Deputy Sheriff, 246, 249, 254, 255
Prockter Productions, 94
Progressive Party, 92

Quinn, Thomas, contempt case (*Quinn v. U.S.* 349 U.S. 155 [1955]), 84, 91, 93, 142–143, 144, 145, 146, 147, 148

Rabinowitz, Victor, 324
Rainey, Sheriff, 246, 249, 254, 255, 269
Randolph, A. Philip, 155, 156, 159
Rap Brown statute, 319
Rauh, Joseph, 259–260, 261, 262, 263, 288
Reagan administration, 329
Reconstruction era: Congress, 67–68, 191, 192, 214, 240, 250; Constitutional amendments, 203, 225, 227; statutes, 250–251
Red baiting: and labor movement, 63, 84–85, 131, 134, 137–141; and civil

rights movement, 216, 218, 221, 225, 227, 229, 230, 278–279
Red Channels (magazine), 95
Reed, John, 41
Rehnquist, William, 9, 12, 13, 14, 18, 20, 27, 33, 34, 38, 39
Reichstag Fire trial, 79, 82
Reid, Herbert, 313, 314–315, 316, 325
Reid, Milton, 196
Reid, Ogden, 248
Reif, Jim, 326
Removal remedy. *See* Federal courts
Reuther, Walter, 259
Ripley, George, 41, 45
Rives, Richard, 171, 172, 173, 239, 242, 244
Robb, Dean, 189
Rodak, Michael, 28, 33
Rogers, 216
Rollins, Aaron, 196
Roosevelt, Franklin, 26
Roosevelt, James, 275, 293
Rosenberg, Julius and Ethel case (*U.S. v. Rosenberg and Sobell*, 195 F.2d 583 [2d Cir. 1952]), 86, 91–92, 96, 115–125, 129
Rubin, Jerry, 302, 317
Rustin, Bayard, 155
Rutgers University School of Law, 2, 53, 264–266, 312
Rutledge, Wiley, 49
Ryan, Sylvester, 98
Ryan, William Fitz, 248, 271, 272–273, 274, 275, 292–293

Sacco and Vanzetti trial, 119
Sacher, Harry, 40, 74, 89
Saunders, Richard, 149–150
Saypol, Irving, 98
SCEF. *See* Southern Conference Educational Fund
Scheiner, Frank, 120, 121
Schenectady (New York) UE struggle, 136, 137
Schine, David, 133, 141
School desegregation, 143, 147, 148. See also *Brown v. Board of Education;* Little Rock
Schwartz, Helene, 2, 318, 319, 321, 323, 325

338

Index